GLASS IN BUILDING

A Guide to Modern Architectural Glass Performance

PILKINGTON

David Button, John Colvin, Joan Cunliffe, Cliff Inman
Ken Jackson, Gordon Lightfoot, Peter Owens,
Brian Pye, Brian Waldron

Editors: David Button and Brian Pye

Pilkington Glass Ltd
Flachglas AG
Libbey Owens Ford
Pilkington Floatglas AB
Pilkington (Australia) Ltd

with
Butterworth Architecture

Butterworth Architecture
An imprint of Butterworth-Heinemann Ltd
Linacre House, Jordan Hill, Oxford OX2 8DP

A member of the Reed Elsevier plc group

OXFORD   LONDON   BOSTON
MUNICH   NEW DELHI   SINGAPORE   SYDNEY
TOKYO   TORONTO   WELLINGTON

First published 1993
Paperback edition 1994

British Library Cataloguing in Publication Data
Glass in Building: Guide to Modern Architectural Glass Performance
  I. Button, David II. Pye, Brian
  721.04496

ISBN 0 7506 2170 2

Library of Congress Cataloguing in Publication Data
Glass in Building: a guide to modern architectural glass performance
  David Button ... [et al]; editors, David Button and Brian Pye.
  p. cm.
  'Pilkington Glass Ltd, Flachglas AG, Libby Owens Ford, Pilkington
  Floatglas AB, Pilkington   (Australia) Ltd with Butterworth Architecture.
  Includes biblographical references and index.
  ISBN 0 7506 2170 2
  I. Glass construction. I. Button, David. II. Pye, Brian.
  NA4140.G57
  721'. 04496-dc20   92–17060
                                                             CIP

Designed by Robert Walster

Printed and bound in Spain

Contents

Contents

Preface

I use light abundantly, as you may have suspected; light for me is the fundamental basis of architecture. I compose with light.

Le Corbusier, *Oeuvre Complète*

Amongst all building materials, glass has the unique property of transmitting light. It is by means of light that we perceive the space in and around architecture. But today, window glass performs many functions additional to its fundamental daylighting role. The advent of new requirements for building, such as the accommodation of information technology, and the development of new glass technologies to meet those requirements, for example the deposition of electroconducting coatings, are generating new glass performances. In this context architectural glass requires a reappraisal and a new understanding.

This book is designed to aid our understanding of the nature and performance of glass used in the windows of buildings today. The primary readers will be architects, designers and other specifiers of glass, so that they may approach its specification with added understanding and confidence. The general reader too will discover a new understanding for this magic material.

The technology of glass, and its relationship with the building occupants, form the body of this work. However, the provision of a guide to window design, or a study in environmental physics, has been avoided; there are many competent specialist books available on these subjects. The authors have also avoided rewriting material found in glass manufacturers' catalogues, since such data are best available locally or nationally.

In serving an international readership, references to national legislation, codes of practice and standards have been avoided. Similarly, references in the text to specific manufacturers' brands have been avoided wherever possible. However, most of the illustrated buildings show Pilkington Group glass products; where this is not the case the manufacturer is identified, if this has been found to be possible.

This book deals with glass *per se*. But window glass cannot be considered wholly in isolation. Its performance is affected by the associated framing, wall and structure, the services and, their controls, and the behaviour of the building occupants. Increasingly in modern buildings, windows are being designed as parts of larger systems and components. Some chapters, therefore, have to deal with these associated matters, such as the window framing, but these are included only where they are essential to the understanding of the glass itself. Shading device technology, which is well documented in other publications, is excluded except where devices are contained within the glazing product.

The technical chapters are divided into separate functional groups – visual, thermal, mechanical and others. The technologies of the chapters overlap and therefore an individual functional group should be read as a whole. Inevitably, there are also important interrelationships between the functional groups which will need to be considered in design: for example, 'daylight' will be considered with 'heat gain', as 'heat loss' will be considered with 'sound insulation'. A complicated cross-referencing of chapters has been avoided, since it is hoped that these interrelationships will be self-evident.

Acknowledgements

The editing of this book has been greatly assisted by many in the Pilkington Group: from Pilkington Glass Ltd, John Alderson, Robert Birch, Richard Chapell, Leslie Clarke, Ray Cross, Mervyn Davies, Reg Dunning, José Gallego, Mike Jenkins, David Johnson, Robin Steere and Howard McKenzie; from Triplex, Robert Wright and David Oakley; from Pilkington Energy Advisers Ltd, Alan Williams and Gerry Shaw; from Flachglas AG, Horst Harzheim, Frank Passmann and many of their colleagues; from Libbey Owens Ford, Peter Gerhardinger and Chris Barry.

We are also indebted to Wendy Wilberforce who organized the word processing and typed innumerable revisions to the text with much fortitude; to Ray Jennings and David Crook for providing much valuable criticism and constructive advice; to Ken Wilson for organizing the artwork, by TIS Publicity, Manchester; and to Alex Smith for photography. Terry Driscoll and Rufus Ide of T.W.Ide Ltd helped greatly with the text concerning decorative glass and the provision of decorative glass samples and photography.

Praeger Publishers in New York generously granted permission for extracts from the English translation of Paul Scheerbart's *Glasarchitektur*, which threads throughout the book.

We are indebted to Petra Hagen-Hodgson for constructive historical criticism and to Margareta Artner for *Gerinnungsdiagnostik*. James Carpenter provided encouragement, photos and the important copy of the English version of Scheerbart's book. Mike Davies of Richard Rogers and Partners provided much encouragement and material support.

The directors of Pilkington Glass Ltd are thanked for their permission and support in providing much of the data.

The preparation of this book has been a team effort but errors and omissions are the responsibility of the editors.

Pilkington Glass Companies

Pilkington Glass Ltd
Prescot Road
St Helens
England
WA10 3TT

Flachglas AG
Auf der Reihe 2
D-4650
Gelsenkirchen
Germany

Libbey Owens Ford Co.
811 Madison Avenue
Toledo
Ohio 43695–0799
USA

Pilkington Floatglas AB
Box 530
301 80 Halmstad
Sweden

Pilkington (Australia) Ltd
420 St Kilda Road
Melbourne
Victoria 3004
Australia

CHAPTER 1

Introduction to the History of Architectural Glass

In 1914, at a time of social conflict and revolution in Europe, the German visionary writer Paul Scheerbart described his dream of a world revivified by glass architecture:

If we want our culture to rise to a high level, we are obliged for better or for worse, to change our architecture. And this only becomes possible if we take away the 'closed' character from the rooms in which we live. We can only do that by introducing glass architecture, which lets in the light of the sun, the moon, and the stars, not merely through a few windows, but through every possible wall, which will be made entirely of glass.

Scheerbart's book *Glasarchitektur*, which vividly expressed that dream, was an inspiration to the then emerging modern movement in architecture, at a time when the potential of glass technology was newly revealed. Today, his vision of an architecture 'made entirely of glass' is almost possible. Society is again at a time of great change, accompanied by much technical innovation; whilst it may be unwise to predict the future relationships between culture and architecture, it is possible to show that newly available technologies will have profound effects on future glass architecture, potentially enabling the full realization of Scheerbart's vision.

The evolution of architectural glass technology can be revealed by tracing several ideas which have established it in the recent history of architecture. These are the building structure, the architect's regard for the crystal quality of glass, the evolving comfort needs of the building occupants, and the flow of natural light to the interior. The future evolution of architectural glass generated from these ideas will encompass new technologies obtaining exciting performances.

THE BUILDING STRUCTURE

The unique and important quality of architectural glass is its ability to transmit daylight. The ancient relationship between daylight and architecture was clarified by Le Corbusier: 'The history of architecture shows an untiring struggle to admit daylight through the heavy obstacles imposed by gravity; this struggle is the history of the

Figure 1.1 *(Opposite)*
German Pavilion, International Exhibition, Barcelona, Spain, 1929
Architect: Mies van der Rohe

The elegant walls of finely framed tinted glass and travertine marble were free of any load bearing function since the roof was independently supported by thin steel columns. These walls created, in this small pavilion, spatial vistas and intimate enclosed spaces. Mies van der Rohe was one of the first architects to demonstrate, at an almost domestic scale, the then new idea of the inside and outside flowing together through crystalline glass spanning uninterruptedly from floor to ceiling.

window (McGraph, 1961). The struggle for the admission of daylight succeeded in spectacular ways at the beginning of the nineteenth century. From this time on the development of framed building structures, superseding the heavyweight load bearing wall, liberated window area.

Throughout history the load bearing wall of brick and stone had been the principal means of construction. Its very nature severely limited the width of opening, although this limitation was at times exceptionally overcome, such as in the developments culminating in the Gothic cathedral. By structural invention, as Le Corbusier pointed out, designers have achieved increasingly larger window openings, and eventually the all glass wall, in order to enhance the visual quality of the building interior by means of daylight. The nineteenth century saw the culmination of post and lintel construction, making available larger window openings, for all types of building. This skeletal framing was promoted by the development first of cast iron, then of wrought iron, and later of steel and reinforced concrete. These materials were the products of the engineering and manufacturing invention of the burgeoning industrial revolution – invention which also found effect in glass manufacture.

Until then the customary 'crown' process manufactured only limited sizes of glass pane, which led to its decline in the 1830s after 150 years of development. It had provided panes of 0.75×0.5 m, but the majority of panes were of smaller dimensions. This showed clearly in the design of the eighteenth and nineteenth century window with its divisions of mullion and transom. In the 1830s manufacturers began to employ the new improved 'Cylinder' process, providing glass of more uniform thickness in sizes up to 1.0×1.3 m. Glass was now available to seal the larger openings in the façades of the new skeletal constructions. This process, which was an early form of mass production, permitted the rapid construction of the Crystal Palace in London in 1851.

Glass was the inevitable material to seal the new, hard won, openings. Glass and the steel skeleton came together as key elements in the modern architectural movement – a movement whose ideals concerned natural light, transparency, health and social well-being. Glass was seen both to provide and to symbolize those ideals.

The early development of cast iron allowed framed constructions of up to eight storeys but initially was only used in industrial buildings. However, these innovative constructions still tended to be shrouded by load bearing wall façades.

Figure 1.2
Oriel Chambers, Liverpool, UK, 1864
Architect: Peter Ellis

Figure 1.3
Fagus factory, Germany, 1911
Architects: Gropius and Meyer

Figure 1.4
Bauhaus, Dessau, Germany, 1925
Architect: Walter Gropius

During the 1860s, the post and lintel structure was revealed on the façade of monumental public buildings, to support panels of brick and glass. Oriel Chambers, an office in Liverpool completed in 1864, is an early example from the UK (Figure 1.2). Thus metal framing and glass eventually became visibly expressed. They symbolized the modern architecture and they became visually acceptable in the then flourishing urban centres such as Liverpool, Berlin and Chicago.

The symbolism of glass and metal was to find a new expression in the form of a glass skin, rather than glazed generous openings in the skeletal structure. In 1911 Walter Gropius designed the Fagus factory in Germany, the first example of a façade completely in glass supported by a thin framework of steel (Figure 1.3), and later his Bauhaus in Dessau in 1925 (Figure 1.4) achieved the modern ideal designers had strived for – the integration of outside with inside by means of a transparent building skin. This skin was a flat continuous surface separated from the building structure – an early form of curtain wall.

A more spectacular façade was the early curtain wall designed by Willis Polk for the Hallidee Building in San Francisco in 1918, which was a product of the development of metal extrusion techniques in the 1890s (Figure 1.5).

Mies van der Rohe's 1922 Glass Sky Scraper project model, shown at the annual Berlin Art Exhibition (Figure 1.6), was a further attempt to design the all glass curtain wall. He intended to reveal the internal structure and at the same time to exploit the glass's reflective qualities, by breaking up the façade surface with angular planes, thus mirroring the adjacent properties (an effect not obtained in this form until Foster Associates' Willis Faber Dumas Building in Ipswich, UK, in 1975). The curtain wall revealed itself as both the leading edge of structural design and a fulfilment of Scheerbart's prophecies.

How did glass manufacturing technology give support to these ambitious structural developments? At the turn of the century various drawn flat sheet processes were introduced which superseded the cylinder process, starting with the Belgian Fourcault process and continuing notably with the Colburn process from the USA. These drew glass approximately 1.9 m wide; thus the larger glass panes much desired by architects were now available. Further processing was required, by grinding and polishing, to produce the distortion free quality plate which was perfected in the 1920s. There was now available the crystal glass quality to which Scheerbart had referred and which constituted another important idea in glass architecture.

THE CRYSTAL QUALITY OF GLASS

Bruno Taut, in a pamphlet produced for the opening of his Glashaus glass pavilion for the Werkbund Exhibition in Cologne in 1914, described the pavilion as having no other purpose 'than to be beautiful' . Glass was no longer only a functional light admitting material; it now embodied an aesthetic and symbolic role (Figure 1.7).

In the pavilion, glass was everywhere; walls, ceilings, floors and staircases were all finished in translucent or transparent glass. Taut's aim was the enclosure of space by means of glass. He also introduced coloured, opaque and clear glass, to create various effects by means of their optical qualities. Whilst being an ephemeral construction, the pavilion had an important influence on architects. This idea of glass as a beautiful material in its own right found a continuing embodiment in the architecture of Gropius, Mies van der Rohe and Le Corbusier. This idea has continued through to the present day, as pointed out by Banham (1981) in discussing Foster Associates' Willis Faber Dumas Building:

In the traditions of the modern movement in architecture, glass is of the party of order and hygiene. It stands for the replacement of the slums of the huddled poor by clean crystal towers. It stands for the illumination of the dark places of vernacular superstition by the pure light of rationality. Worldwide, it has become the symbolic material of clarity, literal and phenomenal.

Figure 1.5
Hallidee Building, San Francisco, USA, 1918
Architect: Willis Polk

Figure 1.6
Glass Sky Scraper project, Berlin Art Exhibition, Germany, 1922
Architect: Mies van der Rohe

Glass has its own material developments which have, and will bring, new aesthetic qualities to architecture (Figure 1.8). In the ebb and flow of human achievement and spirit, generating architectural styles, glass will continue to have its functional place in building, but its future expression will be enhanced by the new technologies, such as holography, electrochromics and electroluminescence.

BUILDING OCCUPANT COMFORT

Today the important relationship between glass and building structure still exists, but the history of architecture has moved on. The building structure is no longer of primary architectural importance; of equal design consideration, and equal financial investment, are the heating, lighting and air conditioning services. Furthermore, in the 1990s, information technology will become the major investment shaping building design.

Alongside this technology, the future building occupants will make new demands for their well-being, which will influence new façade glass performances. These will be achieved by new, innovative glass technologies. By the twenty-first century, glass will have become the dynamic enveloping skin of the building, and an information medium. But its ancient light transmitting quality will still be of primary importance.

At the beginning of the twentieth century the light admitting functional role together with the aesthetic expressionism of the façade created, by the more generous use of glass, new environmental conditions inside buildings. In 1914, even the visionary Scheerbart had his feet on the ground in sounding naïve, but not irrelevant, warnings:

The worst thing though is that glass walls are single and not double; in consequence the expense on heating is enormous. In the first instances it is advisable only to build glass houses in temperate zones, and not in the equatorial and polar regions.

The age old load bearing wall of brick and stone gave relatively high thermal insulation and thermal capacity with low solar admission. Up to 1900 the multi-cellular building was, by modern standards, still heavyweight and able to absorb much of the daily climatic fluctuations; but from this time onwards, building structures became increasingly lighter and the building fabric increasingly permeable to heat transfer, producing potentially a more capricious internal environment. The delicate relationship between skin, structure and the internal and external environments was critical to comfortable living conditions in the building. This delicate relationship can be shown by an analogy with certain animal groups. The lobster and snail, which have their structure on the outside, can be compared with those animals with an internal skeletal structure, such as vertebrates. Each demands very different performance from its outer skin in order to obtain its internal metabolic balance. Equally the metabolic balance of the modern building greatly relies on its own internal services. Building structure has changed from a load bearing façade to an internal skeletal form with changing implications for the building services.

It was Reyner Banham (1969) who first explored the history of building services, and their role in enabling the emergence of a modern architecture complete with a 'well tempered environment'. He showed that air conditioning, as an important contributor to the building's metabolism, also had its roots in the nineteenth century. In its simplest sense the air conditioning system must be able to reduce the temperature of the ventilating air; humidity control and filtration are secondary but important aspects of the design. The role of the building skin is to reconcile the outside climate with the needs of the inside environment, with the support of those service systems. An important landmark in building service history was when networks of meteorological stations were set up in a number of countries in the 1850s to enable the recording of that outside climate. At the same time, compression refrigerating machines were developed in the United States. Research then was directed towards efficient ice production, which until 1890 was used in commercial refrigeration or in primitive methods of air cooling. In the latter, air was blown over racks of ice to cool special buildings such as places of assembly; in 1880 Madison Square Theatre, New York, put four tonnes of ice in the air stream per evening.

In coming to terms with measuring the internal environment, Professor Marvin of the Weather Bureau, Washington, devised in 1900 his *Psychometric Tables for Obtaining the Vapour Pressure, Relative Humidity and Temperature on the Dew Point of the Air*. Then in 1902 Willis Carrier, the 'father of air conditioning', turned his idea for dehumidifying air and holding its temperature constant into reality by designing the first fan coil dehumidifying system for the Sackets-Wilhelms printing company in New York. This installation heralded the beginning of modern air conditioning at a time when the new lightweight building structure and skin provoked an awareness of its necessity.

Architects slowly began to take these new technologies on board. In 1904 the separate developments in air conditioning and architecture came together in Frank Lloyd Wright's Larkin Building, Buffalo, USA, which he claimed as the 'first air conditioned building', and which Banham (1969) claimed as 'the first building to make a masterpiece of its mechanical services'.

Figure 1.8 *(Opposite)*
Interior of bathroom apartment,
London, UK, 1991
Architect: John Young, Richard
Rogers & Partners

9

Figure 1.9 *(Opposite)*
Pieter de Hooch, *An Interior, with a*
Woman Drinking with Two Men,
1658 (National Gallery, London, UK)

As the vertebrate's animal skin partly protects its body from too much heat, cold, moisture and dryness, so too should the building skin perform. Since glass had become a major part of that skin it had new responsibilities in the form of new performance requirements. For example, the need for solar attenuation, because of the solar loading from the glass skin and the low thermal mass of lightweight skeletal structures, became an important issue in the thermal behaviour of buildings. But the consideration of this issue was slow in an architecture devoted to other priorities.

These new performance requirements for the glass skin were revealed in Le Corbusier's pioneer glass curtain wall in La Cité de Refuge in Paris, one of Europe's first air conditioned buildings, and which had a profound effect on architects. However, this façade did not perform well since it had little solar protection, and it was necessary in the 1940s to construct external shading devices. During the 1920s the development of air conditioning for multi-cellular buildings by Carrier and others to some extent obscured these solar overheating problems in the United States.

In the 1930s Scheerbart's environmental warnings (and perhaps his love of 'coloured glass') found effect in glass manufacture. Body tinted glass products were introduced, to attenuate solar energy transmission and to reduce summer overheating. This was a first step towards higher performance glass to meet the emerging environmental requirements. With the sophistication of the building services, and demands for increased occupant comfort, glass products were developed with coatings for solar energy attenuation, as was multiple glazing for thermal insulation. As a result the actual light transmission of window glass changed in both quality and quantity; that is, lower light transmission and coloured transmission were introduced.

Later, other issues influenced window performance requirements. There are many building types and climates where air conditioning is essential. However, with the energy crisis of the 1970s and the present compelling need for a reduction in

carbon dioxide (CO_2) emissions, investment in air conditioning is now being carefully reconsidered. Natural ventilation, natural lighting and other 'green' concepts are having a new effect on building design, building services and the role of the window. The window has become a selective filter of solar energy and, with the advent of low emissivity coatings, a key element in passive solar energy design in energy efficient buildings with reduced carbon dioxide emissions. Glass has therefore obtained many new roles which impinge on its primary light transmitting function and which have consequences for lighting design.

THE FLOW OF NATURAL LIGHT

Previous generations of architects had understood the window opening as a discrete source from which light flowed. They had channelled it, by interior light reflection and inter-reflection, to produce adequate illumination, and in this context to obtain a distinctive modelling of the interior and the objects in the interior. Paintings of the seventeenth century Dutch school, exemplified by Vermeer and de Hooch, exploited these effects. Interestingly, Dutch windows of that period included several shutters to regulate varied internal lighting qualities, as is shown in the painting by de Hooch of An Interior, with a Woman Drinking with Two Men (Figure 1.9).

The modern liberated window had dissolved to become part of a transparent skin potentially admitting an abundant flow of daylight to every corner of the building. Modern architects seemed to have forgotten the age old preoccupation with modelling the interior with natural light, except perhaps for Le Corbusier, Frank Lloyd Wright (Figure 1.10) and Aalto, for whom it remained a vital architectural tool.

But further innovations had arisen to complicate lighting design. Thomas Edison emerged at the end of the nineteenth century as the 'father of electric lighting'. With the growth in electrical power generation and distribution industries, the designer was suddenly provided with new and fascinating means of illumination. They presented problems, however, for

Figure 1.10
Meyer May House, Grand Rapids, USA, 1908
Architect: Frank Lloyd-Wright

the designer who had been trained to model forms by external light and its cast shadows. Architecture had been defined, in Le Corbusier's words, as 'forms assembled in light'. Now the designer has also to model his shapes from artificial sources. Banham (1969) clearly defined these problems:

For the first time it was possible to conceive buildings whose true nature could only be perceived after dark, when artificial light blazed out through their structure. And this possibility was realised and exploited without the support of any corpus of theory adapted to the new circumstances, or even of a workable vocabulary for describing these visual effects and their environmental consequences. No doubt this accounts for the numerous failures of this century to produce the effects and environments desired; equally doubtless it accounts for periodic waves of revulsion against 'glass boxes' and fashionable returns to solid concrete and massive masonry.

From now on the window had to be considered in relation to artificial illumination. On the other hand, today, with the concern for global warming, it is also considered for electrical light saving. These considerations too have influenced the development of new window glass performances.

THE FUTURE: THE DYNAMIC SKIN

The method of suspending glass assemblies as a curtain of glass, and the Planar structural glazing system, symbolize the full liberation of glass from the building structure. But with this liberation, glass bears the full environmental responsibilities of the building skin. Can the glass skin meet the numerous complicated environmental demands upon it, as does the vertebrate's skin? In 1978 Richard Rogers and Partners carried out a research study for Pilkington Glass to aid the definition of future glass research targets, and the following was proposed:

It is no good having a sophisticated mechanical services system for a building and a poor skin performance. It is only even partially effective to have a sophisticated mechanical services installation and high quality fixed performance skin. A time responsive, variable quality skin system is the only logical answer to this problem. A building becomes a chameleon which

Figure 1.11
Stansted Airport, UK, 1991
Architects: Foster Associates

adapts. A properly equipped and responsively clothed building would monitor all internal and external variables, temperature, hygrometry and light levels, solar radiation etc., to determine the best energy equation given these conditions and modify the building and its internal systems accordingly. It is not too much to ask of a building to incorporate, in its fabric and its nervous system, the very basic vestiges of an adaptive capability.

In the last few years there has been much research on variable transmission glass, directed initially to the automotive industry. There are already successful examples at a laboratory level, but there are many major technical tasks yet to be overcome in order to achieve a variable transmission glass for buildings. New technologies in photochromic, thermochromic and electrochromic devices have excited the interest of researchers; their study of variable transmission is driven by a desire for energy saving and improved levels of comfort. Variable transmission will also be used for visual amenity and appearance, and it is likely that these benefits will support its earliest applications. Nevertheless new products which offer more comfort and amenity in the workplace will be in great demand by future employers anxious to increase productivity and attract staff.

Variable transmission can be achieved in several ways, but electrochromic glass, which changes heat and light transmission as the result of an electrical signal, appears to offer the best potential (Figure 1.12). Studies at Lawrence Berkeley Laboratories in California have shown that, for a single given building form and climate, variable transmission glass 'constantly outperforms conventional systems' in savings in the capital and running costs of lighting and cooling equipment. Since the final manufacturing costs of variable transmission glass are not yet known, the important cost effective comparisons cannot be fully made, but such costs are part of the research and development targets.

Variable transmission façades in the future could be controlled personally or by climatic sensors linked to the central services control. This technology will find its place in windows, translucent walls and internal screens; it will also have a dynamic effect on the appearance of the interior and exterior of buildings.

Research work has also been carried out examining glass as a communications medium by means of electroluminescent display technology (Figure 1.13). This could mean that the functions of light transmission and dynamic environmental control combine with communications and moving decoration in the glass. Decoration could be integrated with the information technology and communications function, so that the internal glass walls and external skin become electronic displays of information or simply patterns of colour – creating the possibility of changing instantly the whole character of the building.

The twenty-first century will see a full and rich expression of Scheerbart's prophecies, which concluded:

After all the above, we can indeed speak of a glass culture. The new glass environment will completely transform mankind, and it remains only to wish that the new glass culture will not find too many opponents; to cling to the old is in many matters a good thing; in this way at any rate the old is preserved. We, too, want to cling to the old – the pyramids of ancient Egypt should most certainly not be abolished. But we also want to strive after the new, with all the resources at our disposal; more power to them!

Figure 1.13
Glass as a communications medium, Pilkington Technology Centre, Lathom, UK

An experimental electroluminescent flat glass display with a pixelated matrix structure to create moving patterns activated from its periphery by electrical inputs from a computer.

Figure 1.14
Los Angeles Planar Project with
dichroic coating.
Glass design: James Carpenter.

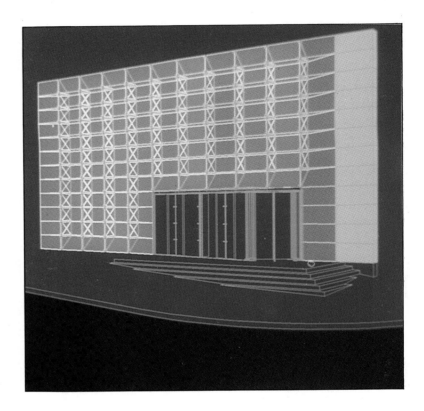

BIBLIOGRAPHY

Banham, R. *The Architecture of the Well-Tempered Environment*, Architectural Press, London, 1969

Banham, R. *Design by Choice*, Academy, London, 1981

Barker, T.C. *The Glass Makers*, Weidenfeld and Nicholson, London, 1977

Button, D. and Dunning, R. *Fenestration 2000: An Investigation into the Long Term Requirements for Glass. Phase I*, Pilkington Glass Ltd and the UK Department of Energy, July 1989

Fischer, W. *Geborgenheit Und Freiheit – Vom Bauen Mit Glas*, Sherpeverlag, Krefeld, 1970 (in German)

Flachglas AG *500 Jahre Flachglas*, Gelsenkirchen, 1987 (in German)

Ingles, M. *Father of Air Conditioning – Willis Haviland Carrier*, Country Life Press, Garden City, USA, 1952

McGrath, R. (ed.) *Glass in Architecture and Decoration*, Architectural Press, London, 1961

Pevsner, N. *Pioneers of Modern Design*, Penguin, Harmondsworth, 1960

Rogers, R. 'Notes on the Future of Glass', (Private report to Pilkington Glass Ltd) Richard Rogers and Partners, London, 1979

Scheerbart, P. *Glass Architecture*, ed. Dennis Sharp, Praeger, New York, 1972 (English translation of *Glasarchitektur*, Verlag Der Sturm, Berlin, 1914)

Selkowitz, E. and Lampert, C.M. 'Application of Large-Area Chromeogenics to Architectural Glazings' in *Large Area Chromogenics: Materials and Devices for Transmittance Control*, ed. C.M. Lampert and C.G. Granquist, Optical Engineering Press, Bellingham, Washington, USA, 1989

CHAPTER 2

Manufacturing Processes and Window Glass Functions

Developments in glass manufacturing and glass processing technologies are designed to achieve better and new window performances. In the early twentieth century the need to attenuate the ingress of solar radiation through windows was met by the introduction of solar control glass, made possible by tinting the base glass. Similarly the early twenty-first century will see the introduction of variable transmission window glass, made possible by the development of new electrochromic technologies. Between these examples is the complicated evolution of glass processing technologies to meet many other needs. The current glass manufacturing and processing technologies are outlined below and the terminology is defined in Appendix C.

Figure 2.1 *(Opposite)*
Float glass manufacture, Pilkington Glass Ltd, St Helens, UK

BASIC MANUFACTURE

There are two main flat glass manufacturing methods for producing the basic glass from which all processed glass products are made.

FLOAT

More than 90% of the world's flat glass is made by the float process (Figure 2.2). Molten glass, at approximately 1000°C, is poured continuously from a furnace on to a large shallow bath of molten tin. It floats on the tin, spreads out and forms a level

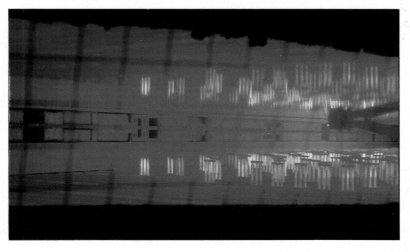

Figure 2.2
Float glass manufacture, Pilkington Glass Ltd, St Helens, UK
View inside the float bath where the ribbon of glass is floated across molten tin.

Figure 2.3
Rolled glass manufacture, Pilkington
Glass Ltd, St Helens, UK

Figure 2.4
Body tinted glass, Swim Centre, Hatfield, UK

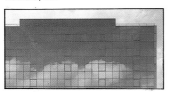

Figure 2.5
On-line coated glass, Levi Strauss Building, London, UK
Architects: Halpern and Partners

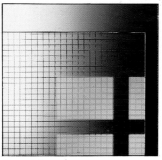

Figure 2.6a
Polished wired glass, Pilkington Glass Ltd, St Helens, UK

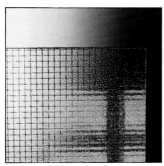

Figure 2.6b
Rough cast wired glass, Pilkington Glass Ltd, St Helens, UK

surface. Thickness is controlled by the speed at which the solidifying glass ribbon is drawn off the bath. After annealing the glass emerges as a 'fire' polished product with virtually parallel surfaces.

ROLLED

The rolling process makes patterned, figured and cast glass products, whereby a semi-molten glass is squeezed between metal rollers to produce a ribbon with controlled thickness and surface pattern (Figure 2.3).

MODIFIED BASIC MANUFACTURE

Broadly, there are three forms of modification to the above basic manufacturing processes.

TINTED

Body tinted glass products are produced by small additions of metal oxides to the float or rolled glass composition. These small additions colour the glass bronze, green, blue or grey but do not affect the basic properties of the glass except for changes in the solar energy transmission (Figure 2.4).

COATED (ON-LINE)

Modified properties are produced from the basic glass by means of surface coatings applied, in this case, on-line during the basic manufacture. They have advantages of hardness and durability over off-line coatings applied after the basic manufacture. Coatings may modify some or all of the solar energy transmission, colour, and thermal insulation properties (Figure 2.5).

WIRED

Wired glass is made by rolling processes. In one such process, a steel wire mesh is sandwiched between two separate ribbons of glass and passed through a pair of consolidating rollers which may also impress a required pattern (Figure 2.6a). The rough cast surface may be polished to obtain clear transparency (Figure 2.6b). Its uses may be in fire resistance and safety glazing.

PRIMARY PROCESSING

This is treatment to the basic glass after its manufacture.

HEAT TREATED

Toughened glass, or tempered glass as it is also known, is produced by heating annealed glass to approximately 650 °C, at which point it begins to soften. Its outer surfaces are then cooled rapidly, creating in them a high compression. Its bending strength is usually increased to a factor of 4 or 5 that of annealed glass. When broken, it fractures into small harmless dice and is deemed a safety glazing material. Heat strengthened glass is similarly produced, but with strengths approximately half that of toughened glass and without the safety glazing characteristic (Figure 2.7).

Figure 2.7
Toughened glass, Sainsbury Art Centre, Norwich, UK
Architect: Foster Associates

Figure 2.8
Bent glass rooflights, Tagungs-
Centrum Messe, Hanover, Germany
Architects: Hinrich Storch and
Walter Ehlers

Figure 2.9
Acid etched glass, factory
manufacture, Pilkington Glass Ltd,
St Helens, UK

Figure 2.10
Screen printed louvre designs, Shell-
Mex House, London, UK

BENT

Bent glass is produced by heating annealed glass to a point where it softens so it can be pressed or sag bent over formers (Figure 2.8).

SURFACE WORKED

Fine surface textures are applied, of varying degrees and varieties, using sand blasting and acid etching (Figure 2.9). Deeper textures, cuts and designs are produced by engraving, using an abrasive copper wheel, a diamond point or a carborundum pencil. They may be factory or hand applied, and the glass may be subsequently heat treated or bent.

SECONDARY PROCESSING

This is defined as adding extrinsic additional materials or components to the basic glass after its manufacture.

PRINTED

Ceramic ink designs are screen printed on to float glass which is then toughened, fusing the ink to the surface and providing a permanent durable finish. These products may meet requirements of aesthetics, solar control and information display (Figure 2.10).

COATED (OFF-LINE)

This coating is applied to individual plates of glass after manufacture and deposited by means of chemical solutions, vacuum evaporation or magnetron sputtering, producing solar optical and thermal insulation properties similar to on-line coatings (Figure 2.11). Silvering is a form of coating, but is not included in this discussion.

MULTIPLE GLAZED UNITS

Multiple glazed units incorporate two (or more) panes, separated by a spacer (or spacers), to create a hermetically sealed gap between each successive pane in the unit. This gap can be filled with air which is subsequently desiccant dried. Low emissivity coatings can be added to one or more interior glass

Figure 2.11
Off-line silver coated glass
Rover Building, Hanover, Germany

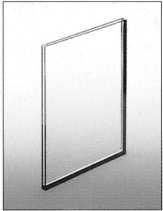

Figure 2.12
Multiple glazed unit

surfaces in a multiple glazed unit to provide improved thermal insulation. To further enhance the thermal insulating properties, low conductivity gases such as argon can be used instead of air in the cavities. Other gases (primarily sulphur hexafluoride) can similarly be used to improve acoustic insulation. The panes are usually connected by a spacer using sealants to give mechanical strength and to resist air or water penetration (Figure 2.12).

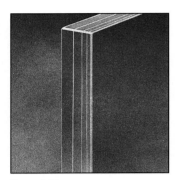

Figure 2.13
Laminated glass composed of 10 mm
+ 6 mm + 4 mm + 4 mm glass

LAMINATED

Laminated glass is produced by bonding two or more panes of glass together with a plastic material, a resin or intumescent interlayers. Laminates can incorporate most thicknesses of glass and plastics to give a selection of products with a range of mechanical, fire resistant and optical properties (Figure 2.13). Laminated glass can incorporate other materials, such as polycarbonates, to achieve specific mechanical performances. When a laminated glass is broken the interlayer tends to hold the fragments of broken glass in place, and it may be deemed a safety glazing material.

PRODUCT PERMUTATIONS

Using the basic float glass product, permutations of the many glass processing technologies generate an extensive range of glass product performances to meet building needs. For example, basic float may be a clear, tinted or coated glass which can then be heat treated or bent. It can be further printed, laminated and double glazed.

There are, however, some combinations that are not feasible to manufacture. The major restrictions are:

- Wired, deeply patterned and deeply worked glass products cannot be heat treated.
- Toughened glass cannot be subsequently surface or edge worked or cut.

Some combinations are feasible only by specialized manufacture. However, given the manufacturing parameters, the permutations are considerable. For example, the variations that might be obtained from the 16 different types of sound reducing glass are shown in Figure 2.16. A more complicated product combining lamination and double glazing to form a bandit resistant product is shown in Figure 2.14.

In order to understand why such permutations are demanded for glazing, the functions of the window itself should be considered.

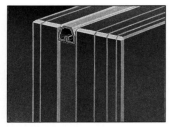

Figure 2.14
Double glazing unit containing laminated glass composed of 4 mm + 15 mm glass, a 10 mm air space, and 15 mm + 8 mm + 6 mm + 4 mm glass

PRIMARY GLASS FUNCTIONS

VIEW OUT, VIEW IN

A primary function of glass is to allow the transmission of light and obtain a view through the window.

APPEARANCE

Appearance is the visual celebration of glass arising from the optical qualities of basic and processed glass.

PASSIVE SOLAR GAIN

Another primary function is to provide the transmission of useful solar radiation for lighting and heating.

INCURRED GLASS FUNCTIONS

In order to achieve the primary functions, the glass must resist the natural forces likely to be imposed upon it, such as wind and weather, and may also be required to keep out man-made attacks such as bullets, vandalism and explosions. It must be safe and secure. It must also act as a complicated filter of light, heat and sound energy to optimize efficiently the primary visual and lighting functions. The general relationship between current processing technologies and glass functions is shown in Figure 2.15.

The following chapters, grouped into visual, thermal and mechanical functions, examine each of the primary and incurred window glass functions.

Figure 2.15
Relationship between glass
manufacturing/processing
technologies and glass functions

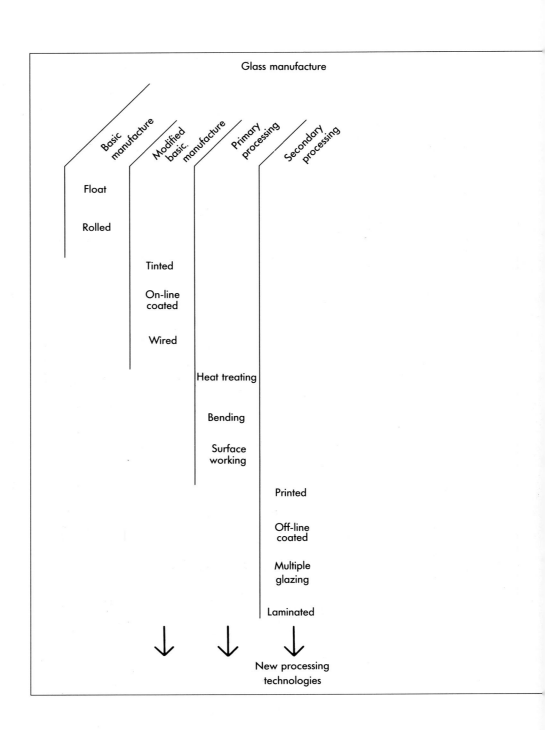

Manufacturing Processes and Window Glass Functions

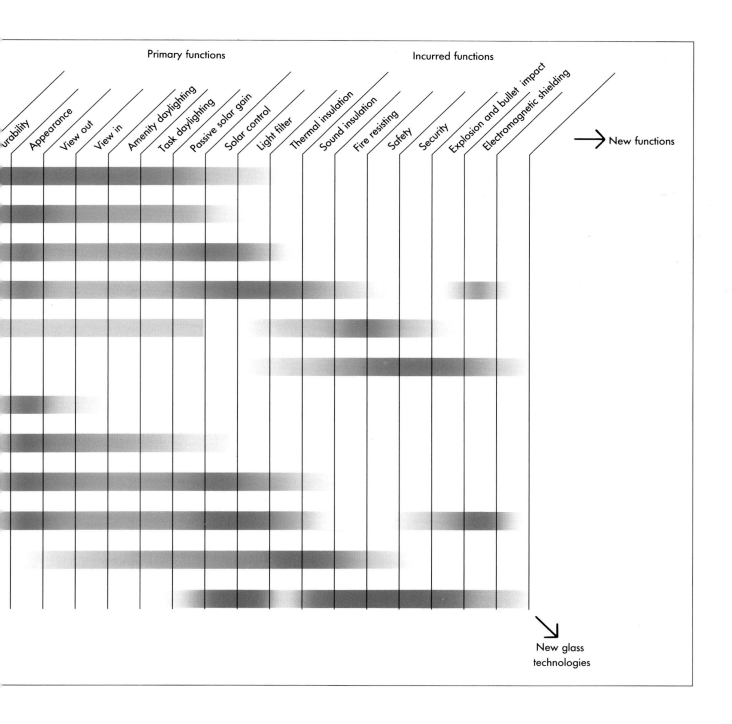

31

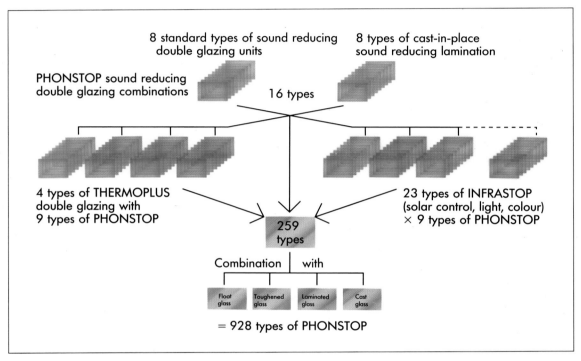

Figure 2.16
Permutations of sound reducing
glass

BIBLIOGRAPHY

BS 6262 *Code of Practice for Glazing for Buildings*, British Standards Institution, 1982

Burgoyne, I. and Scoble, R. *Two Thousand Years of Flat Glass Making*, Pilkington Glass Museum, April 1989

Federal Association of German Sheet-Glass Wholesale Trade *Glasfibel*, Cologne, 1983 (in German)

Flachglas AG. *Glashandbuch*, Gelsenkirchen, 1992 (in German)

CHAPTER 3

Introduction to Heat and Light

Light permeated the universe.
It comes to life in the crystal.
The prism is marvellous.
That is why the glass house is great.

Scheerbart Glasarchitektur, 1914

Electromagnetic radiation is the principal energy source which provides both heat and light. In order to describe the glass functions in the following chapters it is necessary to provide a general description of electromagnetic radiation, in the form of both heat and light, and its behaviour with glass.

PHYSICS OF HEAT AND LIGHT

All bodies emit and absorb energy in the form of electromagnetic radiation. By definition, a body that absorbs all the radiation falling on it is termed a 'black body', and the radiation emitted from such a body is called 'black body radiation'.

The total rate of radiant energy emission (Q, W/m^2) from a black body depends on the temperature of the body and its total emissivity, as defined by the Stefan–Boltzmann law (Figure 3.2b). The emissivity expresses the ratio of the actual radiation emitted by a body to that emitted by a black body at the same temperature. By definition, a black body has an emissivity of unity.

The rate of radiant energy emitted per unit wavelength interval (Q_λ, $W/m^2\,nm$) by a black body is called the spectral energy distribution function (Figure 3.3). This also depends on (absolute) temperature, as defined by Planck's law (Figure 3.2b).

When radiation strikes the surface of a body, it is reflected, transmitted or absorbed. The sum of the reflectance R, the transmittance T and the absorptance A is unity, that is R + T + A = 1; this relationship is described in Figure 3.2b.

The sun is a large, hot star with an effective surface temperature of about 6000 K. The surface of the sun has similar characteristics to those of a black body obeying Planck's law,

Figure 3.1 *(Opposite)*
Structural glass prisms, Christian Theological Seminary, Indianapolis, USA
Glass design: James Carpenter
Architects: Edwards Larrabee Barnes and Associates

'These windows transmit light into the chapel's high spaces, making the room a reflecting vessel. The 30 ft high glass blades are stabilized with horizontal panels or stiffeners of dichroic glass, making an all glass structure. Two reflected and two transmitted images are projected from each glass section, creating reflection and transmission patterns of great and changing complexity over the course of the day. The colours change as natural light moves into the room from the south west, from noon to sunset, tracking a subtle and complicated path through the space'. (James Carpenter)

Figure 3.2b Nature of radiant energy

The total rate of radiant energy Q (W/m^2) emitted by a body at absolute temperature T (K) is given by the Stefan–Boltzmann law $Q = E\sigma T^4$ (W/m^2), where E is the total emissivity of the surface integrated over a hemisphere, and σ is the Stefan–Boltzmann constant, equal to 5.67×10^{-8} W/m^{2}K^4.

Absolute temperature, in degrees kelvin, is measured on the thermodynamic temperature scale. Absolute zero is the theoretical temperature at which all the atomic particles of a material are at rest and have zero thermal energy. The zero point of the Celsius scale, where pure ice starts to melt, coincides with the absolute temperature of 273.2 K.

The distribution of radiant energy with wavelength is given by Planck's law

$$Q_\lambda = C_1 \lambda^{-5}/(e^{C_2/\lambda T} - 1) \quad \text{W/m}^2 \text{ nm}$$

where Q_λ is the rate of radiant energy emission per unit wavelength interval (nm), λ is the wavelength, T is the absolute temperature (K), C_1 and C_2 are constants and e is the exponential number.

The radiation received by a surface is governed by the equation $R + T + A = 1$.

where R (reflectance) is the proportion of the incident radiant energy that is reflected by the body, T (transmittance) is the proportion transmitted through the body, and A (absorptance) is the proportion absorbed by the body.

A corollary of this equation and Kirchhoff's law (which states that, at any given wavelength λ, $A(\lambda) = E(\lambda)$, where E is the emissivity) is that when $T = 0$, $A(\lambda) = 1 - R$; therefore $1 - R = E(\lambda)$.

In the particular case of a black body, $R(\lambda) = 0$; therefore $A(\lambda) = 1$ and $E(\lambda) = 1$.

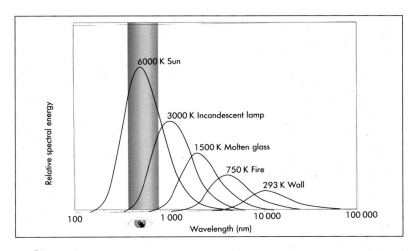

Figure 3.3 Spectral energy distribution for various black body temperature curves

The energy in thermally sourced electromagnetic radiation is governed by the Planck equation for a black body. The figure shows the characteristic spectral energy distributions from surfaces at very high temperatures (6000 K) at short wavelengths down to ambient glass surface temperatures (293 K). The following table gives a range of temperatures corresponding to various 'hot' surfaces:

Temperature		Typical surfaces
K	°C	
6000	5727	sun
3000	2727	incandescent lamp
1500	1227	molten glass
750	477	domestic fire
293	20	wall

The significance of radiation exchange in normal temperature heat transfer processes, where it is conventionally termed long wave radiation exchange, is often unappreciated. Nonetheless, it plays a major role in glazing system heat exchanges, and in other areas such as influencing human comfort.

and emits electromagnetic radiation with the solar spectral distribution shown in Figure 3.4.

A narrow band, between 380 nm and 780 nm, of the solar spectrum received at the earth's surface is visible to the eye, whilst the radiation below 380 nm (ultraviolet) and between 780 nm and about 3000 nm (near infrared) and beyond is invisible. The combined wavelengths of the visible spectrum give a white colour, whilst each individual wavelength has an associated colour.

Figure 3.4
Spectral graph of solar energy

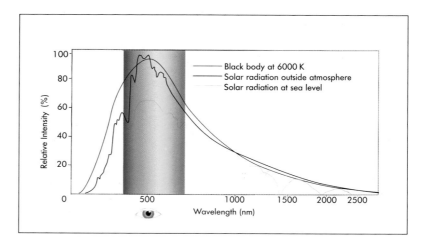

All electromagnetic radiation striking any surface is either transmitted or reflected. The part transmitted through the surface may be absorbed. For opaque materials, all the absorption effectively occurs at, or very close to, the surface. With ordinary clear glass, solar radiation is transmitted with low absorption (Figure 3.5).

Reflected radiation may be diffuse, specular or a mixture of both depending on the nature of the surface and the wavelength of the radiation. Thus, the same surface may reflect diffusely at short wavelengths and specularly at long wavelengths.

With visible radiation, the colour of an opaque surface

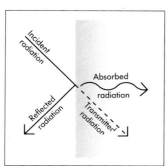

Figure 3.5
Reflection, absorption and transmission at a surface

38

depends on the relative amounts of radiation reflected and absorbed at each wavelength. For example, a red surface reflects the 'red' wavelengths and absorbs the remaining wavelengths.

All the radiation absorbed produces heat (though in some special circumstances certain wavelengths also excite molecular resonances, giving rise to fluorescence). Heat flows from higher temperatures to lower temperatures. Therefore the heat produced by absorption raises the temperature of the material beneath the surface, which is then either conducted into the material or dissipated from the surface to the surroundings by reradiation, conduction and convection. The reradiation will generally be at a longer wavelength than the incident radiation.

LIGHT

Daylight or visible light refers to the narrow band of the electromagnetic spectrum with wavelengths from about 380 nm to 780 nm (Figure 3.6).

The colour of light depends on its spectral composition within this band, which can be plotted as a spectral energy distribution curve (Figure 3.7).

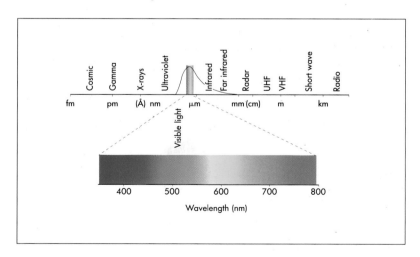

Figure 3.6
Electromagnetic spectrum

Figure 3.7
Spectral energy transmission curve
with a dominant peak in the visible
band

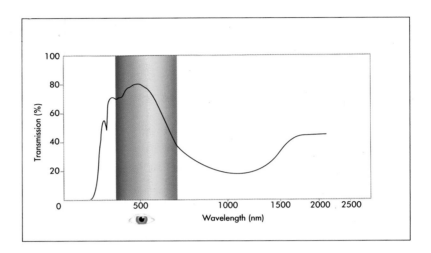

COLOUR TEMPERATURE

Colour can also be described in terms of colour temperature. The colour temperature of a light source is the temperature in kelvin (K) of a black body which, when emitting light, matches the colour of the light source.

CORRELATED COLOUR TEMPERATURE

Colour temperature strictly applies only to black body emitters. The colour of everyday objects can be described in terms of correlated colour temperature (CCT), which is the temperature of a black body emission nearest in appearance to the colour of that everyday object. Colours correspond to the following black body colour temperatures:

- red: 800 to 900 K
- white: 5000 K
- blue: 6000 to 10 000 K

A light source such as a cloudy sky would have a CCT value of 4500 to 6500 K, while that for a clear sky would be in the range 6000 to 10 000 K (because of the scattering of blue light in the atmosphere).

COLOUR MEASUREMENT

The measurement of colour is based on the principle that any

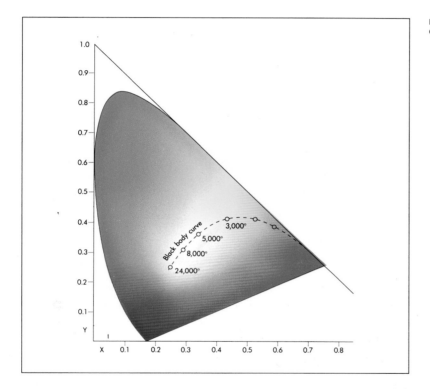

Figure 3.8a
CIE chromaticity chart

The chart provides a graphical means of comparing colours. It was adopted by the CIE in 1931 to standardize the way in which colours could be specified without reference to colour samples.

Colours are specified by their hue, saturation and luminance. The three components, combined via a mathematical formula, determine the chromaticity values. The colour is specified by the proportion of the three primary colours (red, green and blue). The strength of the resulting colour is determined by the saturation. The brightness is determined by the luminance.

Hues are distributed aroun he periphery according to their wavelength spread. The area assigned to each hue (green occupies a larger area than blue or red) takes the spectral sensitivity of the human eye into account. The position occupied by a colour on the diagram indicates the greenness or redness or blueness. White or 'neutral', which is made up of equal proportions of red, green and blue, occupies the centre of the diagram. Every colour can be interpreted in terms of its x, y, z coordinates plotted on the chromaticity chart. These values can be used to evaluate a colour sample which is illuminated by a standard light source. To specify a colour only two of the coefficients need to be known, since $x + y + z = 1$.

Figure 3.8b
CIELAB chromaticity diagram

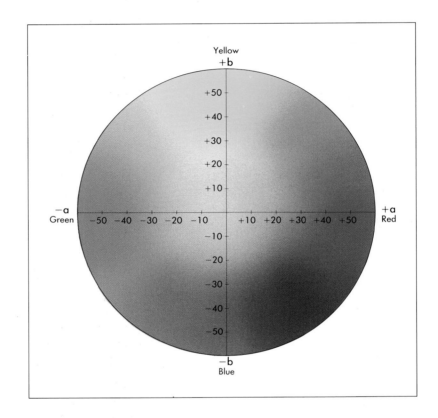

In 1976 the CIE adopted a modified chromaticity diagram, known as CIELAB, in which the spaces allocated to each colour on the diagram are nearly equal. This classification procedure is particularly useful since it has been incorporated in commercially available colour measuring equipment, which will accept a colour sample and produce a virtually instantaneous printout of the colour analysis. It is often used by the glass industry.

colour can be matched by a suitable mixture of light from the three primary sources – red, green and blue.

The definitions of the primary sources and the framework of the measurement method were defined by the Commission Internationale de l'Eclairage (CIE) in 1931. The usual way of representing colour measurement is to use the CIE chromaticity diagrams (Figures 3.8a, b). The centre of the diagram (Figure 3.8a) represents neutral, that is grey or white, and all other points represent colours either close to neutral (unsaturated colours) or further from neutral (more saturated colours) until the pure spectral colours are reached around the periphery of the diagram.

The third dimension of colour which usually goes with the CIE chromaticity diagram is the luminance Y, a measure of the amount of light in the colour.

Light in and around buildings will be modified by reflections from the surroundings, whilst light from the sun will mix with light reflected from buildings, the ground and other landscape features.

Some surfaces have practically the same reflectance for all wavelengths of light and do not change the spectral composition of light after reflection. Most surfaces, however, exhibit selective reflection properties, by absorbing or transmitting certain wavelengths of the incident light. In these instances, the spectral composition of the reflected or transmitted light provides a different colour.

RESPONSE OF THE EYE

The colour sensation experienced by the eye depends on the spectral composition of the light received, and on the sensitivity of the eye to different wavelengths in the visible spectrum. The response of the human eye varies with wavelength according to the 'standard observer response curve' as adopted by the CIE in 1931 (Figure 3.9).

Figure 3.9
CIE luminous efficacy curve

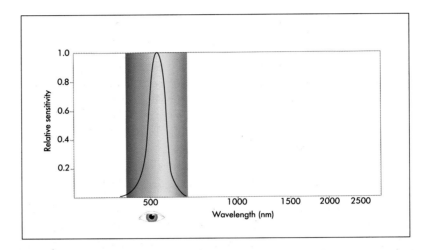

Figure 3.10
Detail in structural glass prism from
Figure 3.1

PERCEIVED COLOUR

The perceived colour of an object is determined by:

- the spectral distribution of the light incident upon it
- the extent to which certain parts of the visible spectrum are reflected, transmitted or absorbed by the object.

The perceived colour is also affected by psychological considerations of eye and brain.

MODIFICATION OF LIGHT BY GLASS

Glass allows the transmission of light. The extent to which this transmission can be modified depends upon the optical properties of the material. The modifying mechanisms occur principally by reflection and absorption.

REFLECTANCE

This occurs when the surface of a material reflects an incident beam of light. As shown in the following, reflections can be specular, diffuse or a mixture of the two.

Reflectance expresses the fraction of incident radiation reflected by the glass.

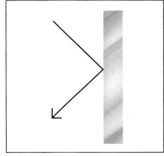

Figure 3.11
Specular reflection

Specular Reflection

If a material surface is microscopically smooth and flat, such as float glass, the incident and reflected light rays make the same angle with a normal to the reflecting surface, producing specular reflection (Figure 3.11).

Diffuse Reflection

If a material has a 'rough' surface, that is if it is not microscopically smooth, diffuse reflections will occur. Each ray of light falling on a small particle of the surface will obey the basic law of reflection but, because these particles are randomly oriented, the reflections will be randomly distributed (Figure 3.12). A perfect diffusely reflecting surface would in practice reflect light equally in all directions, giving a perfect matt finish.

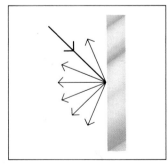

Figure 3.12
Diffuse reflection

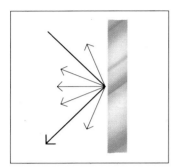

Figure 3.13
Spread reflection

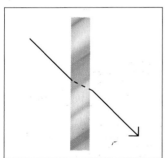

Figure 3.14
Geometry of refraction through glass.

The diagram illustrates a ray of light passing from air with a refractive index of 1.0 into a parallel faced pane of glass having a refractive index of 1.5, and back to air. The emerging ray is parallel to the incident ray but is displaced sideways from it.

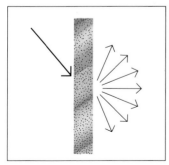

Figure 3.15
Diffusion through glass

Patterned or finely etched glass surfaces produce significant diffuse reflections. Finely textured glass is used in picture framing because its diffusing surface reduces specular reflections which, with normal float glass, can veil perception of the picture.

Spread Reflection

When an incident light beam produces a mixture of diffuse and specular reflections on glass, these are termed 'spread' or 'semi-diffuse' reflections. The incident ray of light is only partly reflected in a random manner, so that most of the reflection occurs in the same direction (Figure 3.13).

Corrugated, dimpled and etched surfaces will usually produce spread reflections.

ABSORPTANCE

This expresses the fraction of incident radiation absorbed. In other words, absorptance is that part of the incident light which is 'lost' in the body of the glass (Figure 3.14).

TRANSMITTANCE

This expresses the fraction of incident radiation directly transmitted through the glass. Transmittance is that part of the incident light remaining after reflection and absorption.

Transmitted light is subject to modification by refraction, diffusion and colouring (Figure 3.14).

Refraction

When light passes through one material and enters another with a different refractive index the velocity of the light changes. Except at normal angles of incidence, this causes a bending in the ray of light at the boundary (Figure 3.14).

Diffusion

This occurs when a transmitted ray of light is spread in many directions, either at the surface of the glass or by irregular reflection from particles within the glass (Figure 3.15).

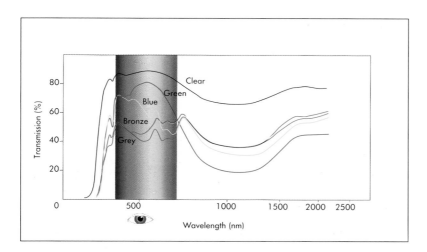

Figure 3.16
Examples of spectra for different
coloured glass

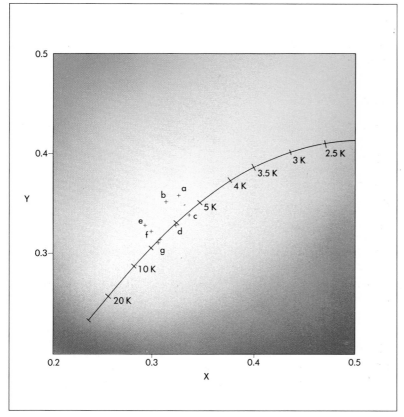

Figure 3.17
Enlarged central portion of CIE
chromaticity chart.

The curve is the Planckian locus
(black body curve) with
temperatures in kelvin.
a	coated azure	47/33
b	coated gold	26/22
c	body tinted bronze	27/47
d	body tinted bronze	50/62
e	body tinted green	61/51
f	body tinted green	72/62
g	body tinted grey	19/45
h	body tinted grey	42/60

Figure 3.18
Window with patterned glass

Colouring

Types of glass with special characteristics of light transmission and solar transmission are invariably coloured, sometimes as a result of changes introduced into the glass composition (body tinted) and sometimes by the application of surface coatings. Typical spectra are given in Figure 3.16.

Some types of glass exhibit strong colour characteristics when viewed by reflection but not when viewed by transmission. If the colour coordinates of the transmitted light for the various glass types are plotted on a CIE chromaticity chart, they cluster in the central area (Figure 3.17). This suggests they would not normally influence situations where internal colour rendering or colour discrimination is important; this is discussed in the following chapter.

BIBLIOGRAPHY

Billmeyer, F.W. Jr and Saltzman, M. *Principles of Colour Technology*, 2nd edn, Wiley, 1981

Feynman, R.P. *The Strange Theory of Light and Matter*, Princeton University Press, Princeton, NJ, 1985

Gobrecht, H., Bergmann and Schaefer, *Textbook of Experimental Physics*, Vol 3, *Optics*, Walter de Gruyter, New York, 1987 (in German)

Gobrecht, H., Bergmann and Schaefer, *Textbook of Experimental Physics*, Vol 1, *Mechanics, Acoustics and Heat*, Walter de Gruyter, New York, 1990 (in German)

Gösele, K. and Schüle, W., *Sound, Heat, Humidity*, Vol 75, 8th edn, Bauverlag GmbH, Wiesbaden and Berlin, 1985 (in German)

Henderson, S.T. *Daylight and its Spectrum*, Adam Hilger, Bristol, 1970

Hopkinson, R.G., Petherbridge, P. and Longmore, J. *Daylighting*, Heinemann, London, 1966

Petzold, Marusch, Schramm, *Glass as a Material*, 3rd edn, Verlag fur Bauwesen, Berlin, 1990 (in German)

CHAPTER 4

View Out and View In

Without a glass palace
Life becomes a burden.
Glass opens up a new age
Brick building only does harm.

Scheerbart, *Glasarchitektur*, 1914

Windows are the eyes of a building; they provide a view out. To the outside observer, windows also provide information on much of the building's character and content. Both view out and view in are included here, because their design involves the same considerations of glass and window (Figures 4.2, 4.3).

Window design for view out is not considered in detail. Briefly, it involves: content of the outside scene, height above ground level, window area, window shape and disposition, and spectator position and activity.

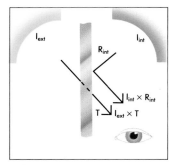

Figure 4.4
Light transmission, reflection and
illuminance, internal (the perception
of the internal viewer)

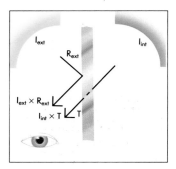

Figure 4.5
Light transmission, reflection and
illuminance, external (the
perception of the external viewer)

Design for view through glass, however, is considered in detail below. It involves:

- light transmission and reflection
- colour
- obscuration.

GLASS LIGHT TRANSMISSION AND REFLECTION

TRANSMISSION, REFLECTION AND ILLUMINANCE

The lower the light transmission of the glass, the more the occupant may become conscious of its presence. However, this transmission may be as low as 5%, and still provide a view out.

Generalizations about view through glass are influenced by properties of light transmittance and reflectance interacting with the luminances (brightness) of the internal and external scenes. That interaction can create veiling reflections on the glass which can, to varying degrees, obscure the view through the glass.

View in and view out may be considered in terms of the following parameters:

- internal luminance I_{int}
- external luminance I_{ext}
- glass internal light reflectance R_{int}
- glass external light reflectance R_{ext}
- glass light transmittance T.

The internal perception of the view out varies in accordance with the expression

$$\frac{I_{int} \ R_{int}}{I_{ext} \ T}$$

For the external perception of the view in, the expression is

$$\frac{I_{ext} \ R_{ext}}{I_{int} \ T}$$

These expressions are shown in Figures 4.4 and 4.5. In the USA, the expressions are termed the masking ratio and the observation ratio respectively.

When the external illuminances are high, such as on a bright day, internal veiling reflections will have little effect on the view out. However, as the daylight fails, the interior illuminances produce increasingly significant internal veiling reflections. This veiling is enhanced by higher internal reflectances and lower light transmittances of the glass. It is diminished by dimming the internal illuminance (turning the light off to view the night scene) and by higher outside illuminances.

When the external illuminances are significantly greater than those inside, external veiling reflections usually obscure the view in; this can occur even with clear float glass. When the lighting conditions are reversed, for example at night, the view

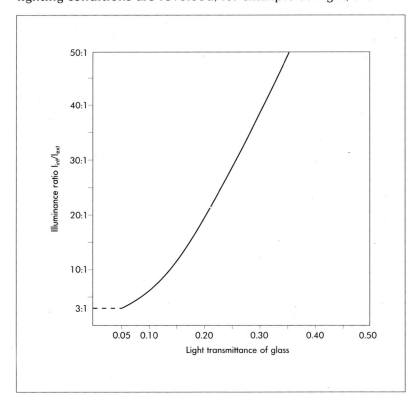

Figure 4.6
Relationship between glass light transmittance and illuminance ratio for view in or view out on either side of a one-way vision condition

The diagram assumes normal incidence, when the effect of veiling reflections on the transmission properties of the glass will be at a minimum. At more oblique viewing angles, the reflective properties of the glass surface will play an increasing part in reducing the visibility through the glass, and as a result the illuminance ratios could be diminished without impairing the one-way vision condition. It is important to realize that the light transmission of windows is determined by a combination of reflection and absorption properties.

Figure 4.7 *(and opposite)*
Stadt Bibliotek, Berlin, Germany
Architects: Moore, Ruble, Yudell

Figure 4.8
One-way observation windows,
Pilkington Glass Ltd, St Helens, UK

One-way transparent security
windows permit observer vision of a
security area (the observed side), yet
the observer remains unseen. For
these applications, the lighting
should be evenly distributed on the
observed side. On the observing
side, lighting should be dim and
shaded from the observed side.

in becomes clearly visible (Figure 4.7).

The approximate relationship between internal and external illuminances is illustrated in Figure 4.6. It enables (for a given ratio of inside to outside illuminances) the glass transmission properties to be determined for the case where the view out would be totally eliminated. This effect is exploited in one-way transparent windows (Figures 4.8, 4.9).

Figure 4.9 Performance of one-way vision glass (Libbey Owens Ford Co.)

Nominal thickness	Glass substrate	Visible T	Visible R	Recommended ratio of illuminances	Correct glazing
6mm	Grey	12%	60%	10:1	Mirror coating towards observed side

REFLECTANCE

The reflectance of most types of glass increases as the viewing angle departs from the normal; the more oblique the angle, the stronger the reflection and the more obscured the view through any glass (Figure 4.10).

Reflections of the sunlight from glass can never be as bright as direct sunlight, but where reflections may be perceived as a problem, computational prediction methods can establish the geometry of the reflected sunlight from the building façade on to adjacent areas and observers (Figure 4.11).

A further consideration is the quality of the reflected image. Float glass is optically very flat, but processing, glazing and mechanical loading can create distortions of reflection which are particularly apparent on the building façade (Figure 4.12).

Where it is important to minimize reflections, the amount of light reflected at a glass surface can be reduced considerably by the application of a thin transparent coating having a thickness comparable with one-quarter of the wavelength of the

Figure 4.10
Oblique viewing angles/reflectance

The more oblique the viewing
angle, the greater the reflectance.

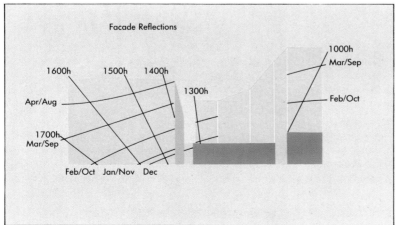

Facade Reflections

1600h   1500h   1400h

Apr/Aug

1300h

1000h
Mar/Sep

1700h
Mar/Sep

Feb/Oct

Feb/Oct   Jan/Nov   Dec

Figure 4.11
Computer prediction output of
reflected sunlight with sunpath
overlays.

Computer programs enable the user
to predict the occasions when an
observer may see the reflected sun
in the windows or reflective
cladding of adjacent buildings. The
user describes the observer's
position, in relation to the building
in question, for the particular
latitude, as an input value to the
program. The program computes the
solar geometry and superimposes
sunpaths and hour lines over the
projection of the building, as seen
from the observer's point of view.

Figure 4.12   Normal distorted reflected images, Weena Huis, Amsterdam, Holland
Architects: Architectenburo Quist BV, Rotterdam, Holland

Distortion may be caused by a variety of normal factors. During toughening (tempering), the induced stresses are not perfectly uniform, and the resulting small mismatches of stress can cause distortion or bowing. Vertically toughened glass is supported by hanging tongs at the top edge during toughening; these grip the heated, softened glass to produce 'tong marks'. Horizontally toughened glass is processed on rollers, which may result in a slight waviness. With laminated glass, distortion may be present as the gap between the leaves may not be parallel (if toughened or curved glass is used) or, in the case of resin interlayers, the applied pressure may deflect the glass before setting. Glass can also be distorted by an imposed load, such as frame clamping pressures, and the distortion is apparent by reflection. It is sometimes possible to minimize this distortion, but it cannot be eliminated completely. There may also be temporary distortions, such as those produced by wind loading.

A double glazed unit is hermetically sealed at a particular pressure. As the normal atmospheric pressure outside the unit changes, this pushes both panes outwards or inwards in the centre, but the edges, restrained by attachment to the edge seal, move little, resulting in bowing or dishing. In addition, the temperature of double glazed units, and the enclosed gas, change due to variations in ambient external temperature and absorbed solar radiation. Such temperature variations cause the enclosed gas to expand or contract (since the unit is sealed at one particular temperature and pressure), again resulting in bowing or dishing. The effects of bowing or dishing can be calculated.

light being controlled. This is known as an 'anti-reflection coating'. Typically, reflection at normal incidence can be reduced from 8% for float glass to below 1%. Owing to the coating, light which is reflected from the glass surface optically interferes with light reflected from the coating surface, resulting in a diminished reflection. However, the amount of residual reflection depends on the angle of view.

GLASS COLOUR

INTERNAL COLOUR APPEARANCE

Transmitted colour is produced from tints in the body of the glass and from coatings, which are usually introduced to attenuate solar radiation.

Tinted glass colours, when plotted on the CIE chromaticity chart, indicate a 'neutrality', and research into occupant satisfaction suggests little comment concerning their effect on the colour of the outside view. This holds true only as long as there is no visual reference to unmodified daylight, such as might be seen through an open window or through clear glass. Without such a reference, the eye adapts rapidly to the colour of light received through glazing (Figure 4.13).

Cooper, Hardy and Wiltshire (1972) of Newcastle University, UK, conducted a series of experiments in existing offices, where occupant response to various types of installed tinted glass was obtained. It was concluded that no major differences in the perceived satisfaction with the view out, or in the perceived attractiveness of the internal environment, were introduced by varying the glass colour (Figure 4.14). Similar conclusions would be expected from transmitted light through coated glass in view of their similar colour locations on the CIE chromaticity chart.

However, a room's interior decorative treatment also has an effect on the recognition and discrimination of colours. This was confirmed by experiments conducted in hospitals, and in experiments to determine the colour rendering and discrimination properties of glass types and artificial light sources.

Figure 4.14 Conclusions from Newcastle University research

'It has been hypothesized that some glass types would distort the perceived range of colours when looking through them. Bronze glass was expected to have a "warming" effect and green glass a "cooling" effect. It was clear that this did not occur even though such differences are clearly visible if the glass types are compared directly together. It would appear that perceptual adaptation is compensating for the distorted spectrum when people's view of the outside is exclusively through tinted glass.'

'The respondents were also required to make judgements of the warmth and attractiveness of colours within the office, both close to the window and well away from it. Tests on the attractiveness of the colours within the office show no differences between glass types, from which it can be inferred that no serious colour distortions were introduced by the glass tints.' (Cooper, Hardy and Wiltshire 1972)

Figure 4.13 (Opposite)
Jacob K. Javits Convention Center, New York, USA
Architects: Pei, Cobb, Freed & Partners
Glass: Pittsburgh Plate Glass Co., USA

This exhibition hall, the world's largest under a single roof, is clad in a solar control glass which is not easily perceived as such by the occupant until the higher transmission glass is revealed as shown here adjacent to the entrance.

EXTERNAL COLOUR APPEARANCE

Most float glass products contain small amounts of iron oxide which produce a green tint usually only perceived when the glass pane is viewed 'on edge'. Additional iron oxide is introduced to produce green tint, cobalt oxide for grey tint and selenium oxide for bronze tint. To produce a blue tint additional cobalt oxide is added to the float glass composition. These products are perceived as giving weak colours by transmitted light. They do not produce high or significantly coloured reflectances. Usually their principal external visual characteristic is their lower light transmission.

Coated glass products with high light reflectances can exhibit stronger exterior colours than those of body tinted glass. Transmitted light through the glass, from the building interior, diminishes the perceived effect of these reflected external colours of coated glass. Conversely, such light increases the perceived transmitted colours. Since most coated reflective glass products also exhibit colour by transmission, the transmitted coloured light from the building interior will also be seen externally in conjunction with the reflected colours (Figure 4.15) producing complicated colour appearances.

For special architectural applications, specialist glass manufacturers change the glass formulations to exclude most of the iron oxides in the mix, with the result that a 'white' glass is produced which also has a proportionately higher light transmission than standard clear float glass. A comparison between standard clear float and 'clear white' glass spectra is given in Figure 4.16, with an application of clear white glass in Figure 4.17.

Figure 4.15
Technologie Zentrum, Dortmund, Germany
Architects: HBA, Walter Koppka

Figure 4.16
Standard float and clear white float spectra

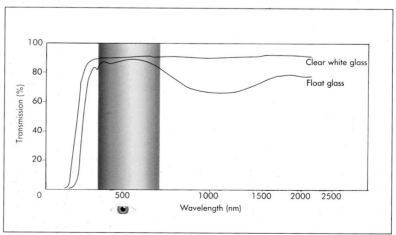

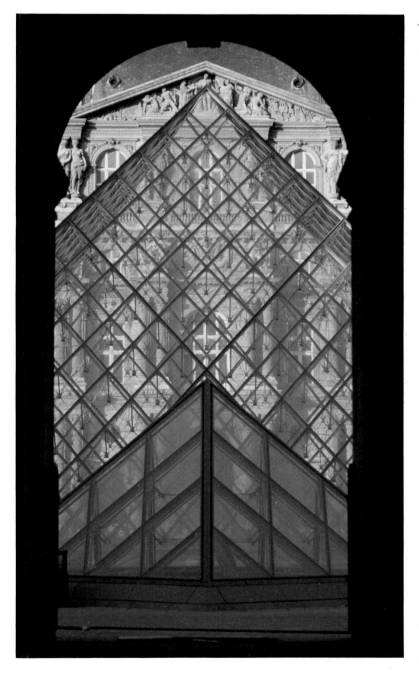

Figure 4.17
Grand Louvre, Paris, France
Architects: Pei Cobb Freed &
Partners
Glass: St. Gobain

Unlike commercially available glass,
in which iron oxides produce a
noticeable green tint, the pyramid is
clad in a specially produced 10 mm
glass using a negligible iron oxide
mix. The glass was subsequently
ground and polished in the UK and
then two panes were laminated to
form the structural silicone fixed
panels.

GLASS OBSCURATION

Obscuration of the view through glass can be achieved either in the body or on the surface of the glass. Obscuration may be required for reasons other than modifying the quality of view (for example, screen printing for solar control), but such applications are dealt with in other chapters.

Various materials are used to produce body effects, such as micro-louvres in a laminate.

Surface based obscuration techniques usually rely on modifying reflections and/or transmissions or introducing surface scattering. They include:

- patterning
- treatment (acid etching and sand blasting)
- printing.

SURFACE PATTERNED GLASS

Reflection and diffusion, in combination, are present in surface patterned glass products. The depth, size and shape of the pattern largely determine the magnitude and direction of reflection. The surface finish determines the degree of diffusion. The interplay between diffusion and reflection influences the degree of 'sparkle' (by specular reflection) and obscuration.

Patterned glass usually transmits only slightly less light than clear glass. The more diffusing the glass, the more the directional properties of light transmitted by the glass will be diminished, and the more likely it might become a glare source, when its whole surface may appear bright.

Patterned glass products may be graded subjectively for obscuration (Figure 4.18).

SURFACE TREATMENTS

Sand blasting and acid etching are examples of surface treatments. They produce uniform, relatively matt appearances and surface reflection properties that approach those of a perfect diffuser. The appearance of a surface treated glass is

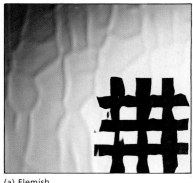

Figure 4.18
Patterned glass with various grades of obscuration, Pilkington Glass Ltd, St Helens, UK

(a) Flemish

(b) Rough cast

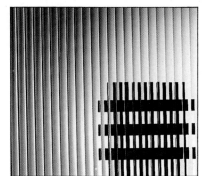

(c) Reeded.

influenced by the relative level of illuminance on either side of the glass. Whilst this appearance is mainly for decoration, such materials can also be graded for their obscuration (Figure 4.19).

SURFACE PRINTING

Surface printing can be typically by screen printed dots, lines or meshes (Figure 4.20). These can contain fine detail which, when viewed from a distance, produces a light veiling effect, like a net curtain. This veiling effect still allows the view to be perceived.

Figure 4.19
Surface treated glass with various
grades of obscuration

Glass: T. W. Ide, London

(a) Bromesh on clear glass

(b) Bromesh on tone

(c) Sponge stipple on clear

(d) Sponge stipple obscured

(e) Medium stipple obscured

(f) Large stipple obscured

(g) Medium bright stipple

(h) Large bright stipple

(i) Satin etched

(j) Semi-tone etched

(k) White acid.

Figure 4.20
Standard patterning designs

(a) 20% dots, 2 mm dia, 2 mm apart

(b) 40% dots, 3.6 mm dia, 1.5 mm apart

(c) 80% mesh, 2 mm dia, 2 mm apart

(d) 60% mesh, 3.6 mm dia, 1.5 mm apart

(e) Table of performance

Light transmission and printed cover for 6 mm single clear float:

Cover (%)	20	40	60	80
Transmission (%)	75	62	49	37

The level of obscuration in this veiling effect depends upon:

- The light transmission, determined by the proportion of surface covered by the printing.

- The pattern design.

- The combination of the light reflectance of the printing and the relative illuminances either side of the glass. A light coloured printing with a high illuminance on the observing side will produce high veiling obscuration, which is used to diminish the daytime view into buildings.

- The distance of the observer from the glass surface. The closer is the observer, the more discernible are the details of pattern. More distant observation results in an overall veiling in light and colour (Figure 4.21).

Screen printing provides the benefit of bespoke design (Figures 4.22, 4.23).

Figure 4.21
Stockley Park, Hayes, UK
Architect: Ian Ritchie

Figure 4.22
Screen printed façade panels,
Frankfurter Messturm, Frankfurt am
Main, Germany
Architects: Murphy/Jahn Inc.,
Chicago/Frankfurt

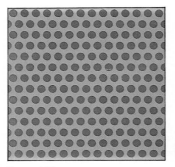

Figure 4.23
Details of panels in Figure 4.22

BIBLIOGRAPHY

CIBSE *Window design*, application manual, Chartered Institution of Building Services Engineers, 1987

Cooper, J.R., Hardy, A.C. and Wiltshire, T.J. *Attitudes towards the Use of Heat Rejecting Low Light Transmission Glasses in Office Buildings*, research project report, School of Architecture, University of Newcastle, 1972

Cuttle, C. *The Use of Special Performance Glazing Materials in Modern Offices*, MA thesis, University of Manchester, 1974

Glass and Glazing Federation, *Glazing Manual*, 1990

Keighley, E.C. 'Visual requirements and reduced fenestration in office buildings', *Building Science*, 8, 311, 1973

Lam William, M.C. *Sunlighting as Formgiver for Architecture*, Van Nostrand Reinhold, 1985

Ludlow, A.M. 'The functions of windows in buildings', *Lighting Research and Technology*, 8, 1976

Waldron, J.M. 'A manual of perspective for lighting engineers', *Lighting Research and Technology*, 14, 65, 1982

Figure 4.24
Paul Birkbeck, *Porky's Last Walk*

CHAPTER 5

Daylight

Light is of decisive importance in experiencing architecture. The same room can be made to give very different spatial impressions by a simple expedient of changing the size and locations of its openings. Moving a window from the middle of a wall to a corner will utterly transform the entire character of the room.

To most people a good light means only much light. If we do not see a thing well enough we simply demand more light. And very often we find that it does not help because the quantity of light is not nearly as important as its quality.

Steen Rasmussen, *Experiencing Architecture*

Figure 5.1 *(Opposite)*
East wall, Ronchamp Chapel, France
Architect: Le Corbusier

Figure 5.2
Sketch by Le Corbusier

The quantity and quality of daylight change with location, time of day, time of year and weather conditions. These changes in the nature of daylight, when exploited, provide interest and variation in the appearance of a building's interior. However, this variable nature creates design difficulties.

Figure 5.3
View of the sky, Jacob K. Javits
Convention Center, New York, USA
Architects: Pei, Cobb, Freed and
Partners

Many prediction methods are available to aid designers in the use of daylight to provide lighting for amenity, for tasks and to contribute to energy efficiency.

SOURCES OF DAYLIGHT

To produce reliable daylight prediction methods, the spectral and luminance distributions of the sky have been measured and standardized for different parts of the world.

In high latitude temperate areas such as Northern and Central Europe, an overcast sky is assumed as a basis of daylighting design because this type of sky occurs frequently in winter and is not uncommon in summer.

In middle latitude temperate coastal areas, such as the Mediterranean, clear skies are experienced in summer, with few overcast days in winter. These areas also experience clear blue skies with high amounts of direct sunshine, and therefore protection from direct sunshine tends to be more important than the admission of daylight (which can rely upon reflected sunshine).

Three types of design sky are in general use, and two of these have been adopted by the Commission Internationale de l'Eclairage (CIE), each with its own spectral distribution and luminance distribution. The three types are:

- the CIE standard overcast sky
- the CIE clear sky
- the blue sky.

SPECTRAL DISTRIBUTIONS

Design sky spectral distributions are shown in Figure 5.4.

LUMINANCE DISTRIBUTIONS

The luminance distributions of the overcast sky and the clear sky have been standardized by the CIE (1972). All of the luminance distributions are based on measurements of real sky conditions at various locations over many years.

The CIE overcast sky is assumed to have sufficient cloud

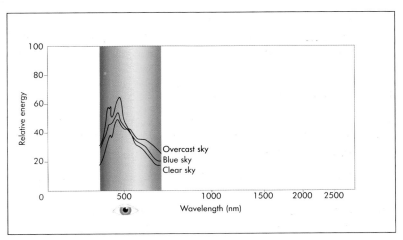

Figure 5.4
Spectral distributions of CIE
standard overcast sky, CIE clear sky,
and blue sky

cover to eliminate any direct sunlight. As a result there are no orientation effects. The overhead (zenith) luminance is three times that at the horizon (Figure 5.5a).

The CIE clear sky has a luminance distribution which varies with orientation, latitude and time of day depending on the position of the sun (Figure 5.5b). The luminance distribution is higher at the horizon than at the zenith.

The blue sky (Figure 5.6) is much the same as the CIE clear sky, and is referred to in some natural lighting publications produced prior to the definition of the CIE clear sky.

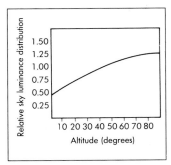

Figure 5.5a
Luminance distribution of CIE
standard overcast sky

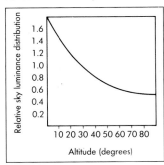

Figure 5.5b
Luminance distribution of CIE clear
sky

DAYLIGHT PREDICTION

Daylight prediction for interior spaces is usually based on 'daylight factor' concepts, although in the United States the 'lumen method' is frequently used. A wide variety of daylight prediction methods exists and there are 58 listed in CIE (1970).

DAYLIGHT FACTORS

The daylight factor is a ratio, expressed as a percentage, of the illuminance at a point on a given internal plane due to light received directly and indirectly from a sky of known or assumed luminance distribution, to the illuminance on a horizontal plane from an unobstructed hemisphere of the sky.

Figure 5.6
Luminance distribution of blue sky,
Stockholm, 2 October 1953, solar time
1425–1450
The unit of luminance (brightness) is
the foot lambert (ft L), a non-metric
unit which has now been superseded
by the candela per square metre (cd/
m²); the conversion is 1 ft L = 3.426
cd/m².

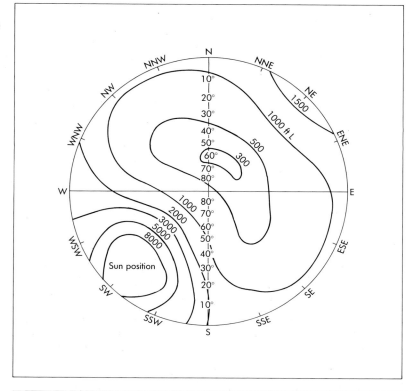

Figure 5.7
View of blue sky, Aquatoll
Neckarsulm, Germany
Architects: Kohlmeier & Bechler,
Heilbronn

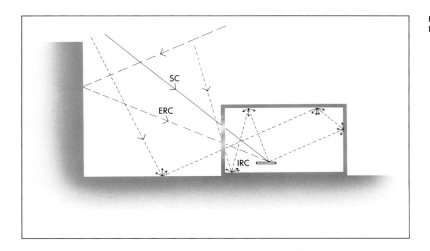

Figure 5.8
Daylight factor components

Sky component (SC): direct light from sky or sun. The ratio is expressed as a percentage of the component part of the illuminance at a point on a given plane that is received directly from a sky of assumed or known luminance distribution, to the illuminance on a horizontal plane due to an unobstructed hemisphere of the sky.

Externally reflected components (ERC): externally reflected light, received after reflection from the ground, building or other external surfaces. The ratio is expressed as a percentage of the component of the illuminance at a point on a given plane that is received directly after reflection from external obstructions under a sky of assumed or known luminance distribution, to the illuminance on a horizontal working plane due to an unobstructed hemisphere of the sky.

Internally reflected component (IRC): internally reflected light, received after being reflected from inside the room. The ratio is expressed as a percentage of the component of the illuminance at a point on a given plane that is received after reflection from interior surfaces under a sky of assumed or known luminance distribution, to the illuminance on a horizontal plane due to an unobstructed hemisphere of the sky.

The daylight factor (Figure 5.8) comprises three components:

- sky component
- externally reflected component
- internally reflected component.

The daylight factor only gives the proportion of daylight from outside that reaches the interior of a building, and does not indicate the absolute level of illumination that will occur. In order to determine whether a particular daylight factor will give adequate illumination, for amenity or task lighting, it is necessary to know how the outdoor illumination varies with time of day, time of year and location.

Windows which have a view of the high altitude (overhead) areas of the overcast sky, with their high luminances, will admit more daylight to the interior. They risk becoming a source of glare, because of the higher luminance. With a clear or blue sky the opposite applies, but orientation effects also come into play.

Data are available in various forms for a variety of locations to assist in the advancement of a design solution; typical examples are given in Figures 5.9, 5.10 and 5.11.

Figure 5.9 Typical outdoor diffuse illumination from sky (excluding direct sunlight)

Latitude N or S degrees	Sky illuminance lux
0	17000
10	15000
20	13000
30	7000
40	6000
50	5000

The lux (or lumen/m^2) is the unit of illuminance of a surface, defined as the luminous flux reaching the surface perpendicularly per unit area.

The effective integration of daylight and artificial light is important to the energy efficiency of buildings. Since the CIE standard overcast sky assumes no orientation effects, the estimates of the daylight contribution can be in error. To correct for this, orientation factors have been derived to be applied to the daylight factors (Figure 5.12).

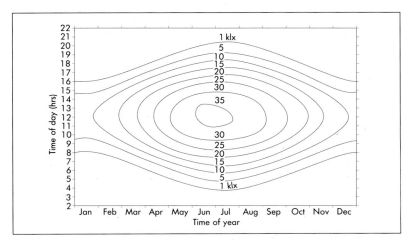

Figure 5.10
Availability of daylight

Measurements of outdoor daylight availability on a horizontal plane (mean horizontal diffuse illuminance from an unobstructed sky) were made at Kew in the UK. The range of daylight illumination was found to vary considerably with time of day and time of year (direct sunlight is excluded from the measurements). This diagram allows daylight factors calculated on the basis of the CIE standard overcast sky to be converted to illumination levels at specific times of the day and year. For example, a daylight factor of 2% provides an illumination level of about $25\,000 \times 0.02 = 500$ lux at noon at the end of March. At 6.30 in the evening on the same day, the illumination level from the same daylight factor is about $1000 \times 0.2 = 20$ lux. (On diagram, klx is abbreviation for kilolux.)

Figure 5.11
Availability of diffuse illumination
at various locations

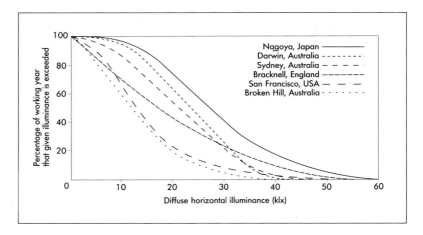

The diagram provides an indication for various locations of the proportion of the working day that a given diffuse illumination is exceeded on a horizontal working plane. The data provide the designer with a rapid indication of the periods of the day when natural lighting will provide adequate illumination, or alternatively the periods of the day when artificial lighting will be needed either as a supplement to natural light or as a replacement.

Figure 5.12 Orientation factors for overcast sky

Orientation	Correction factor	
	total	diffuse
North	0.77	0.97
East	1.02	1.15
South	1.67	1.55
West	1.08	1.21

The diffuse factor should be used when movable shading devices are incorporated in the window design.

USER REQUIREMENTS FROM DAYLIGHT

The building occupant has traditionally required daylight to work by, to enhance the visual quality of the interior and latterly to conserve electric lighting. Thus there are three user requirements:

- for task lighting
- for amenity lighting
- for energy conservation.

TASK LIGHTING

This involves the provision of adequate amounts of light to enable tasks (reading, machine operation, component assembly) to be performed.

The standards of daylight provision for task lighting are set out in various national codes of practice, or similar documents, and most are based on the provision of illumination on the working plane. Computational prediction techniques are available (Figure 5.13a, b). Task lighting cannot be provided by daylight alone for the entire working day throughout the year, and some form of artificial lighting is required to supplement the available daylight. The more demanding the task, the better the quality of the lighting should be.

The use of excessive glazed areas in an attempt to admit more daylight may give rise to solar overheating. The alleviation of this problem involves orientation, solar control and other key factors dealt with in Chapters 9 and 10.

AMENITY LIGHTING

Amenity lighting is concerned with the appearance of an interior and its contents.

Figure 5.13
Computational prediction of daylight factor

(a) The screen image shows a coloured array of daylight factors in plan, calculated for a given window area.

(b) Computer graphics allows the three-dimensional representation of natural lighting in both quantity and quality.

Amenity and task lighting may be provided simultaneously by daylighting or separately. Levels for amenity daylighting will generally be lower than those required for task lighting. Emphasis is placed on creating light, shade and interest to reveal shape and texture (Figure 5.14).

Figure 5.14
Church in Vuoksenniska, Finland,
1952.
Architect: Alvar Aalto

ENERGY CONSERVATION

The effective use of daylight through good window design can, by reducing reliance on artificial lighting, be one of the largest single means of saving energy.

Lighting design for energy conservation will involve the use of window specifications to admit daylight in an effective manner, whilst successfully integrating daylight and artificial lighting. This needs to take account of room shape, window orientation, occupancy patterns and tasks. The relationship of windows with surrounding buildings and other obstructions will be critical. As with task lighting, possible solar overheating may result and similar precautions must be taken.

GLASS PROPERTIES AND THEIR INFLUENCE ON DAYLIGHT QUANTITY AND QUALITY

GLASS LIGHT TRANSMISSION FOR TASK LIGHTING

The quantity of task lighting achieved is determined principally by the light transmission of glass (Figure 5.15) and the extent and size of the glazed area. However, the quality of the lighting, and its distribution, depend on the shape of the glazing, its position, its orientation (Figure 5.16) and the nature of the space to be daylit.

Clear glass with a light transmission of 87% when correctly positioned in a window wall, with little obstruction and light coloured interior decoration, will provide adequate daylighting to a depth of about 6 metres from the window (Figure 5.17). Changes in glass light transmission affect useful daylight penetration (Figure 5.18). If windows are placed in opposite walls then more than 12 metres of space can be effectively daylit.

Reducing the height of the window reduces the depth of daylight penetration, and changing its shape and distribution influences the lighting levels and quality (Figure 5.19).

If glass is used in a roof then a fairly even daylight distribution at the horizontal working plane is obtained providing that the spacing and profile of the rooflights are correctly specified (Figure 5.20).

Figure 5.15 Light transmission and daylight factor correction for various glazing materials

Glass type	Light transmittance	Correction factor
Clear 6 mm	0.87	1.00
Body tinted 6 mm:		
bronze	0.46	0.57
grey	0.39	0.48
green	0.66	0.83
Highly reflecting 6 mm	0.18	0.23
Double glazed units:		
6 mm clear + 6 mm clear	0.65	0.82
6 mm clear + 6 mm Low E	0.63	0.79
6 mm reflecting + 6 mm clear	0.26	0.33
6 mm highly reflecting		
+ 6 mm clear	0.15	0.19
Wired cast 6 mm	0.74	0.92

These correction factors are used in determining daylight factors when glazings other than clear 6 mm glass are specified.

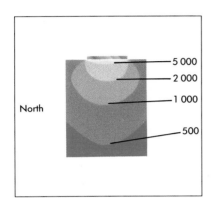

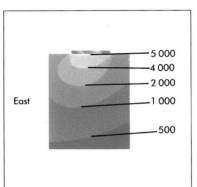

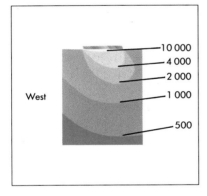

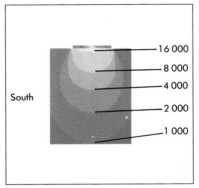

Figure 5.16
Effects of orientation on daylight distribution in a room when clear sky conditions prevail

The diagram shows different daylight distribution contours (illuminance in lux) experienced at noon in a room with differing window orientations, when illuminated by a CIE clear sky. The daylight distributions vary significantly with orientation, particularly the south facing example compared with the others. It is interesting to note the near symmetry of the east and west facing distributions. At other times of day the daylight contours vary still further.

Whenever the daylight distributions within a space are determined, it is important that regard is paid to the need for uniformity or variation, and whether the daylight provision is for amenity, task lighting, or a combination of the two. The need to supplement the available daylight with artificial lighting must also be considered.

Figure 5.18
Influence of glass transmission on
useful daylight penetration

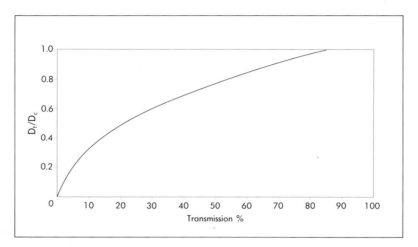

Figure 5.17
Daylight factor array from side window

(a)

(b)

The two diagrams above illustrate
how the penetration of daylight
factor (%) is influenced by the
width of a window in one wall.
When the window occupies the full
width of one wall as in (b), a much
more uniform distribution of
daylight occurs within the width of
the room, with less risk of dark or
gloomy corners, and with a deeper
penetration of useful daylight.

Window dimensions: (a) 1.71 m
wide, 1.95 m high (b) 3.45 m wide,
1.95 m high.
Room dimensions: 3.6 m wide, 3.1 m
high, 6.3 m deep.
Daylight factor contours are from a
CIE overcast sky.

A change in glass transmittance affects daylight levels in two ways.
First, the level of daylight illumination is reduced in strict ratio to the
light transmittance of the glass. Thus a point in an interior which
receives a daylight illuminance of 2.0% daylight factor with clear glass
(transmittance 0.84) only receives daylight factor1.0% if a glass with a
transmittance of 0.42 is used (the level is reduced by the factor 0.42/
0.84 = 0.5). Second, the penetration of daylight is affected but, as
halving the glass transmittance does not halve the depth of
penetration, the graph must be used.

For any glass transmittance a factor can be determined from the graph,
which can be applied to the distance from a window at which a given
daylight factor is achieved with clear glass. (D_t is depth of useful
daylight penetration with tinted glass, D_c is depth of useful daylight
penetration with clear glass.) For example, if a 2.0% daylight factor is
achieved 5 metres from a window glazed with clear glass, changing to
glass with a transmittance of 40% results in a 2.0% daylight factor being
achieved 3.5 m from the window (from the graph, for transmittance
40%, $D_t/D_c = 0.7$; new distance at which a 2% daylight factor is achieved
is 0.7 × 5.0 = 3.5 m).

Both the effects described above are related to the CIE standard
overcast sky, but could equally apply when a clear sky is used in
design. However, when a clear sky is used, the orientation of the
glazing additionally influences the daylight distribution.

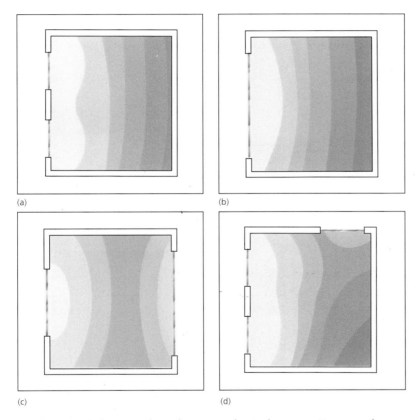

Figure 5.19
Daylight factor distribution under
overcast sky with varying window
positions in window wall

(a)

(b)

(c)

(d)

The area of glazing in these four examples is the same. However, they produce quite different daylight distributions in a room, depending on how the glazing is positioned and shaped.

(a) Shows the daylight factor distribution for glazing which is predominantly vertical and symmetrically positioned on either side of the centre line of the room, with relatively high window head.

(b) The glazing is arranged horizontally, with a lower window head than (a).

(c) The glazing is split between two opposite walls, resulting in a much more uniform distribution of daylight.

(d) The glazing is divided between two adjacent walls producing an asymmetrical distribution of daylight with a much lower daylight factor in one corner. As a result, the daylight distribution might be regarded as unsatisfactory for task illumination.

Figure 5.20
Daylight factors for different rooflight systems

Depending on the type of roof glazing profile, a particular glass to floor area ratio provides different average daylight factors. The simple 'shed' profile allows maximum daylight entry for a given glazed area. Sawtooth and monitor rooflight profiles generally allow less natural light into the interior for a given area of glazing, because arrays of such rooflights are likely to obstruct each other, resulting in the glazing not giving a 'clear view' of the sky.

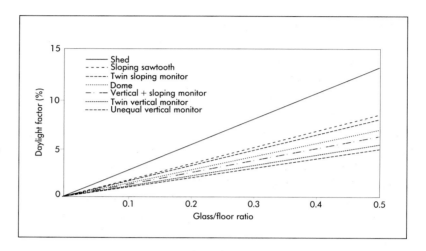

Figure 5.21
Jan Vermeer, *A Young Woman Standing at a Virginal* (National Gallery, London, UK)

'It is in Jan Vermeer's paintings that the lighting of Dutch interiors is best documented. Many of his pictures were painted in a room with windows stretching from one side wall to the other. Vermeer worked experimentally with the problems of natural light. His easel almost always stood in the same spot, with light coming from the left, and his usual background was a white washed wall parallel with the picture surface. In some of his paintings you see no more of the room than that one wall but nevertheless you are conscious of the entire room because it is reflected in the objects depicted. You are aware of the strong light coming from the left and reflections from the other walls give light and colour to the shadows, which are never colourless. Even when the painting shows only one figure against a light rear wall you experience an entire room.' (Rasmussen 1964)

GLASS LIGHT TRANSMISSION FOR AMENITY LIGHTING

The successful implementation of amenity lighting depends on the occupant's subjective judgement. Hence quantitative recommendations based on visual performance requirements may be irrelevant.

An observer's subjective judgement of acceptability of an interior, where recreation and social contact predominate, is based on the appearance of the furnishings and the other occupants. This is determined by the areas of light and shade giving shape and detail. Thus, the 'flow' of light within the interior and its intensity and distribution are particularly relevant.

An office worker's ability to do desk work is catered for if the correct design illumination level for task lighting is provided. However, the quality of the lighting (ranging from the intimate to the dramatic) will influence attitudes to colleagues, communication with them and general well-being.

Light may be considered as flowing through an interior (Figures 5.22, 5.23 and 5.24). If this flow is strong, an object which intercepts the flow appears modelled, that is it shows highly contrasting areas of light and shade (Figures 5.25, 5.26).

How this modelling appears depends on the direction of view and the relative strengths of shadow and highlight. A room with a side window, glazed with a glass of high light transmission, is regarded as adequately daylit, subject to the room depth and decorative treatment. In these circumstances, a strong flow of light and a variation in lighting pattern will be perceived. When the light transmission of the window glass is low, the level of natural lighting may be considered inadequate and the appearance of objects will be judged differently.

The variations in illumination pattern give daylight its unique desirable characteristics. The visual success of the overall lighting system is judged by the balance between 'directional'

Figure 5.22
Light flow due to natural lighting from a window

When the light transmission of the glazing is sufficiently high to provide adequate natural light, the flow characteristics are shown. The contour lines indicate the directional properties of the daylight, at different positions within the space.

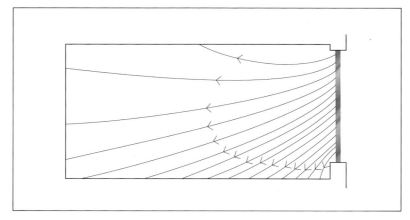

Figure 5.23
Light flow due to one row of fluorescent diffuse fittings

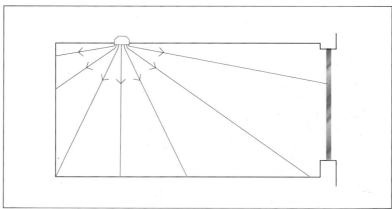

Figure 5.24
Light flow from a combination of daylight from a window and a ceiling mounted diffusing light fitting

When natural light and artificial light are used in combination, a compromise should be attempted by careful choice of luminaire, its position in relation to the glazing and its light contribution.

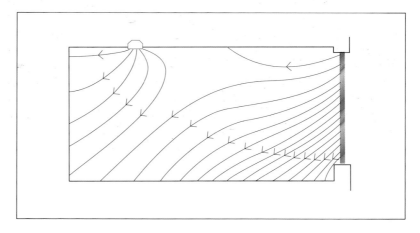

(a) (b)

Figure 5.25
Human head and modelling effects,
Pilkington Glass Ltd,
St Helens, UK

(a) Shows a human face illuminated
from above by a conventional
luminaire, the areas in shadow being
under the eyebrows, under the nose
and under the chin.
(b) Shows the same face, illuminated
from the side by daylight from a
window. The areas of light and
shade are quite different, and more
acceptable than in the previous
situation.

Figure 5.26
Sparkasse Geseke, Germany

light, which flows over and around the interior and its contents, and the 'non-directional' diffuse light reflected from the walls, floor and ceiling.

Methods of predicting the flow of light and its visual effects have been developed (Lynes *et al.* 1966; Cuttle *et al.* 1967).

ENERGY CONSERVATION

Daylight and artificial light may need to be integrated for two main reasons:

- Artificial lighting may be needed to supplement an inadequate supply of daylight.
- Daylight is used as the main form of lighting to achieve a high level of energy efficiency within the building interior.

The methods used to integrate the two forms of lighting are, however, the same, and procedures for integrating daylight and artificial lighting are defined in various national publications.

In the UK, four distinct situations are considered:

- interiors where the average daylight factor is greater than 5%
- rooflit interiors where the average daylight factor is less than 2%
- rooflit or shallow sidelit interiors having average daylight factors of 2% to 5%
- deep sidelit rooms.

When the average daylight factor exceeds 5%, natural lighting should be adequate for most purposes during daylight hours.

In rooflit areas with average daylight factors less than 2%, permanent supplementary lighting is usually required. Lighting controls should be arranged to switch or dim individual luminaires at fixed steps of illumination.

When the average daylight factor is between 2% and 5%, the electric lighting should be planned to take full advantage of available daylight. The provision of automatic controls for switching results in significant energy savings. The position of luminaires, and their switching regime, is arranged in relation to the position of windows, in order to preserve the daylit character. In most situations, this means rows of light fittings parallel to the windows, with selective switching of those rows. It is often advantageous to use local artificial task lighting and to use daylight to provide general background lighting.

In deep sidelit spaces the electric lighting must be carefully zoned. The switching zones close to the window can be defined by the daylight contour.

Before any lighting system is satisfactorily specified, either as a totally daylit system or as an integrated daylight/artificial system, it is necessary to predict the amount and distribution of natural light, using one of the many methods currently available.

Figure 5.27
State of Illinois Centre, Chicago, USA, 1979
Architect: Helmut Jahn

GLARE

Glare results from the excessive contrast of illumination or from an excess of illumination in an occupant's field of view. Reaction to it is subjective. When correctly designed, natural lighting does not give a glare problem. However, the point at which glare becomes a nuisance cannot be stated in a hard and fast way since occupant regard of what constitutes glare varies greatly.

The human eye adapts to the average luminance (brightness) over the whole field of view, but when large contrasts occur between the brightest and darkest areas, the excessively bright areas may cause discomfort, whilst the darker areas may not be visible at all. Contrasts in excess of 10:1 in illumination in different parts of the field of view may give rise to glare in some form.

Outdoor illumination levels can vary from 100 000 lux in bright sunlight on a clear day, to 2000 lux on a dull overcast day. On a sunlit day, it may be pleasant to experience 100 000 lux when the visual task consists of viewing distant scenery, but unpleasant when the task is to read a newspaper or to perform some exacting visual task.

Glare can be experienced in two main forms. Disability glare can be so intense, owing to either excessive contrasts or high illumination/brightness levels in the field of view, that a person subjected to it will not be able to carry out a task such as reading or writing. It is usually caused by the presence of a direct beam of sunlight or reflected sunlight within the field of view (within 45° of the principal viewing direction).

Discomfort glare is a less severe form of glare and, as its name suggests, it causes discomfort and irritation rather than incapacity. It is caused by bright surfaces and objects within the field of view, but with lower luminances than those which cause disability glare. White clouds in a blue sky, high brightness areas in overcast skies, reflection of sunlight from the ground or the surfaces of surrounding buildings, and the contrast between high internal decorations, can all cause discomfort glare.

DISABILITY GLARE AND GLASS

Reducing the light transmission of glass from 87% to 60% produces a just perceptible reduction in disability glare caused by direct sunlight. Even when the light transmission of the glass is as low as 10%, some 10 000 lux can still be experienced and glare will almost certainly occur (Figure 5.28).

Figure 5.28 Typical luminances (cd/m^2) from clear cloudless sky

Sun position	No glass	Clear float	Body tinted float	Coated double glazed float
Facing sun:				
midsummer	7500	6675	5400	5250
equinox	6000	5340	4320	4200
midwinter	4000	3560	2880	2800
Opposite sun:				
midsummer	3500	3115	2520	2450
equinox	2000	1780	1440	1400
midwinter	1000	890	720	700
90° to sun:				
midsummer	3500	3115	2520	2450
equinox	2500	2225	1800	1750
midwinter	2000	1780	1440	1400

In some instances, a solution may be achieved by redirecting the solar beam away from the direct line of sight. A more satisfactory solution might be some form of mechanical shading, for example a canopy, an overhanging floor, a balcony or a louvre system. Alternatively, internal screening can be provided by louvres or blinds. Any fixed shading system will reduce the amount of natural light entering the building throughout the year, irrespective of whether there is a glare problem at any particular time.

At the design stage, it may be possible to reorientate the glazing to avoid entry of direct solar radiation. Alternatively, the interior layout may be suitably designed to eliminate glare. Prediction methods, based on sunpath diagrams and perspective views of the glazing, are available to aid the designer (Figure 5.29).

Figure 5.29
Sky vault in projection

A parallel perspective of the
window and the obstructions are
plotted. The appropriate vertical
sun-dial overlay is superimposed and
oriented, showing annual and
hourly sun positions.

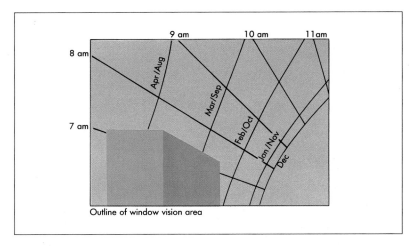

Figure 5.29
Sky vault in projection

A parallel perspective of the
window and the obstructions are
plotted. The appropriate vertical
sun-dial overlay is superimposed and
oriented, showing annual and
hourly sun positions.

DISCOMFORT GLARE AND GLASS

Glass products with light transmission lower than 50% ameliorate discomfort glare. These glass products will decrease the sky luminance component but permanently reduce the admission of daylight. Alternatively, shading devices, internal or external, movable or fixed, may be used.

Other methods of easing the problems of glare are available:

- windows in more than one wall to raise the general back ground adaptation illumination and, in so doing, to reduce the contrast between a window and its surrounding surfaces
- light coloured matt finishes for the window frames and the surrounding surfaces
- splayed reveals, to assist in reducing the contrast between the window and its surroundings
- slender glazing bars and transoms of high reflectance
- lower window sills to allow increased illumination to enter, which increases the adaptation level and reduces the likelihood of discomfort glare.

GLARE AND ROOF GLAZING

Glare from roof glazing in the normal field of view requires some form of shading system so that bright areas cannot be seen directly, at angles of 35° or less above the horizontal.

The nature of some glass products (for example, patterned or acid etched) can cause the direct incident solar beam to be scattered diffusely. Hence the window may assume an uncomfortably high brightness and become a discomfort glare source in its own right. Because it is a diffusely scattering material, the glare source can be observed from a wide range of angles in the room.

FADING

Glass transmits both light and heat radiation across a wide spectrum. These transmissions can, in some circumstances, cause a chemical change to occur in some pigments, dyes and colourants resulting in their visual degradation and fading. Most materials can fade when subjected to either daylight (particularly direct sunlight) or artificial light. Some may also fade naturally with time.

Fading is a complex phenomenon. Many chemical reactions are involved, initiated or accelerated by light of different wavelengths. Generally the better quality dyes and pigments fade relatively slowly and react only to the shorter wavelengths of light (blue and violet). Other materials can fade quickly and do so even under light of much longer wavelengths (visible light from blue to red).

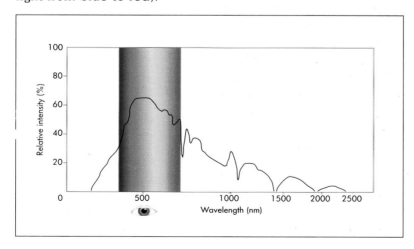

Figure 5.30
Solar radiation spectrum at the earth's surface

Negligible amounts of radiation of wavelengths less than 300 nm reach the earth's surface. The ultraviolet region as a whole accounts for less than 3% of the total solar radiation, but the amount of light received increases very rapidly with increasing wavelength around 400 nm which, in fading, is of most relevance (Figure 5.30). The 'changeover' point from ultraviolet to visible is in the range 370 nm to 400 nm, but is generally accepted as 380 nm. It is also in this region that most types of glass have a steeply rising transmission curve (Figure 5.31). Therefore the specification of the UV transmission of the glass should be considered carefully if a level of fading control of materials is important.

However, it can be misleading to relate only the UV transmission figure to the anti-fade qualities of the glass, because the transmission over the rest of the spectrum, particularly the blue end of the visible range, plays an important part. Glass with low UV but high visible transmission (with a steeply rising transmission curve around 380 nm) may be less effective at reducing fade than one with a higher UV transmission but a lower visible transmission. Generally, shorter wavelengths cause most fading of materials, but the shorter the wavelength, the less light there is available, and proportionately less will be transmitted by the glass. It is the combination of these three factors – wavelength, available light and transmission – which determines glass selection to minimize fading, not simply the UV transmission.

For these reasons, it is clear (Figure 5.31) that a significant reduction in fading should be expected from some clear laminated glass compared with clear float glass and even more from some of the coloured or reflective glass products. In fact, while no glass can completely prevent furnishings and fabrics from fading, tests have confirmed these generalizations.

The only way to completely eliminate radiation induced changes in materials is to protect them from all light. In museums and art galleries, rather elaborate precautions are taken. In shops and homes, only some of the following are possible:

- Reduce overall levels of illumination, both daylight and artificial, and in particular avoid direct sunlight. Use shades (curtains) and control the glazing, artificial lighting and orientation.

- Reduce the time for which the object is exposed to the light. Halving the time of exposure has the same effect as halving the light intensity.

- Reduce the temperature. All the changes involved in fading proceed more rapidly at higher temperatures.

- Reduce the UV and blue end of the spectrum in lighting by fitting appropriate glazing and artificial light sources.

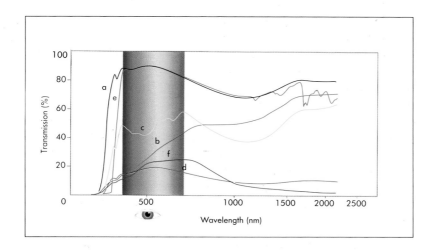

Figure 5.31
Spectrum of representative glass products showing UV transmission
a clear float
b reflective coated
c body tinted bronze
d gold reflective double glazing
e clear laminated
f reflective solar control double glazing

BIBLIOGRAPHY

The Architects Journal, Editorial 'Designing in the tropics', *The Architects Journal*, 16, November 1977

Aydinli, S. 'The calculation of available solar radiation and daylight', *Proceedings of CIE Symposium on Daylight*, Berlin, 1980

Becker-Epsten, D. *Daylight and Architecture*, C. F. Müller, 1987 (in German)

Bensasson, S. and Burgess, K. *Computer Programs for Daylighting in Buildings*, Design Office Consortium, Cambridge, 1978

Biesele, R.L., Arner, W.J. and Conover, E.W. 'A lumen method of daylighting design', *Illuminating Engineering*, January 1953

BRE 'Lighting Control and Daylight Use,' D*igest* 272, Building Research Establishment,1985

BRE 'Estimating Daylight in Buildings', Parts 1, 2, D*igests* 309, 310, Building Research Establishment, 1986

British Standard Draft for Development, B*asic Data for the Design of Buildings*: S*unlight*, DD67, British Standards Institution, 1980

British Standard Draft for Development, B*asic Data for the Design of Buildings*: D*aylight*, DD73, British Standards Institution, 1982

British Standard, Code of Practice for Daylighting, 1992

CIBSE *Window Design*, application manual, Chartered Institution of Building Services Engineers, 1987

CIE Publikation (E-32) *International Recommendations for the Calculation of Natural Daylight*, Commission Internationale de l'Eclairage, 1970 (in German)

CIE *Daylighting*, publication 16, Commission Internationale de l'Eclairage, 1970

CIE *Standardization of Luminance Distribution of Clear Skies*, publication 22, Commission Internationale de l'Eclairage, 1972

Crisp, V.H.C., Littlefair, P.J., Cooper, I. and McKennan, G.T. *Daylighting as a Passive Solar Energy Option: an Assessment of its Potential in Non-domestic Buildings*, report, BR129, Building Research Establishment, 1988

Cuttle, C. 'Lighting patterns and the flow of light', *Lighting Research and Technology*, 3(3), 1971

Cuttle, C., Valentine, W. B., Lynes, J.A. and Burt, W. 'Beyond the working plane', *Proceedings of the CIE Conference*, Washington, 1967

DIN 5034 *Daylight: Inside Lighting with Calculation of Daylight*, Deutches Institut für Normung e.V., 1983 (in German)

DIN 67507, *Degree of Light Transmission and Total Energy Transmission through Glazing*, Deutches Institut für Normung e.V. (in German)

Evans, B.H. *Daylight in Architecture*, McGraw-Hill, 1981

Fischer, M., *Daylight Technology*, C.F. Müller, 1982 (in German)

GEPVP *Natural Lighting in Architecture*, Groupement Européen des Producteurs de Verre Plat, Brussels, 1986

Griffith, J.W. *Predicting Daylight as Interior Illumination*, Libbey Owens Ford Glass Co., Toledo, Ohio, 1976

Heusler, W., 'Experimental Investigation of Available Daylight and the Model's Effect on the Internal Room Illumination', Dissertation, Technische Universitat Berlin, 1991 (in German)

Hunt, D.R.G. 'Simple expressions for predicting energy savings from photo-electric control of lighting', *Lighting Research and Technology* 9(2), 93–102, 1977

Littlefair, P.J. 'Daylight availability for lighting control', *Proceedings* CIBSE *National Lighting Conference*, 1984

Littlefair, P.J. 'Innovative daylighting systems – a critical review', *Lighting Research and Technology*, 22(1), 1–18, 1990

Littlefair, P.J. 'Predicting annual lighting use in daylit buildings', *Building and Environment*, 25(1), 43–54, 1990

Longmore, J. BRS *Daylight Protractors*, HMSO, London, 1968

Lynes, J.A. *Principles of Natural Lighting*, Elsevier, London, 1968

Lynes, J.A., Burt, W., Jackson, G.K. and Cuttle, C., 'The flow of light into buildings', *Transactions of the Illumination Engineering Society*, London, 31(3), 65–91, 1966

Olgyay, A. and Olgyay, V. *Solar Control and Shading Devices*, Princeton University Press, Princeton, NJ, 1957

Rasmussen, S. *Experiencing Architecture*, Chapman and Hall, London, 1964

Robbins, C. *Daylighting Design and Analysis*, Van Nostrand, New York, 1986

Scidl, M., 'Daylight in the Living Area', *Light*, 31, 371–373 and 426–429, 1979 (in German)

Secker, S.M. and Littlefair, P.J. 'Geographical variation in daylight availability and lighting use', *Proceedings* CIBSE *National Lighting Conference*, Nottingham, 1986

Szermann, M., Erhorn, H., 'Daylight Calculation by 'Superlite' Calculation Programme', Lichtechniche Geseltshaft, *Daylight Report, Light* '88, Vol 2, p. 531–544, 1988 (in German)

Szokolay, S.V. *Environmental Science Handbook*, Construction Press, 1980

Thomson, G. *Conservation and Museum Lighting*, Museums Association information sheet, May 1970

Turner, D.P. (ed.) *Windows and Environment*, Pilkington Bros. Ltd, 1969

Turner, D.P. (ed.) *Window Glass Design Guide*, Architectural Press, London, 1977

CHAPTER 6

Appearance

Many experiments could be imagined; the choice is almost unlimited ... it would look like a piece of jewellery on a large scale. Much of glass architecture concerns the jeweller, and jewels should be transposed from necks and arms on to walls.

Scheerbart, *Glasarchitektur*

Amongst all building materials, glass has unique optical qualities. Its presence provides a special visual endowment to spaces inside and outside the building.

Glass artists, architects, glass manufacturers and patrons have roles to play in exploring that visual endowment, using modern glass products in buildings. Through the history of architecture, decoration has drawn inspiration and material from new technologies. Today, new technology is introduced at a rate greater than before, and architects are seeking to exploit this expanding opportunity.

There are two contributors to glass decoration, the glass artist and the architect:

The decorative glass crafts are divided between those who believe that the full artistic potential of glass can be realized only by the glass artist, and those who maintain that the proper role of decorative glass is still as an architectural element; that is the survival of glass crafts depends upon closer collaboration with architects.

(Jenson and Conway, 1982)

The glass manufacturer, however, is also involved and has several considerations. First, through the glass artist, glass is able to reconcile the conflicting demands for natural, craft based materials and for the exploitation of new sophisticated technologies for decoration. The traditional glass decorative methods, such as stained glass, acid etching, coloured laminates, screen printing and colour, are combining with the new technologies, such as holography.

Second, since much of new decoration is directed towards individual or corporate expression, products are capable of providing a variety of colours and textures through a custom service. This places a constraint on the manufacturers as they will be required to produce lower volume orders. These are not necessarily commodity products and processes.

Figure 6.1 *(Opposite)*
Lake Sagami Country Club, Yuzurihara, Yamanashi, Japan, 1989
Architects: Arata Isozaki and Associates
Glass design: Brian Clarke

'Every element in the design of this lantern and skylight window exists by virtue of its relation and reaction to a feature in the building. Isozaki designed an internal lighting system that when functioning by night transforms the cylindrical tower into a beacon visible from the surrounding roads and landscape.'
(Brian Clarke, 1990)

Figure 6.2a
Victoria Quarter, Leeds, UK
(decorative glass installed 1990)
Architect: Frank Matcham, 1901
Architects to the conversion:
Derek Latham & Associates
Glass design: Brian Clarke

*'The Prudential Group commissioned
Clarke to design a 125 metre long
(1000 m²) stained glass roof to span
the whole of Queen Victoria Street,
Leeds ... it was decided to retain
clear glass on the edges of the
composition in order to keep white
light on the buildings.'* (Brian
Clarke, 1990)

Figure 6.2b
Design for roof canopies in Figure
6.2a

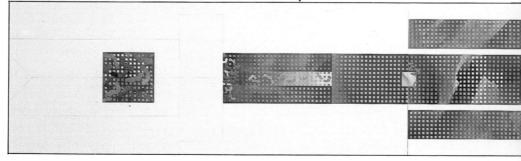

Third, decorative effects will in the future be more readily accepted in combination with other glass functions. For instance, in solar control and glass cladding they will be part of the weather skin; in internal partitions they will offer transparency, translucency and information.

The architect Adolf Loos (1870–1933) spoke about decoration and ornament at the beginning of the century, encapsulating the then current ideals:

Not only is ornament produced by criminals, but also a crime is committed through the fact that ornament inflicts serious injury on people's health, on the national budget and hence on cultural evolution.

In his introduction to Brian Clarke's book *Into and Out of Architecture* (1990), Sir Norman Foster identifies a more pragmatic approach to glass art:

There seems to be a generally held misconception that the modern movement not only excludes art from its buildings but consciously rejects the idea...But surely modern architecture, in the broadest sense, can with the right kind of collaboration go beyond the tokenism of art in architecture and lead to a genuine liaison in the spirit of past ages. Such future possibilities will only be realised when there is a shaped language of awareness between patrons, architects and artists.

This chapter does not attempt to provide guidance on design for decorative glass appearance, but illustrates some of the best works combining contributions from glass artists, architects and industry, including an experimental electroluminescent display glass referred to in Chapter 1.

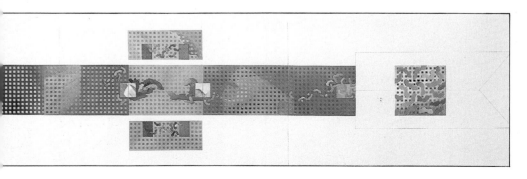

Figure 6.3
Detail of horse, Lime Street station,
Liverpool, UK
Glass designer: Radford and Ball
Partnership

*'It was the largest glass commission
to be undertaken in a public
building. This vast glass curtain was
constructed from seventy-eight glass
panels fixed with the Pilkington
Planar system. The themes relating
to time, man and travel are etched
on both sides of the glass to give
the images a third dimension.'*
(Diane Radford)

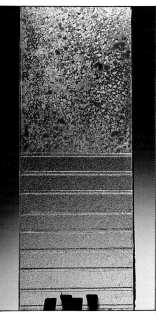

Figure 6.4
Detail of desing for private client,
New York, USA
Glass designer: Radford and Ball
Partnership

*'By combining acid etching and
sandblasting with applied enamels
the colours and textures were
specifically developed to match the
interior designer's schemes.'* (Diane
Radford)

Figure 6.5
Postmuseum, Frankfurt, Germany

Standard solar control glasses have
been used for decorative effects

Figure 6.6
These horizontal gratings have coatings which are microscopically etched to form serrations. Gratings also perform a solar attenuating function as shading devices.
Glass designer: James Carpenter (model proposal with Pei, Cobb, Freed and Partners)

Figure 6.7
Dichroic Project Glass Spine,
Chiswick Park, London, 1993
Architect: Foster Associates
Glass designer: James Carpenter

*'This organic structure for the main
entance to a Norman Foster building
captures elements of the landscape
and brings them into the building
itself, using dichroic glass panels and
a tensile stainless steel structure.
The suspended form of the 70 ft
high sculpture restates the sloping
curtain wall of the atrium.
The dichroic glass coating varies
from intense red reflection at an
oblique angle to a transparent blue
in transmission, allowing for vision
out to the surrounding parklands
and reflecting elements of the
landscape into the interior.
Machined aluminium components
and custom designed stainless steel
fittings bolt through the toughened
glass panels and are in turn
threaded to the main parabolic
cables. A pure tensile structure, this
work continues the studio's
exploration of unique glass and
steel structures'.*
(James Carpenter)

Figure 6.8
Ecology Gallery, Natural History
Museum, London, UK
Architect: Ian Ritchie

'The exhibition envelope is a fragile and delicate "hands-off" conversation with Waterhouse's (1839–1905) architecture.'

'The central vista of the exhibition draws the visitor subtly into the context of the ecology, by means of a layered, curved glass wall on the right which feels like the edge of a glacier (representing water). This effect is created by the use of Optiwhite (low iron oxide glass) with the back face sand blasted and lit from above and behind by cool, coloured temperature lamps. Opposite, the straight glass wall is also back lit similar to the curved wall, but utilizing warm colour temperature lamps to emotionally convey energy (fire). For both walls the use of Optiwhite glass was essential. The individual glass sheets were toughened and fixed via toughened glass lugs UV bonded, resulting in invisible fixed suspended panels. The base of the straight wall gently undulates and flickers, alluding to a lava flow coming from the floor (recycled rubber floor, representing earth). The visitor's attention will be drawn to the first bridge above him made from 2 × 19 mm laminated glass plates (with a leaf pattern) set into an organic structural frame and registering this fragile element and the image of people in the air. Thus the aim of this very low key introduction is to convey the four elements with man.' (Ian Ritchie)

116

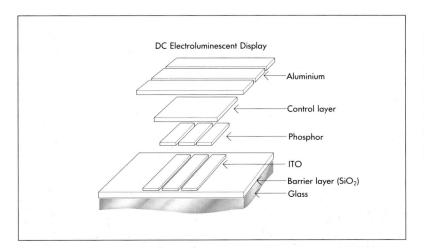

DC Electroluminescent Display

Aluminium

Control layer

Phosphor

ITO

Barrier layer (SiO₂)

Glass

Figure 6.10

Figure 6.9
An experimental flat glass display with a pixelated matrix structure to create moving patterns activated from periphery by electrical inputs from a computer.

Electroluminescent displays are part of the family of 'active' flat panel diplays. The construction consists of a stack of five thin films 1μm in thickness on a sheet of glass. Light is emitted when a voltage of around 200 V is applied between the two outer thin film layers using dedicated driving circuitry.

The normal construction of the device incorporates a reflective film of aluminium as one of the electrodes. The latter is the only opaque film in the stack and could be (in principle) changed to a transparent material, such as Indium-Tin-Oxide (ITO) to produce a transparent display.

The active material is the same as used in TV technology and provides these rugged displays with potential of multicolour operation.

Figure 6.11
Meyer May House, Grand Rapids,
USA, 1908
Architect: Frank Lloyd-Wright

BIBLIOGRAPHY

Clark, B. *Into and Out of Architecture*, Mavor Gallery, London, 1990

Clarke, B. (ed.) *Architectural Stained Glass*, John Murray, London, 1979

Glüser, H. Y., 'Insulating Glass with Heat, Sun and Sound Protection – Properties for Architectural Design Methods', (Seminar: Multi Functioning Windows) 1983 (in German)

Jensen, R. and Conway, P. *The New Decorativeness in Architecture and Design: Ornamentalism*, Clarkson N. Potter, New York, 1982

Petzold, Murusch and Schrumm, *Glass as a Material*, 3rd edn, Verlag F. Bauwesen, Berlin, 1990 (in German)

Wigginton, M. *Glass Today – Report and Proceedings of the Glass in the Environment Conference*, Crafts Council, London, April 1986

Loos, A. *Gravaenolo Benedetto*, Idea Books Edizioni, Milan, 1982

McGrath, R. and Frost, A. C. *Glass in Architecture and Poloration* (new edition revised by R. McGrath) Architectural Press, London, 1961

CHAPTER 7

Introduction to Thermal Comfort

Demands for improved comfort by the building occupants will increase in industrialized countries during the 1990s for several reasons. First, the older working population will have higher comfort expectations. Second, competition for employees will generate incentives by employers; a healthy comfortable working environment will be just such an incentive in the United States, where the number of young adults will fall by 40%, creating a shortage of entry level employees. Third, there will be more personal and individual control over working environmental conditions. Finally, greater affluence will produce higher investment for better environmental performance.

In this context thermal comfort is of great importance in glass specification.

OCCUPANT COMFORT

The sensation of thermal comfort, and the occupant's satisfaction or dissatisfaction, depends on their interaction and response to certain physical influences.

The human body has a thermo-regulating system which tries to maintain its temperature at about 37 °C. Thermal comfort depends on this metabolic system being in balance with the surroundings. The physical factors influencing the sensation of thermal comfort are those which affect the ability to balance the loss of metabolic heat. Since no two individuals are exactly alike, there is always a statistical spread in expressed satisfaction of thermal comfort. The physical factors are:

- activity level and its value of metabolic heat generation
- clothing and its thermal insulation
- air movement relative to the individual, and air humidity
- air temperature and the radiant temperatures of the surroundings.

Window glass design for comfort purposes mainly relies on influencing the radiant and air temperatures.

Activity level and clothing are important influences on

Figure 7.1 (*Opposite*)
Einfamilienhaus Beutelschmidt,
Frankfurt, Germany

121

thermal comfort. The higher the rate of activity, the greater the generation of metabolic heat. Clothing has the effect of thermally insulating the body and modifying the rate of body heat loss. To estimate thermal comfort in environmental design, physical factor values (Figures 7.2, 7.3) can be incorporated in formulae to give a single index of thermal comfort.

Figure 7.2 Typical metabolic heat generated for various activities

Activities	W/m²
Reading	55
Typing	65
Walking	100
Lifting	120

As a guide, a typical male would have 1.7 m² of surface area.

Figure 7.3 Thermal insulation values for typical clothing ensembles for work for daily wear

Clothing	clo
Underwear, socks, shoes	0.70
Underwear, shirt, trousers, jacket, socks, shoes	1.00
Underwear, shirt, trousers, jacket, heavy quilted jacket and overalls, socks, shoes	1.85

The clo is a relative value, with 1.00 being the measure for normal indoor clothing for a man.

Figure 7.4
Relationship between operative temperature, clothing and activity for a man

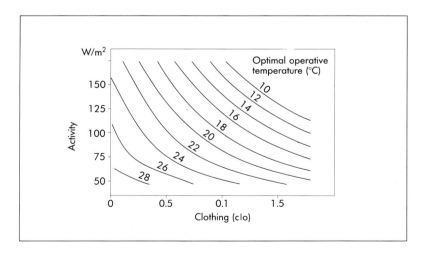

122

Figure 7.4 - *continued*

The body has two mechanisms for losing heat: sensible heat loss and latent heat loss. Sensible heat loss occurs by conduction through the skin, then by convection to the air and by long wave radiation to surrounding surfaces (radiation is an important mechanism for low activity levels, because the body surface temperature is usually higher than that of the surroundings). Latent heat loss occurs by the evaporation of moisture at the surface of the skin and by breathing. In the case of high activity levels, this mechanism is important.

Both sensible and latent losses are influenced to a greater or lesser extent by the physical factors outlined.

GLASS CONTRIBUTION TO COMFORT

Window glass influences occupant comfort by:

- heat gain or heat loss through the glass, which either raises or lowers the room air temperature
- radiation exchange between glass and occupant.

For an occupant close to a window, the internal glass surface temperature influences thermal comfort as a result of heat loss produced by long wave radiation exchange between the occupant and the window. There may be a marked difference in sensation of comfort between the two sides of the body according to the proximity to and the size of the window, and its surface temperature.

In winter, the glass surface can be much colder than other room surfaces, producing a loss of heat from the occupant's body surface, by long wave radiation, to the colder glass surface and contributing to a sensation of cold discomfort.

In summer, the internal surface of glass can be much hotter, for example owing to the absorption of solar radiation in a body tinted glass. This contributes long wave radiation which, in addition to any direct short wave solar radiation received through the glass, is absorbed by the occupant and contributes to a sensation of hot discomfort.

These summer and winter environmental comfort conditions can be calculated as illustrated in Figures 7.5 and 7.6. Guidance on discomfort zones adjacent to a window in winter can be seen in Figure 7.7.

Figure 7.5
Summer condition for a person
seated in an office next to a window

Figure 7.5
Summer condition for a person
seated in an office next to a window

A person in light clothing is sitting 1 m from a window (2 × 2 m) single glazed with a solar heat absorbing body tinted glass. The window receives 750 W/m² solar radiation with a 25 °C outside air temperature and 21 °C inside temperature.

The dry resultant temperature t_{res} is commonly used to describe the environmental conditions. It represents the temperature at any point in the room as influenced by the mean radiant temperature of the surrounding surfaces t_r, the air temperature t_{air} and the air velocity v (m/s).

In order to calculate the principal physical factors influencing comfort, it is necessary to apply the formula

$$t_{res} = \frac{t_{air}\sqrt{(10v)} + t_r}{1 + \sqrt{(10v)}}$$

For indoor still air conditions $v < 0.1$ m/s, $t_{res} = 0.5t_{air} + 0.5t_r$.

The window surface temperature contributes to t_r in the given situation. The glass temperature is 38 °C, which arises from the absorption of solar radiation and the higher temperature of the outside air. Long wave radiation from the glass produces, at a distance of 1 m, a dry resultant temperature of 22.7 °C, an increase of 1.7 °C above room temperature.

The transmitted solar radiation also contributes to the dry resultant temperature. The solar radiation of 750 W/m² is attenuated by the glass, resulting in 345 W/m² of short wave directly transmitted radiation received by the occupant. With an absorptance of light coloured clothes of 0.6 (dark coloured clothes 0.9), then with 345 W/m^2 incident radiation the dry resultant temperature is increased by about 5 °C.

When these increases are combined, they produce a dry resultant temperature of 27.7 °C, which is in excess of a reasonable comfort temperature with light clothing.

If an alternative design is considered, using low emissivity coated glass in a double glazed unit, then the following modified temperatures result:

t_{res} increase due to radiation from the glass surface = 1.2 °C;

t_{res} increase due to direct solar radiation through the glazing = 3 °C.

When these increases are combined, they produce a dry resultant temperature of 25.2 °C which might be deemed reasonably comfortable when compared with the temperature (27.7 °C) from the previous design.

Figure 7.6
Winter condition for a person seated in an office next to a window

A person is sitting 1 m from a window (2 × 2 m) single glazed with clear glass, which is receiving no solar radiation, with −10 °C outside air temperature and 21 °C inside temperature.

The temperature of the internal glass surface will be 1 °C, producing a t_{res} of 19 °C. This is below reasonable comfort temperature for light clothing.

If the window is double glazed, then the internal glass surface temperature becomes 10 °C, which produces an acceptable t_{res} of 20 °C.

Figure 7.7
Discomfort zones adjacent to the window in winter

This illustrates how discomfort zones occur near a window. The examples show single glazed, double glazed, and double glazed Low E windows with external temperatures of −1 °C and −20 °C. At −1 °C, no discomfort zone is distinguishable for double glazed and double glazed Low E windows.

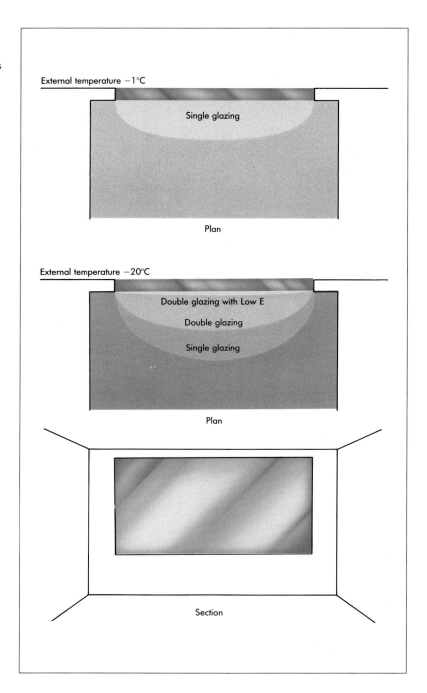

BIBLIOGRAPHY

Button, D. and Dunning, R. *Fenestration 2000: an Investigation into the Long Term Requirements for Glass. Phase 1*, Pilkington Glass Ltd and the UK Department of Energy, July 1989

CIBSE *Environmental Criteria For Design*, Vol. A, Section A.2, Chartered Institution of Building Services Engineers, 1980

DIN 33403 Part 1 and 2 *Climate in the Workplace*, Deutches Institut für Normung e.V. (in German)

ISO 7730 *Conditions for Thermal Comfort*, International Standards Organisation, (in German)

Owens, P.G.T. 'Air conditioned comfort and sunshine', *Journal of the Institute of Heating and Ventilation Engineers*, 37, 92–96, 1969

Recknagel, Sprenger and Hönmann, *Pocketbook for Heating and Ventilation 88/89*, Munich, 1987 (in German)

CHAPTER 8

Heat Loss

As air is one of the worst conductors of heat, the double glass wall is an essential condition for all glass architecture.

Scheerbart, *Glasarchitektur*, 1914

Although double glazing was recognized at the beginning of the century as an essential requirement, in the 1960s the single glazed window was still common in many countries and regarded as a liability in energy conservation and the achievement of comfort conditions. The window is now regarded as a contributor to conservation and comfort; this is largely due to the development of high performance glass products for insulation and passive solar energy technology. Concern for global warming and the reduction of carbon dioxide emissions has created a new impetus for researching glass products of higher insulation to limit heat loss. This is because a major contributor to carbon dioxide emissions is the burning of fossil fuels associated with the servicing of buildings.

HEAT LOSS QUANTIFIED

Heat loss is quantified by the thermal transmittance or U value, normally measured in $W/m^2 K$ (Btu/ft^{2}h°F). The U value is the rate of loss of heat per square metre, under steady state conditions, for a temperature difference of one kelvin or degree Celsius between the inner and outer environments separated by the glazing.

Heat loss can also be quantified in terms of thermal resistance, abbreviated to R value. This is the inverse of the U value:

$$R = \frac{1}{U} \quad m^2 K/W \ (ft^2 h°F/Btu)$$

Values of U and R for typical glazings are shown in Figure 8.2.

There are three stages of heat loss through glass products described in Figure 8.22 and illustrated in Figure 8.3 and 8.4:

- to the internal glass surface from the room surfaces
- through the glass product
- from the outer glass surface.

Figure 8.1 *(Opposite)*
DG Bank, Hanover, Germany
Architects: Bahlo-Köhnke-Stösberg, Hanover

129

Figure 8.2 U and R values for four glass combinations using 4 mm thick glass and, where appropriate, 12 mm air spaces

	U value W/m² K	R value m² K/W
Single	5.4–5.8	0.18–0.17
Double	2.8–3.0	0.36–0.30
Double with Low E coatings	1.7–2.0	0.59–0.50
Triple with two Low E coatings	1.0–1.2	1.00–0.80

Figure 8.3
Mechanism for heat loss through single glass

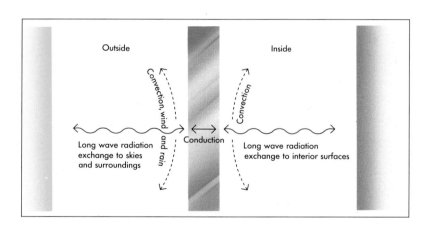

HEAT LOSS TO INTERNAL GLASS SURFACE

Heat is lost to the internal glass surface, from the room, whenever the glass surface is at a lower temperature than the internal air temperature and the room surface temperature. The heat is lost in two ways:

- by exchange of long wave radiation between the glass surface and the room surfaces
- by convection/conduction from the room air moving over the surface of the glass.

Usually, the heat loss by radiation exchange is the greater heat loss (unless the glass surface has a low emissivity coating, explained below).

HEAT LOSS THROUGH THE GLASS PRODUCT

With single glass there is relatively little resistance to loss of heat, because glass readily conducts heat and is a poor insulator. To increase the resistance, one effective method is to add a second pane of glass separated from the first pane by an air space, to form an additional resistive layer. This layer of enclosed air provides extra thermal resistance by virtue of the low thermal conductivity of air (compared with glass) while the second pane provides additional thermal resistance to long

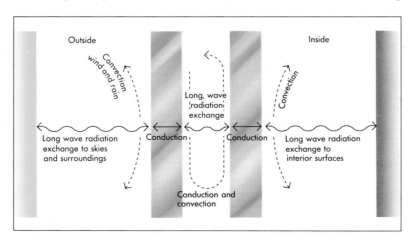

Figure 8.4
Mechanism for heat loss through double glazed units

131

wave radiation exchange (Figure 8.4).

The provision of an air space provides several opportunities for increasing glazing thermal resistance:

- increasing the width of the air space
- incorporating low emissivity coatings
- using gases of lower conductivity
- inhibiting convection in the air space
- evacuating the air space

INCREASING THE WIDTH OF THE AIR SPACE

By increasing the width of the air space, extra resistance is provided. There is a limit due to convection within the air space, which occurs at about 15 mm width, after which little extra thermal benefit is obtained (Figure 8.5). Adding a third glass pane to give a second air space provides further improvement.

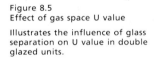

Figure 8.5
Effect of gas space U value

Illustrates the influence of glass separation on U value in double glazed units.

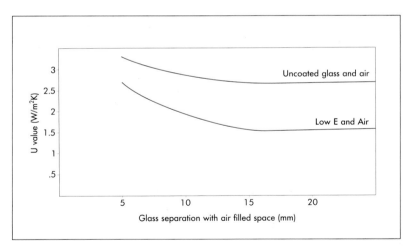

INCORPORATION OF LOW EMISSIVITY COATING

The use of a low emissivity (Low E) coating on the glass provides the possibility of reducing the long wave radiation exchange between the panes. In air spaces with uncoated surfaces, the long wave radiation exchange between those enclosing glass surfaces is high, amounting to about 60% of the total heat exchange across the space. With one of the glass surfaces having a coating with emissivity less than 0.2 (compared with 0.84 for the uncoated glass surface), the radiation exchange is reduced by approximately 75% and consequently the U value is reduced. The term 'Low E' is now generally taken to refer to coatings with an emissivity less than 0.2. The change of U value with coating emissivity is illustrated for air filled double glazed units in Figure 8.6. At ambient tempratures, the long wave radiation lies between 5000–50000 nm where the reflection of Low E coating is high – extending beyond the wavelength coordinate of Figure 8.7.

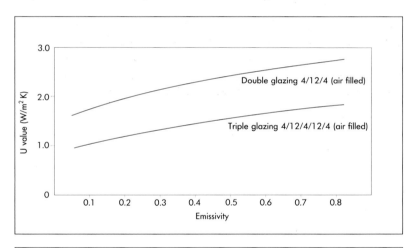

Figure 8.6
Effect of emissivity on U value

The effect of coating emissivity U value in double glazed and triple glazed units with air in spaces 12 mm wide. For uncoated double glazing the U value is about 2.8 W/m² K, reducing to around 1.8 W/m² K with typical Low emissivity coatings. The theoretical absolute limit in this case is 1.5 W/m² K (where there is zero long wave radiation exchange).

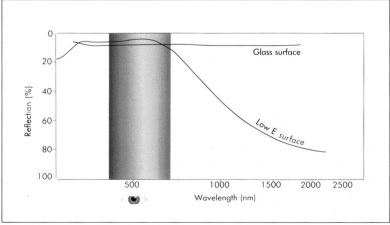

Figure 8.7
Spectral reflectance properties of Low E and clear glass

Comparison shows that in the visible part of the spectrum the reflectance curves are close, diverging at 1600 nm. In the far infrared the Low E coating has a high reflectance.

133

The higher insulating effect (lower U value) provided by a Low E coating in a double glazed unit is due to the high reflectance of long wavelength radiation at ambient temperatures (Figure 8.7).

Emissivity and reflectance in the far infrared are related by Kirchhoff's law (Figure 3.2).

The development of hard low emissivity coatings widens the possibility of including coated monolithic glazing in secondary frames applied to existing windows; the earlier, softer low emissivity coatings were restricted to protected use in sealed glazed units only. Metallic surfaces, including some metallic oxides, provide low emissivity.

Water on the coated surface of the glass, perhaps as a result of condensation, will cancel out the effect of the Low E coating because of the high emissivity of water.

The present technology of on-line, hard Low E coatings can provide slightly higher solar heat transmission than that exhibited by soft coatings, giving improvements to passive solar gain applications. In cold climates the higher temperature of the inner glass surface of double glazed units using Low E coatings diminishes the effect of colder long wave radiation causing discomfort near the window.

GASES OF LOWER THERMAL CONDUCTIVITY

Sealed Low E double glazed units may also contain gases with lower thermal conductivity than air such as argon, providing further improvement in U value (Figures 8.8, 8.9).

INHIBITING CONVECTION WITHIN THE AIR SPACE

Convection within the air space may be inhibited and thus reduced by cellularizing the air space (breaking down the enclosed space into cells) using, for example, thin plastic materials (Figure 8.10).

Transparent and translucent highly insulating materials, such as Aerogel, may be placed within the sealed space.

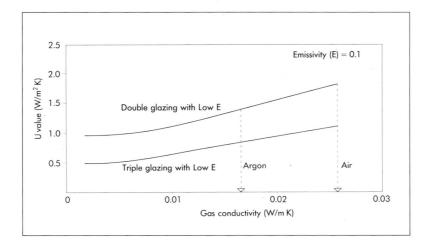

Figure 8.8
Influence of gas conductivity on glazing U values

This shows the reduction in U value of sealed double and triple Low E glazed units when gases with lower thermal conductivity than air occupy the gas space. The most effective gases are those in the argon series, which have low thermal conductivity and little tendency to convect. In a Low E double glazed unit in which air is replaced by argon, the U value is typically reduced from 1.8 W/m² K to 1.5 W/m² K.

Figure 8.9
Filling double glazed units with argon during manufacture, Flachglas AG, Germany

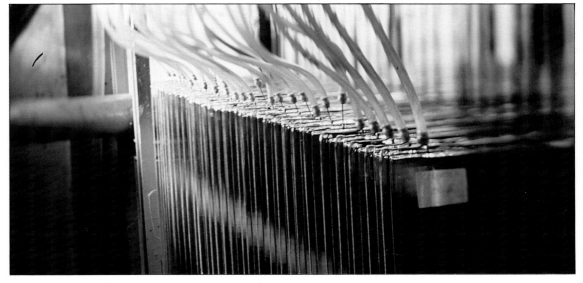

EVACUATING THE AIR SPACE

The air space may be fully or partially evacuated. The technology is currently being developed to overcome the problems of:

- air pressure on the outside, causing the panes to deflect and collapse inwards
- maintaining the vacuum for long periods, which places new demands on edge sealing of the unit.

HEAT LOSS FROM THE OUTER GLASS SURFACE

The final stage of heat loss is from the outer glass surface. As with the inner glass surface, the two modes of heat transfer are by long wave radiation exchange and by convection/conduction. The balance and magnitude of heat transfer at this surface vary considerably, and are climate dominated. The long wavelength radiation exchange depends on the temperature of the surrounding outside surfaces and the sky temperatures. With clear skies, sky temperatures can be extremely low; this effect is demonstrated by the formation of dew and frost on surfaces exposed to clear skies due to their cooling below ambient air temperature.

The rate of heat loss by convection/conduction is usually high

Figure 8.10
U values for a representative sample of glass products

These diagrams characterize the U values (W/m² K) for a range of commercially available and developing technologies for insulating glass products.

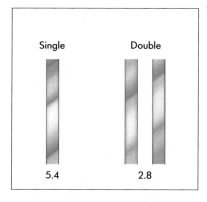

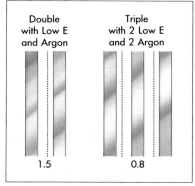

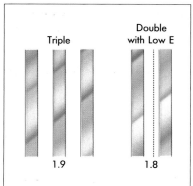

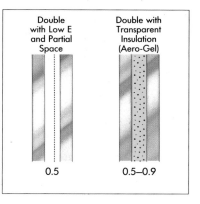

owing to the influence of wind, which is particularly important on exposed sites. Wind driven rain will further increase the heat loss, owing to contact cooling and evaporation.

The overall heat exchange coefficient of the glass can typically vary between 10 W/m^2 K (still and cloudy conditions) and 50 W/m^2 K (clear and windy conditions). Performances for a representative range of glass products using the various opportunities for increased insulation are shown in Figure 8.10.

The mechanism of heat loss from the outside surface of a building is a function of its temperature, and can be illustrated by thermograms showing the long wave radiation loss (Figure 8.11).

Present research is targeted to achieve U values below 0.35 W/m^2 K for glass products of less than 30 mm total thickness. Such values are equivalent to those generally required in legislation for wall insulation.

GLASS DETAILING AND THERMAL INSULATION

Double glazed units containing high performance glass require a compatible high insulation in their edge spacer. Equally high insulation in the framing is required. If this is not achieved, then the insulation benefits of the glass can be significantly diminished. Whilst conventional double glazing with Low E and argon achieves U values between 1.3 and 1.8 W/m^2 K, poorly insulated frames of wood, plastic, aluminium or steel may achieve U values ranging from 2.8 to 7.0 W/m^{2}K. Better insulating frames are therefore necessary.

The thermal transmittance of the complete window is made up of three components:

- the glass product (which has been dealt with above)
- the spacer in double glazed units
- the framing.

The thermal technology of spacers and framing is discussed

Figure 8.11
Infrared thermogram showing long
wave radiation loss from a building,
Pilkington Energy Advisers Ltd, St
Helens, UK

This infrared thermogram shows the non-visible radiation (800 to 1300 nm) from an old hospital building.

The spread from black (cold) to white (warm) covers about 40 °C in black body radiation. At these wavelengths, glass is a selective radiator. At normal temperatures, the radiation is dominated by reflection, as typified by the right hand window, in which cold sky and warmer building reflections can be distinguished. The left hand window is much warmer and its surface temperature, especially in its middle pane, is the dominant feature. The right hand pane shows the reflection of the three thermography engineers.

Elsewhere, edge effects, frame leakage and cold bridging (actually warm bridging when observed from outside) can clearly be distinguished on the windows. The central feature (characteristic of the UK) is an external soil stack which appears warm. A cold drainpipe can be seen on the right. An air brick at bottom right is seen to draw cold air into the wall cavity. The ground floor rooms are clearly warmer than the upper floors, especially as the room on the upper right has the heating controls set at a lower temperature. Wind effects, eddying round the building, can be seen having a cooling effect on the upper left.

below in terms of calculation procedures and future developments.

THE SPACER IN DOUBLE GLAZED UNITS

Multiple glazed units are factory made, hermetically sealed combinations of glass where the space between the glass panes contains dry (dew point <–40 °C) air or other gases. The presence of an aluminium spacer in double glazed units increases the overall U value of the glass and frame owing to a thermal short circuit at the unit edge. This affects the overall U value and also gives rise to local low temperatures at that edge region, often causing condensation on the glass or, in severe winter climates, frost and ice.

The thermal effect of the spacer (the linear thermal transmittance) may be calculated (Figure 8.12) and the resulting value used in the overall window U value calculation (Figure 8.16). The spacer effect can add as much as 10% to the U values of the window. The flow of heat loss through a spacer is shown by the energy flux lines in Figure 8.13.

Figure 8.12 Spacer insulation in double glazed units

This is evaluated in terms of a linear thermal transmittance. For conventional sealed double glazed units of U value 2.8 W/m² K, in which the internal spacer is roughly level with the frame, the values given in the table may be used in the calculation of the overall window insulation. Values for Low E coated double glazed units with U value 1.8 W/m² K are shown in brackets. The three conditions of exposure are those for the UK. The internationally agreed values are drafted in ISO 6946.

Spacer correction for sealed double glazed units:

Glass thickness mm	Linear thermal transmittance for stated conditions of exposure W/m K			
	Sheltered	Normal	Severe	ISO 6946
4	0.03 (0.04)	0.04 (0.06)	0.04 (0.06)	0.04 (0.06)
6	0.05 (0.08)	0.05 (0.08)	0.06 (0.09)	0.06 (0.09)
10	0.07 (0.11)	0.08 (0.12)	0.09 (0.14)	0.09 (0.14)
12	0.09 (0.14)	0.10 (0.15)	0.11 (0.17)	0.11 (0.17)

Figure 8.13
Isothermals and energy flux lines in
a section through the edge of a
wooden frame

This diagram shows a finite element
analysis of the edge region of a
sealed double glazed unit glazed in
a wooden frame. The effect of the
spacer is demonstrated by the
isotherms, showing localized
temperature depression, and by the
energy flux lines being bunched
together through the spacer.

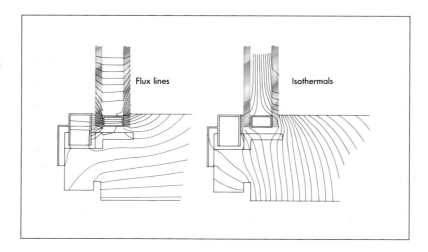

The edge effect of the glazing system, below the glazing lines
of the frame, can be substantially improved if the overall thermal resistance through the spacer is at least as good as the
thermal resistance of the frame. New spacer materials with low
thermal conductivity are being developed such as hollow
polycarbonate extrusions and rigid silicone foams.

Figure 8.14 Typical frame U values

Frame material	U value W/m² K
Wood: average thickness > 80 mm	1.6
50–80 mm	2.0
< 50 mm	2.8
Plastic: without metal reinforcement	2.8
: with metal reinforcement	3.6
Aluminium: with thermal barrier*	
thermal path length >10 mm	3.6
<10 mm	5.0
Aluminium or steel: without thermal barrier	7.0

*Thermal barrier must be continuous and totally isolate the interior
side of the frame or frame sections from the exterior side.

THE FRAMING

The thermal insulation value is important as the overall percentage area of the framing in elevation can be 10–20% of the
opening area.

140

Wooden frames provide insulation because of their relatively low thermal conductivity (approximately 0.16 W/m K). Plastics have a higher conductivity, but their performance in a frame may be improved by designing it to have two or more enclosed chambers. They may also have reinforcing steel included to improve the strength, but the high conductivity of steel diminishes overall insulating performance.

Extruded aluminium has a high conductivity which is much greater than wood. In order to improve insulation, a thermal break is used, which isolates the inner and outer faces of the frame from each other. The improvement can be considerable, depending on the design and material used in the thermal break.

The typical frame U values in Figure 8.14 are based on data given in Norwegian Standard NS 3031. These values were obtained either experimentally or by finite element analysis, and take into account the fact that the total frame area is greater than the projected area (Figure 8.17).

The total overall U value of the window can be calculated taking into consideration the insulation of the glazing, the unit spacer and the framing. The calculation procedure is set out in Figure 8.16.

The life expectancy of double glazed units is dependent on the framing and glazing design (Figure 8.15).

Figure 8.15 Unit life and frame design

The durability of sealed units is strongly influenced by the unit design and specification, the workmanship during manufacture, and the glazing system into which the unit is to be fitted. The glazing system is of critical importance in ensuring that maximum durability is obtained from the sealed unit. If the seal of a unit is in contact with water for a long period, that unit may fail prematurely. Moisture can appear in the rebate area due to rain water penetration either directly from the outside, or through frame joints and into the glazing system. All glazing systems must protect the edge seal of the unit, either by preventing ingress of water into the glazing area or by ensuring that any water which penetrates to the edge of the unit is soon removed by drainage and/or ventilation. Some unit seal materials do deteriorate if exposed to sunlight; it is vital therefore to ensure that frame rebates are deep enough to fully cover the complete seal on a unit.

THE THERMAL INSULATION OF COUPLED WINDOWS

Coupled windows make use of the insulating effect of entrapped air by glazing each pane in a completely separate sash. This thermally isolates the internal and external sashes which are coupled and fit as a single frame. The space between the glass panes in the frames is usually between 50 and 100 mm and must be vented to the outside air to minimize condensation.

Venting does not mean ventilating, in which substantial air movement is obtained. In an appropriately vented space, the air is virtually static. However, owing to pressure and temperature changes, causing contraction and expansion of the entrapped air, a small amount of air is forced in or out through the vent. Commonly, in manufactured windows, the venting is provided by a small gap between the sash members amounting to only a fraction of a millimetre. The venting allows equalization of air pressure between the space and the exterior and also equalization of moisture vapour pressure preventing condensation on the inner face of the outer sash.

HIGH INSULATION WINDOWS

In Scandinavia, overall window insulation levels (frame and glass) as low as 0.8 $W/m^2 K$ are targeted. This is approaching the limit which might currently be achieved with conventional technology, using quadruple glazing, low emissivity coatings and insulating gases (Figure 8.18).

The frame and sashes must have substantially improved levels of insulation. Currently, the better frames achieve U values for wood of 1.4 $W/m^2 K$ and for plastic (UPVC) of 2.0 $W/m^2 K$.

Figure 8.16 Overall window U value calculations

The thermal transmittance of windows is made up of three components: glass or double glazed unit (excluding frame or sash); frame or sash; and spacer between panes (double glazed units). These component values are determined separately as shown by the following formula:

$$U_w = \frac{A_g U_g + A_{wf} U_{wf} + P_{wf} U_s}{A_g + A_{wf}}$$

where

U_w = thermal transmittance
A_g = projected areas of glazing (m^2)
A_{wf} = projected area of window frame or sash (m^2)
U_g = thermal transmittance of glazing (W/m^2 K)
U_{wf} = thermal transmittance of window frame or sash (W/m^2 K)
P_{wf} = length of inner perimeter of window frame or sash (m)
U_s = linear thermal transmittance due to spacer in multiple glazing units (W/m^2 K)

The frame and glass area definitions are set out in Figure 8.17.

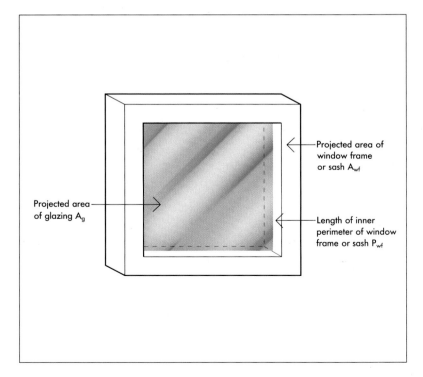

Figure 8.17
Frame and glass area definitions

Figure 8.18
The Scandinavian window

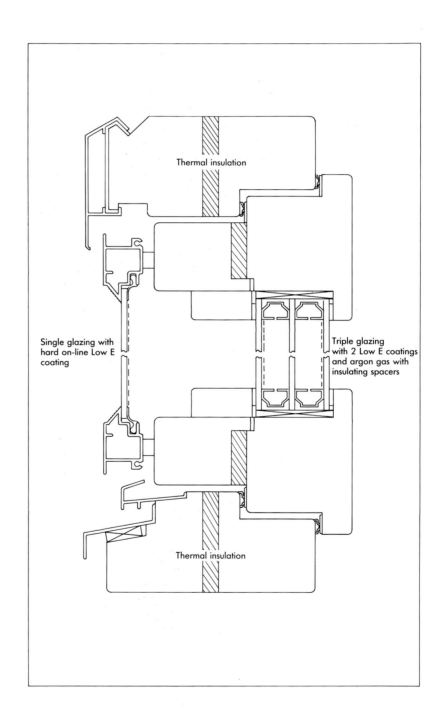

Thermal insulation

Single glazing with hard on-line Low E coating

Triple glazing with 2 Low E coatings and argon gas with insulating spacers

Thermal insulation

TESTING, MEASUREMENT AND STANDARDS

The development of simple codes to categorize the insulation of the whole window depends on the use of standardized measurement methods. International standards are currently under development by the International Organization for Standardization (ISO) and in Europe by the Commission Européenne de Normalisation (CEN). These standards concern direct measurements of U value which are obtained by the use of a hot box method. In this method, the window is fixed into a test aperture in a wall between a hot box and a cold box (Figure 8.19).

In the cold box, typical external design temperatures and standardized air movement (2–4 m/s wind velocities) are provided. The hot box is maintained at typical internal design

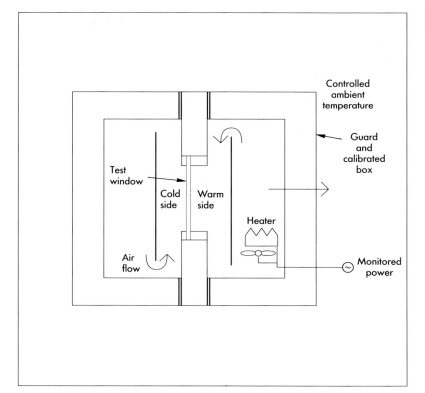

Figure 8.19
Section of a hot box

temperatures, with air movement occurring only by natural convection. The energy provided to maintain steady conditions is measured, and comparison is made with calibrated and standardized samples to determine the U value of the window in the test aperture.

The standards specify exactly how these tests should be done so that comparison of measured values between different test facilities is possible, within prescribed limits of accuracy (Figure 8.20).

CONDENSATION

Air is a mixture of gases including water vapour. The water vapour exerts a partial pressure which increases proportionally as the water concentration increases. At any given temperature there is a limiting maximum vapour pressure, called the saturated vapour pressure, where the air cannot hold any more water vapour.

If air, containing water vapour, comes into contact with a cooler surface, it is cooled locally to the temperature of the surface. If the saturated vapour pressure of the cooled air is less than the original vapour pressure, the excess moisture is deposited on the surface as condensation. The surface temperature at which condensation begins to form is called the dew point.

The ratio of the water vapour pressure at room temperature to the saturated water vapour pressure at that temperature is known as the relative humidity, and is expressed as a percentage. This is a measure of the water content of the air at a given temperature, and many domestic activities (such as cooking and washing) which liberate water vapour increase the relative humidity and thus the occurrence of condensation.

In all cold and temperate climates, condensation can occur on the inside of windows when the external temperature falls significantly below the internal temperature and cools the glass. At times of high external humidity, condensation can also occur on the outside glass surface when its temperature falls due to long wave radiation to clear skies.

Figure 8.20
Hot box, Pilkington Glass Ltd, St
Helens, UK

The onset of condensation on the interior glass surface can be controlled either by reducing the humidity, thereby lowering the dew point, or by raising the inside glass surface temperature. The latter can be achieved by increasing the insulation of the window, for example by the use of a double glazed unit.

Nomograms for the prediction of the conditions under which condensation will start are based on four parameters:

- inside air temperature
- outside air temperature
- indoor relative humidity
- U value of the glazing.

If any three are known, the fourth can be derived (Figure 8.21).

Figure 8.21
Condensation prediction chart

When the internal air temperature is 20 °C and the relative humidity is 60%, condensation will not form on double glazed units with U value 2.8 W/m² K until the external temperature falls below −5 °C. Under the same internal conditions, condensation will form on single glass with U value 5.4 W/m² K when the external temperature falls below 7 °C.

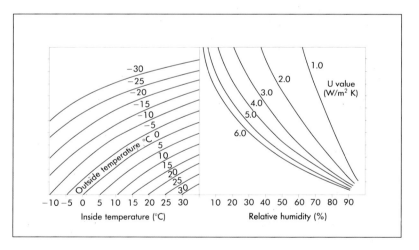

Figure 8.22 Basic equations for thermal transmittance

The thermal transmittance U of glazing is given by the equation:

$$u = \frac{1}{\left[\frac{1}{h_e}+\frac{1}{h_t}+\frac{1}{h_i}\right]}$$

where

h_e and h_i are the external and internal heat transfer coefficients h_t is the conductance of the multiple glazing unit:

$$1/h_t = (\Sigma_N 1/h_s) + dr,$$

where

h_s is the gas space conductance
N is the number of spaces
d is the total thickness of glass used
r is the thermal resistivity of glass (1 m K/W).
$h_s = h_g + h_r$, where h_g is the gas conductance
h_r is the radiation conductance.

Gas conductance
The gas conductance (h_g) is given by the equation:
$$h_g = Nu\, \lambda/s$$
where
s is the mean width of the space (m)
λ is the thermal conductivity W/(mK)
Nu is the Nusselt number
$$Nu = C(GrPr)^n$$
where
C is a constant
Gr is the Grashof number
Pr is the Prandtl number
n is an index

$$Gr = \frac{g\, s^3\, \Delta T\, \rho^2}{T_m\, \mu^2}$$

$$Pr = \frac{\mu\, c_\rho}{\lambda}$$

where

ΔT = temperature difference between gas space bounding surfaces (K)
ρ = gas density (kg/(m^3))
μ = dynamic viscosity (kg/(m s))
c_ρ = specific heat of gas (J/(kg K))
g = gravitational acceleration (9.81 m/s^2)

149

Constant and exponent values

The Nusselt number is calculated from equation above. The values of the constant C and exponent n are given in the table below.

Radiation conductance

The radiation conductance (h_r) for each gas space is given by the equation:

$$h_r = 4\sigma \left[\frac{1}{\varepsilon_1} + \frac{1}{\varepsilon_2} - 1 \right]^{-1} T_m^3$$

where

σ is Stefan's constant

ε_1 and ε_2 are the corrected emissivities at mean temperature T_m absolute.

Values of constant C and exponent n

Direction of heat flow	Space	C	n	Nu=1 for GrPr less than:
Horizontal	Vertical	0.035	0.38	6780
Upward	45°	0.10	0.31	1680
Upwards	Horizontal	0.16	0.28	696

Values at intermediate angles are obtained by linear interpolation.

For values of GrPr less than the value of the last column of the table, the Nusselt number is unity, corresponding to a heat transfer regime of conduction only.

Where the heat flow is downwards convection can be considered suppressed for all practical cases and the value of the Nusselt number is unity.

BIBLIOGRAPHY

ASHRAE, ASHRAE *Handbook of Fundamentals*, American Society of Heating, Refrigeration and Air Conditioning Engineers, Atlanta, GA, 1989

BS 874 *Determining Thermal Insulating Properties. Part 3, 1987: Tests for Thermal Transmittance and Conductance. Section 3.1: Guarded Hot Box Method*, British Standards Institution

BS 6993 *Thermal and Radiometric Properties of Glazing. Part 1, 1989: Method for Calculation of the Steady State U Value (Thermal Transmittance). Part 2, 1990: Method for Direct Measurement of U Value (Thermal Transmittance)*, British Standards Institution

CIBSE *Guide*, Vol.A, Section 3, 'Thermal properties of building structures', Chartered Institution of Building Services Engineers, 1980

DIN 4108 Part 4 *Heat Protection in Highrise Buildings, Heat and Damp Conditions, Technical Characteristic Values*, Deutches Institut für Normung e.V., (in German).

DIN 52619 Part 2 *Regulations of Heat Transfer Resistance and Heat Transfer Coefficients of Windows from Glazing Measurements*, Deutches Institut für Normung e.V., (in German).

Hartmann, H. -J. Heat Transfer in Windows and Parts of Facades, *Windows and Facades*, 17, Vol 2, 39–45, 1990 (in German).

ISO 6946 *Thermal Insulation Calculation Methods. Part 1, 1983: Steady State Thermal Properties of Building Components and Building Elements*, International Standards Organisation

Johnson, T.E. *Low-E Glazing Design Guide*, Butterworth, Boston, 1991

NBR NS3031, *Thermal Insulation: Calculation of Energy and Power Demand for Heating and Ventilation in Buildings*, Norges Byggstandardiseringsrad, 1986

Owens, P.G.T. 'Heat reflective coatings on glass', *Building Services Engineering Research and Technology*, 5, (2), 1984

Owens, P.G.T. and Barnett, M. 'Reducing glazing U values with low emissivity coatings and low conductivity gases', *Building Services Engineer*, 41, (11), 250–252, 1974

Pilkington Glass Ltd *Windows and Environment*, Part 3, 'Windows and heat', Section 2, 'Condensation', Pilkington Environmental Advisory Service, 1969

CHAPTER 9

Heat Gain

In the first instance it is clearly advisable to build glass houses only in temperate zones, and not in the equatorial and polar regions as well.

Scheerbart, *Glasarchitektur*, 1914

An improved understanding of environmental physics, the development of building services and new product technologies are now available to solve the problems implied in Scheerbart's warnings. Heat gain – mainly solar heat gain – through windows can usefully contribute to the heating of the building. On the other hand it can cause thermal discomfort, or unnecessary loading on any refrigeration and air conditioning equipment. Solar control glass, usually either body tinted (absorbing) or coated (reflecting), is often used to reduce unwanted solar gain. Window area, orientation and shading devices are other efficient means of control which may be used in combination with these types of glass, but except for blinds and louvres they are not dealt with in this book.

The effect on internal air temperature of solar heat gain through the windows of a naturally ventilated office may be reduced by substituting solar control glass for clear glass. This effect and the effect of a similar substitution on air conditioning load is shown in Figures 9.2 and 9.3.

Figure 9.1 *(Opposite)*
The Sun

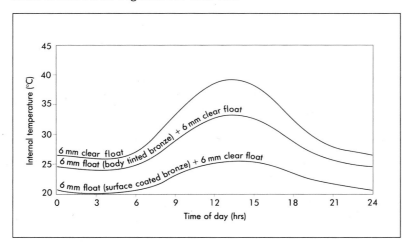

Figure 9.2
Hourly summer internal air temperatures in a typical office building in a temperate climate

For a natural ventilation rate of three air changes per hour in July, a solar control glass (with a shading coefficient of 0.18) maintains the internal temperature below 27 °C, which is a typical upper limit of comfort temperature for lightly clothed sedentary occupants.

Figure 9.3
Effect of solar heat gain through
windows in air conditioned offices

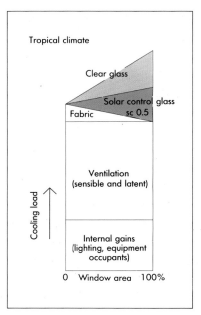

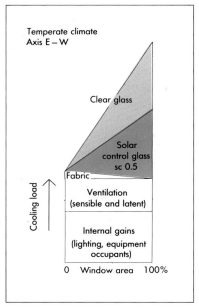

These diagrams show the influence of area and type of glass on the total cooling load in temperate and tropical climates. The glass has greater effect in the temperate climate, because the lower altitude of the sun has a large effect on the south facing zones of the building. In a tropical climate the sun's altitude is much higher, giving a correspondingly smaller effect on the south facing zone. This would not apply for buildings with their main axis lying north–south. With this orientation the glazing loads are much higher, for both the temperate and the tropical climates, because the morning sun causes high loads on the east facing windows, while the afternoon sun produces high loads on west facing windows. In both climates, the preferential orientation of the building is usually with the main axis lying east–west. This principle applies in both southern and northern latitudes.

THE MECHANISM OF SOLAR CONTROL

Chapter 3 identifies the effect of glass on electromagnetic radiation as consisting of three mechanisms, reflection, transmission and absorption, which for solar control purposes are defined in terms of the following parameters:

- reflectance: the fraction of solar radiation at normal incidence that is reflected by the glass
- absorptance: the fraction of solar radiation at normal incidence that is absorbed by the glass
- direct transmittance: the fraction of solar radiation at normal incidence that is transmitted directly through the glass.

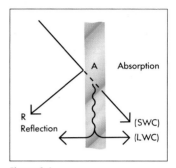

Figure 9.4
Transmission, reflection and absorption

The total solar heat transmittance is the fraction of solar radiation at normal incidence that is transferred through the glass. It is composed of the direct transmittance, also known as the short wave component, and the part of the solar absorptance dissipated inwards by long wave radiation and convection, known as the long wave component (Figure 9.4). The proportions of the absorbed energy which are dissipated either inside or outside depend on the glazing configuration and the external exposure conditions (Figure 9.5). Where the inner glass surface has an emissivity different from that of ordinary glass, the internal surface heat transfer is reduced.

Figure 9.5 External exposure values

The part of the absorbed energy which goes to heat the glass is dissipated inside and outside according to the external exposure conditions. These relate external surface heat transfer coefficients (W/ m^2 K) to the wind speeds. Typical nominal exposures assumed in different countries vary somewhat, giving rise to small differences in published figures of total solar heat transmittances for the same glass:

	External exposure W/m^2 K
Germany	23
UK	16.7
USA: summer	23
winter	34

The solar radiant heat transmission properties of solar control glasses can also be described by their shading coefficients (Figure 9.7).

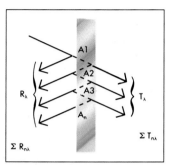

Figure 9.6
Transmission, reflection and
absorption in single glass

Figure 9.7 Shading coefficients

The shading coefficient is derived by comparing the properties of the solar control glass (or any glazing system) with a clear float glass having a total solar heat transmittance of 0.87 (such a glass would be between 3 mm and 4 mm thick). There are two components: the short wave shading coefficient (the direct transmittance divided by 0.87); and the long wave shading coefficient (the fraction of the absorptance that is dissipated inwards, divided by 0.87).

The total shading coefficient (the total solar heat transmittance divided by 0.87) is the sum of the short and long wave shading coefficients.

Shading coefficients are calculated for radiation at normal incidence. For other angles of incidence, the glass is compared with clear glass in the same situation. As a result, the shading coefficients are substantially constant at all incident angles of solar radiation.

Transmission is measured in terms of the transmittance $T_{(\lambda)}$ for each relevant wavelength λ of the incident radiation. Integrated over the whole spectrum, this is abbreviated to T for all the solar energy directly transmitted.

Reflection occurs at each separate surface. For a single glass, reflection from its first surface is reinforced by transmitted radiation reflected back by its second surface. There are multiple internal reflections, and the sum of these reflections at each wavelength is the spectral reflectance $R_{(\lambda)}$. The solar reflectance R is also a weighted integral over all wavelengths of the spectral reflectance.

Absorptance is the solar energy remaining in the glass (after reflection and transmission) and raises the glass temperature. The absorptance A is given in the equation $A = 1 - R - T$, and the sum of T, R and A is illustrated for single glazing in Figure 9.6.

When two or more glass panes comprise the window, the mechanism is more complex. Transmission, reflection and absorption are defined by T, R and A but are now compounded to account for the absorption in each pane, for example $A = A_1 + A_2 \dots A_x$.

All the foregoing properties are angle dependent. The incident solar radiation usually comprises a direct beam, a background diffuse component from the sky and a diffuse component reflected from the ground and/or surroundings. All these embody angle dependent contributions (Figure 9.8). The sun angle can be readily predicted. It is dependent on the time of day, the time of year and the orientation and inclination of the glass surface. Taking into account this angular effect, the incident solar intensity can be calculated sufficiently to quantify the solar energy transmitted through the glazing. These considerations are integrated in the formula for calculating total instantaneous heat gain through glass (Figures 9.9a, b). This is for a notional glass of total solar transmittance of 0.87. All other glass products can be compared with this value by their total instantaneous heat gain factors.

Computational methods are available for calculating solar gain through glass and windows (Figure 9.9c).

MODIFYING THE GLASS PERFORMANCE FOR SOLAR CONTROL

By taking advantage of modifications in transmission, reflection and absorption properties, it is possible to specify glass and glass combinations which control the total solar transmittance to desired levels. Such control can be achieved by the use of:

- body tinted glass products (with increased absorption)
- reflective coated glass (with increased reflection and usually also increased absorption)
- combinations of body tinted and reflective coatings in a single glass
- single and double glazed units and laminated glass incorporating blinds and louvres.

Variable light transmission products are also discussed later as a future development.

Reduction in total solar transmittance will usually decrease the transmission of the visible part of the solar spectrum. Some body tints and coatings are able to preferentially attenuate the non-visible solar radiation, leaving the transmission of the

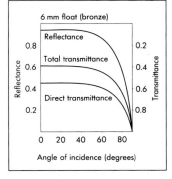

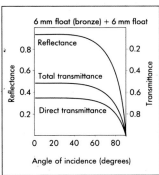

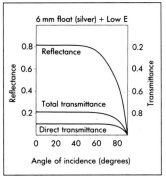

Figure 9.8
Angular dependence

Figure 9.9a Solar gain through 4 mm clear glass

Total instantaneous heat gain is calculated for a clear single glass that has a total solar transmittance of 0.87 for radiation at normal incidence. It includes both the directly transmitted short wave radiation and the fraction of the absorbed energy that is released inwards when the outdoor wind velocity is 2 m/s. The basic equation is:

$$Q = I_a T_i \cos i + T_{60} (I_s + I_g)$$

where

Q = total solar heat gain per unit area of glazing

a = angle of altitude of the sun

b = angle of the glazing to the horizontal (for backward sloping glass b < 90°, for forward sloping glass b > 90°)

c = window–sun azimuth (the horizontal angle of the sun with respect to the normal to the window wall)

i = angle of incidence: $\cos i = \cos a \sin b \cos c + \sin a \cos b$

r = ground reflectance

I_a = intensity of direct solar radiation for the sun at altitude a (see I_s and I_g)

I_{ad} = intensity of sky diffuse radiation for the sun at altitude a (see I_s and I_g)

I_s = intensity of sky diffuse radiation impinging on the glass :
$$I_s = I_{ad} (1 + \cos b) / 2$$

I_g = intensity of ground reflected radiation impinging on the glass: calculated for ground reflectance, r, from $I_g = (I_a \sin a + I_{ad}) r (1 - \cos b) / 2$

T_i = total transmittance of clear single glazing for angle of incidence i

T_{60} = total transmittance of clear single glazing for angle of incidence 60°, which is found to be close to the value of diffuse transmittance.

$T_i \cos i$ is often calculated from a polynomial in $\cos i$ fitted to an experimentally derived curve. For the nominal glass, I_a and I_{ad} are calculated from a polynomial fitted to standardized values of solar radiation at various altitudes.

The position of the sun depends upon the time of the day, the time of year and the latitude of the site. It is derived from:

$$\sin a = \sin L \sin d + \cos L \cos d \cos h$$

$$\sin z = \sin h \cos d + \cos d$$

where

a = angle of altitude of the sun

L = latitude of the site

d = declination of the sun, according to the time of year

h = hour angle of the sun: it is zero at solar noon and changes by 15° per hour

z = horizontal angle of the sun with respect to its noon position.

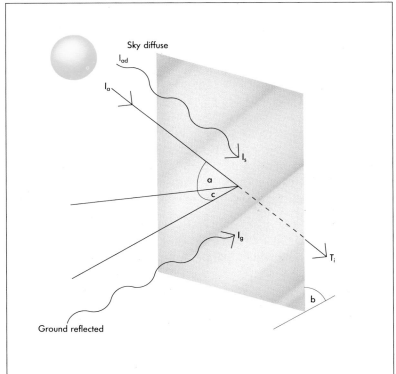

Sky diffuse

I_{ad}

I_a

I_s

a

c

I_g

T_i

b

Ground reflected

Figure 9.9b
Factors influencing total solar heat gain Q

For notation see Figure 9.9a.

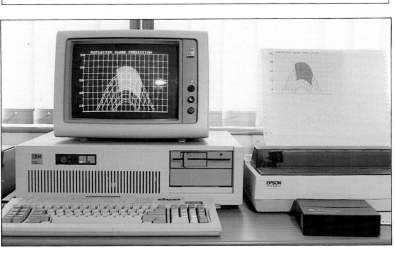

Figure 9.9c
Computational methods for calculating solar performance, Pilkington Glass Ltd, St Helens, UK

greater proportion of the visible radiation largely unchanged (discussed below under body tinted and reflective coated glasses). Such preferential performances are preferred for passive solar applications.

The relationship between light transmission and total heat transmission is referred to as the light/heat ratio. Some manufacturers use it as a descriptive code, quoting a light transmission figure followed by a total heat transmission figure (for example: 72/62, 6 mm green body tinted glass; 89/86,4 mm clear glass). The performance of typical glass products showing the relationship between light transmission and total solar heat transmission is illustrated in Figure 9.10.

Some North American manufacturers adopt a 'coolness index' which is daylight transmittance divided by the shading coefficient. For example, a glass with 0.66 light transmission and a total shading

Figure 9.10
Performances of different glass products showing relationship between light transmission and total solar heat transmission

The green area represents the envelope enclosing most practically available architectural glass products.

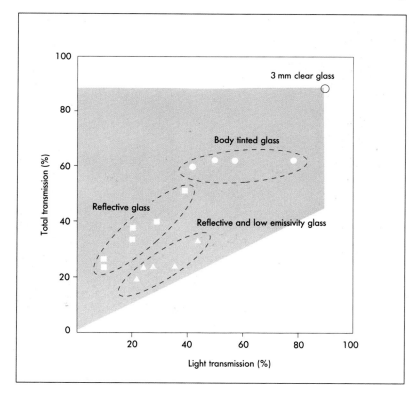

coefficient of 0.58 would have a coolness index of 1.14.

The reflection from glass can be increased if the window is tilted, with the top outwards to make use of the distinct curvature of the reflection factor curve at angles of incidence of about 60° (Figures 9.8). This practice is particularly favourable in temperate latitudes for buildings with a predominantly north–south orientation. At 54°N, for example, the maximum solar altitude at midday is 60°. On south facing vertical glazing the angle of incidence is 60° and the direct transmission factor is 0.73. Tilting the glass outwards by 15° would increase the angle of incidence to 75° and reduce the direct transmission factor to 0.51. The values of direct transmission factor that occur at the solar zenith in midsummer for various latitudes and glazing angles are shown in Figure 9.11b. The values are for 4 mm glass facing north or south. An energy efficient building using this principle is shown in Figure 9.11a.

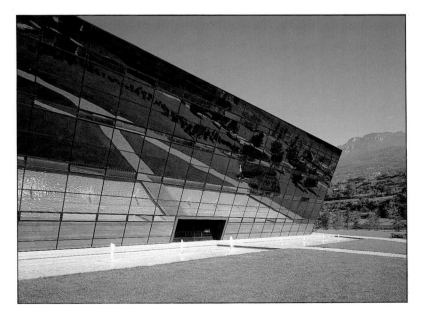

Figure 9.11a
Volani Building, Trento, Italy
Architects: Armani-Trento

Figure 9.11b Transmission factor of sloping glass for radiation direct from the sun at its zenith

Latitude	Angle of window from vertical			
	0°	5°	10°	15°
50°	0.70	0.64	0.56	0.43
55°	0.74	0.70	0.64	0.53
60°	0.76	0.73	0.69	0.63

BODY TINTED GLASS

These types of glass are normally tinted grey, green, bronze or blue throughout their thickness. Their solar control properties and colour vary with thickness whilst their reflectances are slightly less than clear float. When used in double glazed units they are best positioned as the outer pane because the heat due to the absorbed radiation is more easily dissipated to the outside.

Performances of a typical range of clear and body tinted glass products are shown in Figure 9.13. The spectral behaviour of green body tinted glass is illustrated in Figure 9.12 and a comparison can be made with that of float glass in Figure 9.14. Body tinted glass is limited in the amount of solar attenuation which can be obtained by its absorption.

Figure 9.12
Green body tinted glass: solar spectrum

The transmission curve peaks in the green band of the visible region, giving the glass its colour. Absorption is the main means of radiation attenuation. High absorption in the infrared and relatively high transmission (low absorption) in the visible region means low heat transmission with high light transmission (light/heat ratio favouring light transmission). Reflection is slightly less than clear glass.

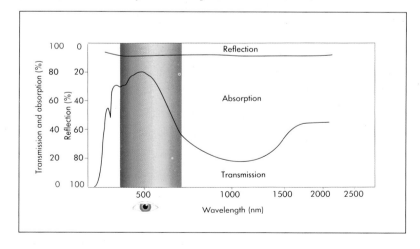

Figure 9.13 Body tinted glass performances compared with clear float

Glass type and thickness	Light		Direct solar radiant heat			Total	Shading coefficient		
							Short	Long	
	T	R	T	R	A	T	wave	wave	Total
Float									
4 mm	0.89	0.08	0.82	0.07	0.11	0.86	0.94	0.04	0.98
6 mm	0.87	0.08	0.78	0.07	0.15	0.83	0.90	0.05	0.95
10 mm	0.84	0.07	0.70	0.07	0.23	0.78	0.80	0.09	0.89
12 mm	0.82	0.07	0.67	0.06	0.27	0.76	0.77	0.10	0.87
Body tinted									
6 mm 72/62 green	0.72	0.06	0.46	0.05	0.49	0.62	0.53	0.19	0.72
6 mm 54/62 blue	0.54	0.05	0.46	0.05	0.49	0.62	0.53	0.19	0.72
4 mm 61/70 bronze	0.61	0.06	0.58	0.06	0.36	0.70	0.67	0.13	0.80
6 mm 50/62 bronze	0.50	0.05	0.46	0.05	0.49	0.62	0.53	0.19	0.72
10 mm 33/51 bronze	0.33	0.04	0.29	0.04	0.67	0.51	0.33	0.26	0.59
12 mm 27/47 bronze	0.27	0.04	0.23	0.04	0.73	0.47	0.26	0.28	0.54
4 mm 55/68 grey	0.55	0.05	0.55	0.05	0.40	0.68	0.63	0.16	0.79
6 mm 42/60 grey	0.42	0.05	0.42	0.05	0.53	0.60	0.48	0.21	0.69
10 mm 25/49 grey	0.25	0.04	0.25	0.04	0.71	0.49	0.29	0.27	0.56
12 mm 19/45 grey	0.19	0.04	0.19	0.04	0.77	0.45	0.22	0.29	0.51

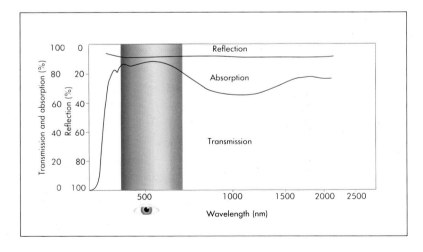

Figure 9.14
Clear float glass: solar spectrum

The transmission curve does not peak significantly at any point in the visible region, indicating a lack of any dominant colour. The absorption and reflection are small. There is a relatively high light transmission (averaging 84% in the visible region).

REFLECTIVE COATED GLASS

To maximize solar heat attenuation, increased direct reflection has to be used, and this is achieved by means of reflective coatings. Their application also increases absorption of solar energy compared with clear glass. These coatings are sometimes 'soft', and in order to prevent their damage they are protected by lamination or more commonly in sealed double glazed units.

Figure 9.15
Hotel Maritim, Bonn, Germany
Architects: Hentrich-Petschnigg and
Partners, Düsseldorf

The use of coatings in solar control provides:

- greater production flexibility and performance range than body tinted glass
- higher performances (greater solar heat attenuation)
- light/heat ratios nearer theoretical optimum values
- a range of colour appearances in transmission and reflection.

The numerous coating compositions available provide a wide range of performances, which is further increased by their combination with body tinted glass products. Thus glass with a particular performance may be selected for specific applications.

It is convenient to consider two areas of application, since hot climates and temperate climates have different requirements for glass performance.

The main requirement for the use of glass in hot climates is to provide high levels of solar control to minimize solar heat gains and air conditioning load, and to avoid overheating. Related to this requirement are the needs to insulate the building from heat conducted to the interior from outside and to provide some control of glare arising from reflection from the ground, surrounding buildings and bright areas of sky (excluding direct sunlight). There will also be a need to provide some natural lighting and sunlighting and a view of the outside.

To meet some or all of these needs, the solar transmission of glass products for hot climates will be wide ranging (in some cases, light and solar heat transmissions are less than 10%). For improved solar control, low emissivity glass, glazed as the inner pane of a sealed double glazed unit, acts as a second line of defence. Heat absorbed by the solar control glass is reflected back out by the low emissivity coating, to provide better solar control.

In hot climates the improved U value reduces the conduction heat gains across the glazing – an important factor in extensively glazed air conditioned buildings. In hot humid climates condensation can form on the outside of windows in air conditioned buildings. The higher insulation of double glazed units incorporating low emissivity glass means that in air conditioned buildings the outer glass is warmer and the incidence of condensation is reduced.

Glass performance in temperate climates has to balance the need to provide solar control, to reduce the risk of summertime overheating, against the need to provide, by glass transmission, high levels of natural illumination and the benefits of passive solar heating. The required total solar transmission and light transmission will not be quite as low as those demanded in hot climates. To allow passive solar design the performance range could be: total transmission 20% to 70%, light transmission 35% to 90%, and a U value in the range 1.0 to 2.0 W/m² K.

These performance parameters for glass must be related to the specific application. There is no one ideal product for all applications. The spectral performance determines the combinations of heat and light transmission which are possible, as illustrated by the envelope in Figure 9.10. This shows that if 100% light transmission was possible the minimum total transmission would be 54%. Since there will almost always be a desire for daylight, a family of ideal fixed performance glass products could be loosely defined depending on whether full daylighting, passive solar heating or solar control is the main objective.

High thermal insulation with solar control is a requirement for the temperate climates. Since some solar control coatings exhibit low emissivity it is possible to combine these functions in the same product.

The performances of reflecting glass products are compared with those of clear float in Figure 9.16. A comparison of a selection of reflecting glass products indicating their shading coefficient versus U value is shown in Figure 9.17, and the spectral performance of two reflecting glass products is given in Figures 9.18 and 9.19. There are, however, many other glass types with a great variety of performances and colours.

Figure 9.16 Table of reflecting glass performances compared with clear float

Glass type and thickness	Light		Direct solar radiant heat			Total	Shading coefficient		
	T	R	T	R	A	T	Short wave	Long wave	Total
Float									
4 mm	0.89	0.08	0.82	0.07	0.11	0.86	0.94	0.04	0.98
6 mm	0.87	0.08	0.78	0.07	0.15	0.83	0.90	0.95	0.95
10 mm	0.84	0.07	0.70	0.07	0.23	0.78	0.80	0.09	0.89
12 mm	0.82	0.07	0.67	0.06	0.27	0.76	0.77	0.10	0.87
Reflecting									
6 mm 10/23 silver	0.10	0.38	0.08	0.32	0.60	0.23	0.09	0.17	0.26
10 mm 10/23 silver	0.10	0.37	0.08	0.30	0.62	0.23	0.09	0.18	0.27
6 mm 20/34 silver	0.20	0.23	0.16	0.18	0.66	0.34	0.18	0.21	0.39
10 mm 20/34 silver	0.20	0.22	0.15	0.17	0.69	0.34	0.17	0.22	0.39
6 mm 10/24 bronze	0.10	0.19	0.06	0.21	0.73	0.24	0.07	0.20	0.27
10 mm 10/24 bronze	0.10	0.18	0.05	0.19	0.76	0.24	0.06	0.21	0.27
6 mm 20/33 blue	0.20	0.20	0.15	0.21	0.64	0.33	0.17	0.21	0.38
10 mm 20/33 blue	0.20	0.20	0.15	0.19	0.66	0.33	0.17	0.21	0.38
6 mm 30/39 blue	0.30	0.16	0.21	0.18	0.18	0.39	0.24	0.21	0.45
10 mm 30/38 blue	0.30	0.15	0.20	0.17	0.63	0.38	0.23	0.21	0.44
6 mm 40/50 blue	0.40	0.10	0.32	0.10	0.58	0.50	0.38	0.19	0.57
10 mm 40/49 blue	0.40	0.09	0.31	0.09	0.60	0.49	0.36	0.20	0.56

Compared with a float glass surface, these reflecting coatings, owing to their composition, exhibit lower levels of emissivity which improves their U value.

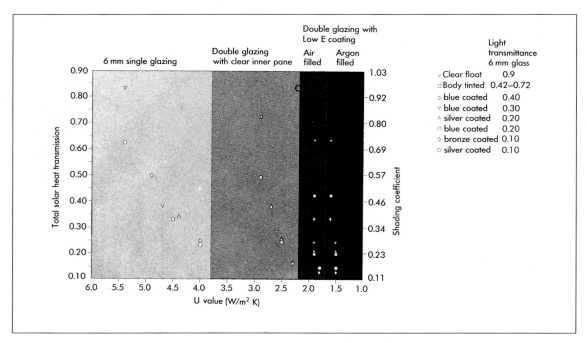

Figure 9.17 *(Above)*
Comparison of shading coefficient
versus U value in reflecting
glass products

Figure 9.18
Reflecting coated glass: solar spectrum

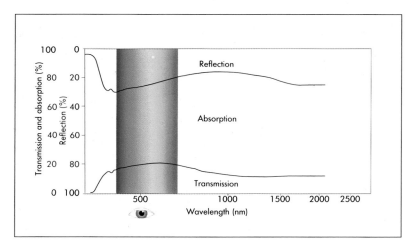

There is high reflection (20–25%) in
the visible region. Absorption and
reflection jointly provide the means of
solar attenuation. There is low visible
light transmission (15–20%) and low
UV transmission. Visible transmission
peaks near the green part of the
visible region of the spectrum (the
glass appears greenish in
transmission). The glass appears blue
by reflection because the reflection
curve is high at the blue end of the
visible region.

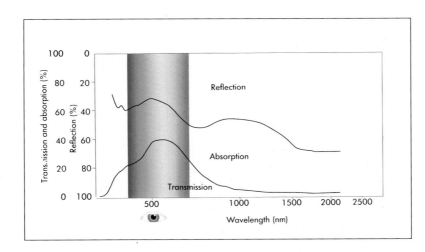

Figure 9.19
High performance glass (gold): solar spectrum

Reflection is the main means of solar attenuation. It continues to increase in the far infrared, producing low emissivity and thus providing an increased thermal insulation potential in multiple glazing. Transmission peaks in the blue/green part of the visible spectrum. Reflection curve peaks towards the red end of the visible region, giving a golden colour by reflection. The transmission is mainly in the visible region, providing a light/heat ratio favouring light transmission.

Figure 9.20
Flachglas AG, Germany

Solar control glass

169

Figure 9.21
Weena Huis, Amsterdam, Holland

SINGLE AND DOUBLE GLAZED UNITS AND LAMINATED GLASS INCORPORATING BLINDS AND LOUVRES

The use of blinds in windows will affect the window shading co-efficient. This will depend upon the solar optical properties of the glass and the material of the blind, on the coefficients of heat transfer at the window surfaces, and on the geometry of the blind and the angular position of the sun.

The relevant solar optical properties are the reflectance, absorptance and transmittance of the material to solar radiation. Some typical values are tabulated in Figures 9.22 and 9.23. These only apply to the blind as a whole when the material is flat and parallel to the plane of the window, that is when curtains are drawn together without folds or when louvres are completely closed. When louvres are partly open the solar optical characteristics are modified by inter-reflections, and the effect can now be assessed by computer routines that calculate the angle factors on which the interchange of radiant energy between adjacent louvres depends.

Figure 9.22 Solar optical properties of typical blind materials and glass products

Blind material	Reflectance	Absorptance	Transmittance
Opaque materials:			
high performance blind	0.70	0.30	0.00
medium performance blind	0.55	0.45	0.00
low performance blind	0.40	0.60	0.00
Translucent materials:			
high performance blind	0.50	0.10	0.40
medium performance blind	0.40	0.20	0.40
low performance blind	0.30	0.30	0.40
Clear glass	0.07	0.13	0.80
Body tinted glass	0.05	0.51	0.44

A typical arrangement, especially with horizontal louvres, is to set them at 45° to the plane of the window and this condition was assumed in calculating the modified values in Figure 9.23.

Figure 9.23 Solar optical properties of blinds with louvres set at 45°

Blind material	Reflectance	Absorptance	Transmittance
Opaque materials:			
high performance blind	0.50	0.39	0.11
medium performance blind	0.40	0.53	0.07
low performance blind	0.30	0.65	0.05
Translucent materials:			
high performance blind	0.50	0.14	0.36
medium performance blind	0.40	0.27	0.33
low performance blind	0.30	0.40	0.30
Clear glass	0.09	0.13	0.78
Body tinted glass	0.07	0.53	0.40

Shading coefficients have been computed (Figure 9.24) for a range of blind materials used in the air space of a double glazed unit and compared with single glazing. The short wavelength and long wavelength shading coefficients are important because they reveal the characteristics of the solar heat gain process. For example, the addition of medium reflectance louvres to a single glazed heat absorbing glass reduces the total shading coefficient from 0.69 to 0.50, an improvement of 28%, but the long wavelength shading coefficient is increased from 0.18 to 0.35, which more than doubles the immediately sensible heat load. Only the short wavelength component of the solar heat gain is subject to the delaying and reducing effect of the thermal capacity of the structure. Care is therefore needed in the application of total shading coefficients to the estimation of the capacity of air conditioning plant.

One effect of high performance blinds is to reflect a large proportion of the transmitted energy for a second pass through the glazing so that the energy absorbed in the glass is increased and the temperature of the glass rises. With some glass products in some glazing systems this increased temperature can introduce a risk of thermal fracture of the glass, discussed in Chapter 15.

As the position of the sun changes continually it is usually impracticable to keep louvres in the most efficient position. It is general practice to make an initial setting, probably to somewhere near the 45° position, and then leave the blind unchanged until the sun is off the façade. Because the apparent motion of the sun is predominantly vertical at sunrise and sunset and horizontal at noon, the practice of leaving blinds in one position favours the choice of vertical louvres for east and west facing windows and horizontal louvres for windows facing towards the equator.

VARIABLE TRANSMISSION GLASS

Experimental variable transmission (VT) glass was introduced in Chapter 1 as a developmental product enabling the future building envelope to be used dynamically. This means the building skin would be constructed in such a way that it is able to respond automatically to the variable nature of the external climate and to the needs of the internal environment. To date this has only been partially achieved by mechanical means.

Figure 9.24 Shading coefficients of glazing systems with blinds or louvres

Window design	Blind perform-ance	Opaque louvre material Shading coefficient			Translucent louvre material Shading coefficient		
		Short wave	Long wave*	Total	Short wave	Long wave*	Total
Single glazing without blind							
Clear glass	-	0.92	0.05	0.97	0.92	0.05	0.97
Body tinted glass	-	0.51	0.18	0.69	0.51	0.18	0.69
Double glazing without blind†							
Clear glass	-	0.52	0.12	0.64	0.52	0.12	0.64
Body tinted glass	-	0.41	0.14	0.55	0.41	0.14	0.55
Double glazing with louvres between, closed†							
Clear glass	High	0.00	0.15	0.15	0.32	0.10	0.42
Clear glass	Medium	0.00	0.21	0.21	0.31	0.14	0.45
Clear glass	Low	0.00	0.26	0.26	0.31	0.18	0.49
Body tinted glass	High	0.00	0.19	0.19	0.17	0.16	0.33
Body tinted glass	Medium	0.00	0.21	0.21	0.17	0.17	0.34
Body tinted glass	Low	0.00	0.23	0.23	0.17	0.19	0.36
Double glazing with louvres between, at 45°†							
Clear glass	High	0.09	0.19	0.28	0.28	0.12	0.40
Clear glass	Medium	0.05	0.24	0.29	0.25	0.16	0.41
Clear glass	Low	0.04	0.27	0.31	0.23	0.20	0.43
Body tinted glass	High	0.04	0.20	0.24	0.14	0.16	0.30
Body tinted glass	Medium	0.03	0.22	0.25	0.13	0.18	0.31
Body tinted glass	Low	0.02	0.23	0.25	0.11	0.20	0.31

* Includes long wavelength radiation and convected heat

† In all the double glazing systems the inner glass is clear

For example, in the façade of the Arab Institute, Paris (Figure 9.25), shading devices perform like an iris in a camera, continually opening and closing to control solar attenuation. Work on non-mechanical methods is in the main confined to research into VT glass involving photochromic, thermochromic and electrochromic materials; the latter are likely to provide the full range of solar attenuating responses necessary for architectural glass applications.

Figure 9.25
The Arab Institute, Paris, France
Architect: Jean Nouvel

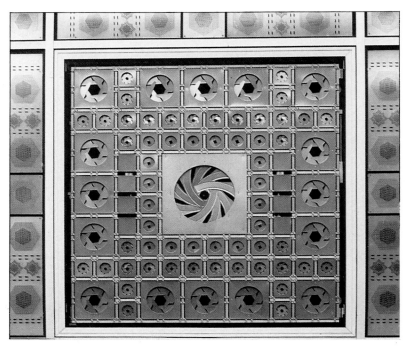

Electrochromism is the property of a material or system to change transmission reversibly under an applied electrical potential. Coatings that can be actively controlled are preferred since they can be continuously adjusted over a range of performances. Electrochromic coatings are transparent multi-layer coatings which are more complex than coatings currently available. A small electrical voltage activates the electrochromic layer, changing the tint and thus the total solar transmittance and light transmittance. Reversing the voltage restores the original transmittance. The voltage may be generated from the building services control or manually by the occupant (Figure9.26).

Figure 9.26
    The Lawrence Berkeley Laboratory in California (Selkowitz and Lampert 1989) has proposed a list of ideal performance properties for Variable Transmission glass products:

Solar transmittance:	bleached	50–70%
	coloured	10–20%
Visible transmittance:	bleached	50–70%
Near infrared reflectance:	bleached	10–20%
	coloured	below 70%
Switching voltage		1–5 volts
Memory		1–24 hours
Switching speeds		1–60 seconds
Cyclic lifetime		above 10^6 cycles
Lifetime		20–50 years
Operating temperature		−30 to +70 °C

The R&D necessary to achieve these properties is currently the recipient of significant investment amongst glass manufacturers and research institutes, supported by the advanced glazing work of the International Energy Agency and the EC Joule programme.

However, products being developed will probably have to compromise on their ability to respond to heat and light transmissions across a wide spectrum, as they will be required to save both on cooling load and on electrical lighting load. It may be that there is no universal single VT glass, and several glass products may be developed for separate uses and climates (Figure 9.27).

Preliminary estimates by the Solar Energy Research Institute in 1986 indicated a relatively small benefit-to-cost ratio when measuring solely the energy advantages of the VT glass, whilst the previously mentioned Lawrence Berkeley Laboratory study indicated significant cost savings when set against the incremental cost of variable transmission glazing. Both studies point to the variety of material options for variable transmission and suggest

Figure 9.27
Variable transmission glass
Pilkington Group Research, Lathom,
UK.

that it would be a serious mistake to believe that 'energy cost payback' alone will drive this new market. However, since the costs of variable transmission glass products are not yet known, the final cost effective comparisons cannot be made.

Initial calculations based on the temperate UK climate indicate that variable transmission glass may have less energy saving advantage than in the USA, but the conclusions from both studies must be further explored in the context of local climate, the specific building form and services design. More work is required before firm cost targets are set for final material development.

Other factors which will affect the market demand are the need for higher comfort levels, personal control by the occupant, office productivity, amenity and novelty. Personal control, whilst being of benefit to the building occupant, runs the risk of inattentive or mismanaged control, as occurs with many mechanical systems. The dilemma of having personal or centralized control can be overcome, however, by providing manual override to the centralized control system for the variable transmission window. Occupants want personal control over the local environment, but it must be reliable and simple.

In cellular buildings with unitized systems the variable transmission window has a clear advantage (especially when the unitized heating and air conditioning system is integrated into the wall), since both local services and the window can be under the control of the individual local occupant.

BIBLIOGRAPHY

ASHRAE *Passive Solar Heating Analysis: a Design Manual*, American Society of Heating, Refrigeration and Air Conditioning Engineers, Atlanta, GA, 1984

Pilkington Glass Ltd *Windows and Environment*, Part 3 'Windows and heat', Section 3 'Climate', section 5 'Heat transfer through windows', Pilkington Environmental Advisory Service, 1969

Pilkington Glass Ltd *Glass and Solar Heat Gain*, Pilkington Environmental Advisory Service, March 1989

Pilkington Glass Ltd *Glass and Transmission Properties of Windows*, Pilkington Environmental Advisory Service, February 1991

Selkowitz, S. and Lampert, C. 'Application of Large Area Chromogenics to Architectural Glazings', in *Large Area Chromogenics: Materials and Devices for Transmittance Control*, ed. C.M. Lampert and C.G. Grangvist, Optical Engineering Press, Washington, USA, 1989

SERI/PR-255-2627 'Solid-State Electrochromic Switchable Window Glazing FY 1984 Progress Report', Solar Energy Research Institute, Colorado, USA, April 1986

Shurcliff, W.A. *Solar Heated Buildings of North America: 120 Outstanding Examples*, Brick House, Harrisville, NH, 1978

CHAPTER 10

Heat Balance

In houses with a south aspect the sun's rays penetrate into the portico in winter but in summer the path of the sun is right over our heads and above the roofs, so there is shade. If, then, this is the best arrangement we should build a south side loftier to the winter sun, and the north side lower, to keep out the cold winds.

Xenophon (quoting Socrates), *Memorabilia*

Figure 10.1 *(Opposite)*
Neoplan, Stuttgart, Germany
Architect: Herbert Gergs

USING SOLAR RADIATION

Since early times, building designers have sought to exploit solar energy. It was the Romans, however, rather than the Greeks who first used glass for window openings.

Since glass is transparent to solar radiation its influence on energy use is more complicated than just its effect on heat loss. The single regard of heat loss has undoubtedly led to some misunderstanding of the role of the window in the energy balance of buildings.

Passive solar gain from the window is a term used to describe both the useful energy that may be provided in reducing some or all of the heating requirements, and the daylighting which can offset electric lighting loads. All buildings with glazings can be described as passive solar buildings to some degree.

Over the last 15 years, the benefits of passive solar gain for energy conservation have been included in building legislation for countries in cold, temperate and hot climates. Regions as diverse as Switzerland and California included passive solar gain in legislation after the energy crisis of the 1970s.

Maximizing passive solar gain presents a challenge for window designers because reducing unwanted solar gains in summer may also reduce beneficial heat gains in winter. In addition, because daylight contains roughly half of the energy in the solar spectrum, rejection of solar gains also leads to a reduction of daylight available to the occupant. As a general rule, glass products with a more favourable light/heat ratio (proportionally higher light than solar heat transmission) are preferred in passive solar applications.

However, attempts in isolation to optimize glass properties to admit passive solar gain and provide winter insulation will not succeed unless the building in question is fully designed for its particular climate and location. For this same reason, the following discussion of passive solar gain can only be a generalized one, providing guidance for the use of glass in the context of national practices, research and experience.

THE WINDOW AS A SOLAR COLLECTOR

Glass loses heat by conduction, but also admits solar heat by transmission. Even in high latitudes, solar gains can outweigh heat losses during the heating season. The periods when a predominantly sun facing window acts as a form of solar collector are shown in Figure 10.2. Other orientations admit less but still significant amounts of solar radiation.

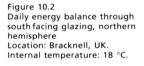

Figure 10.2
Daily energy balance through south facing glazing, northern hemisphere
Location: Bracknell, UK.
Internal temperature: 18 °C.

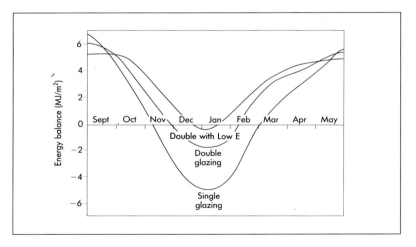

However, assessment of the annual energy balance (Figure 10.2) gives a broad indication. The designer needs to know if the solar gain is useful (offsetting heat losses), or if the solar gain occurs mainly on the milder days of the heating season, when rooms already adequately heated by lighting and occupants may become overheated. For domestic accommodation the following generalizations may be applied to a room with a sun facing window.

If passive solar gain is efficiently utilized:

- Energy consumption increases, although proportionally less so, with increasing single glazed window areas.
- Energy consumption does not increase with increasing double glazed window areas.
- Energy consumption decreases with increasing double glazed Low E window areas.

If passive solar gain is not utilized:

- Energy consumption increases with increasing window areas.

These generalizations are represented by Figure 10.3.

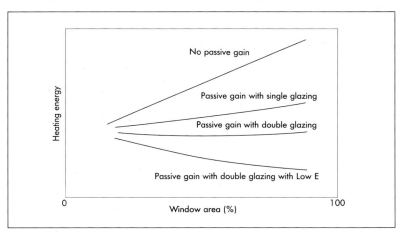

Figure 10.3
Energy consumption, passive gain and window area

In temperate climates calculations have shown that, in a typical office, passive solar gains can be used to significantly offset most annual heat losses. The greater the window insulation, the more closely are heat losses offset.

Using daylight to save artificial lighting can be a substantial means of saving energy. The deeper the daylight penetrates into a building, the more the artificial lighting can be reduced. Large windows and shallow buildings offer potential for significant savings, especially in offices, where the provision of artificial lighting often expends more energy than the heating.

Figure 10.4
Thermostatic radiator valve

It is reasonable to generalize that energy consumption in offices can be independent of window area.

If larger windows are designed to save energy, they may improve the view out, but there is also the possibility of over-heating in summer. Shading devices can be designed to let in the daylight and winter sun, but keep out the summer sun. Solar control glass can help to keep a building cool in summer, and admit enough light and heat to give a positive energy balance in winter.

WINDOWS CANNOT DO IT ALONE

Passive solar gains through windows are wasted if all the lights are permanently on and the radiators in sunny rooms continue to provide heat, irrespective of the levels of daylight and solar heat admitted. Heating and lighting systems must be controlled so that they respond to variations in heating and lighting levels if the energy provided by the window is to be used effectively.

The technology required is simple, readily available and can be cost effective. Good thermostatic controls, such as thermostatic radiator valves (Figure 10.4), ensure that heat is not provided when solar radiation can provide it instead. Photocell controls reduce the use of electric lights when enough daylight is available. Dimming controls may be more acceptable to occupants than on–off controls. Using these simple principles, windows are rarely an energy penalty.

COMMERCIAL BUILDINGS

In temperate climates, the general relationship between window area and electric lighting is that lighting energy consumption decreases as window area increases when suitable controls are used. With heating energy, a similar general conclusion cannot be drawn; sometimes energy consumption rises with increased window area, sometimes it falls. When heating energy reduces as window size increases, the total energy consumption for heating and lighting will show the same trend. When heating energy increases with window size, the total energy consumption may increase, or decrease, while in some

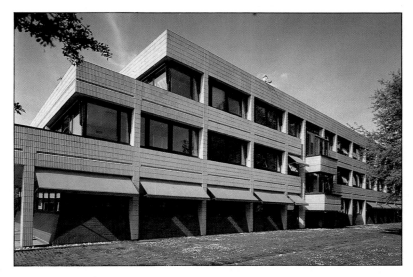

Figure 10.5
Building Research Establishment
office, Watford, UK

Crown copyright 1992

instances there will be an optimum intermediate window area providing minimum energy consumption.

This is shown in calculations by the UK Building Research Establishment for a new office. The least energy consumption for the south elevation occurs at about 45% glazing (Figure 10.5). The total energy consumption at about 60% glazing is slightly less than at 30%. A similar study for the north elevation shows an optimum window area of about 30%. It is possible, therefore, for an increase in window area to reduce energy consumption. However, changes in the window area produce only small changes in energy consumption compared with the effects of other parameters. Two important influences are the level of artificial lighting (the design illuminance) and the requirement for air conditioning. The results of a range of office studies using the Pilkington Interactive Program are shown in Figures 10.6a, b.

For both hot and cold climates, reductions in electricity usage in commercial office buildings by means of passive gain for various glazing types, when using a single clear pane as a base comparison, have been reported by Sullivan *et al.* (1987) of the Lawrence Berkeley Laboratory. They presented a comparative study in which commercial perimeter zone electrical energy (with cooling and fan energy) and peak electrical demand

Figure 10.6a
Predicted energy consumption of an office

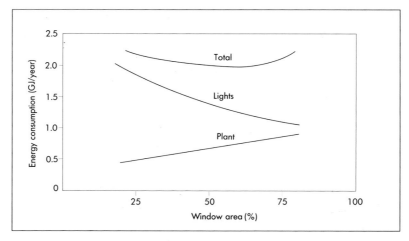

Figure 10. 6b
Variation of energy consumption with glazing area for various lighting loads in shallow plan offices

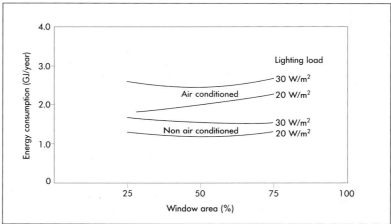

were analysed as functions of glass, with a particular emphasis on the use of products with various solar optical properties.

This study showed the potential for substantial savings through combining solar load control and lighting energy reduction by the admission of daylight. Incremental solar gain (total solar heat gain) and daylighting induced peak electrical demands (daylight transmission), for four glazed orientations of a commercial building, were examined as functions of the

184

product of shading coefficient and window area. Seven glass types were analysed over an area of 50 m² for comparison. The relative effectiveness in passive solar utilization of the seven glass types shows that, in this building case, the most effective glass is the one with the highest insulation and the most favourable light/heat ratio (Figure 10.7).

Figure 10.7 Passive solar utilization for different types of glazing

Window type	U value W/m² K	Shading coefficient	Visible transmittance %	Passive utilization %
G	5.11	0.95	0.88	0
G_g	5.45	0.72	0.75	23
G–G	3.31	0.82	0.78	13
G_g–G	3.37	0.58	0.66	40
G_y–G	3.37	0.55	0.38	42
G E–G	1.94	0.67	0.74	29
G_gE–G	1.83	0.35	0.47	63

G, clear glass; G_g, glass tinted green; G_y, glass tinted grey; E, a Low E coating on the inner surface of the outer panel. Glass thickness is 6 mm; air space is 12 mm.

ESTIMATING PASSIVE GAIN

The more detailed calculations of energy use made possible by computers enable the windows and their influence in energy consumption to be properly evaluated. However, for most building designs, such computer analyses are not always undertaken.

A simple rule of thumb method has been devised which identifies, in a single figure, the influence of the window on total energy use. This figure is the 'effective U value', which is the conventional U value modified to take account of useful solar radiation falling on the window during the course of the heating season (Figure 10.8). The method of calculating effective U value is standardized so that a comparison of products can be made. A wide range of effective U values is produced by the interaction of various factors (Figure 10.9). Effective U value has been proposed for standardization in Europe.

In the United States, the energy rating index (ERI) is used. The ERI is designed to compare products for their heating season efficiency under average conditions, for the northern United States of America. The ERI employs data provided by the National Oceanic and Atmospheric Administration. It permits a convenient standard comparison for all glass products. The index uses average winter temperatures and sunlight intensity over the northern USA and Canada. The sunlight intensity is an average of four elevations and assumes about 30% clear skies over the heating season. Window energy performance in this index is a function of three variables: heat loss (U value), solar gain (shading coefficient) and air infiltration (considered to be zero for glass and most fixed windows). The energy rating index is calculated (Figure 10.10) by deducting heat loss and air infiltration from solar gain:

energy rating index = solar gain – heat loss – air infiltration

When the energy rating index formula is applied to some of the window glass products used today, it shows the wide variation that can be achieved (Figure 10.11).

Figure 10.8 Effective U value formula

The equation for effective U value is

$$U_e = U - \frac{1000\, T_g T_d f I}{24\, DD}$$

where

U = conventional U value (W/m^2 K)

T_g = total solar transmittance

T_d = dust, dirt and/or shading factor

f = utility factor

I = solar radiation incident during heating season (kW h/m^2)

DD = number of degree days with internal room temperature as basis (kelvin days)

The utility factor f is necessary because all the solar radiation passing through the window may not be able to displace an equivalent heating load, especially at the beginning and end of the heating season. During warmer days there may be a surplus of solar heat after the heating requirements of the building have been met.

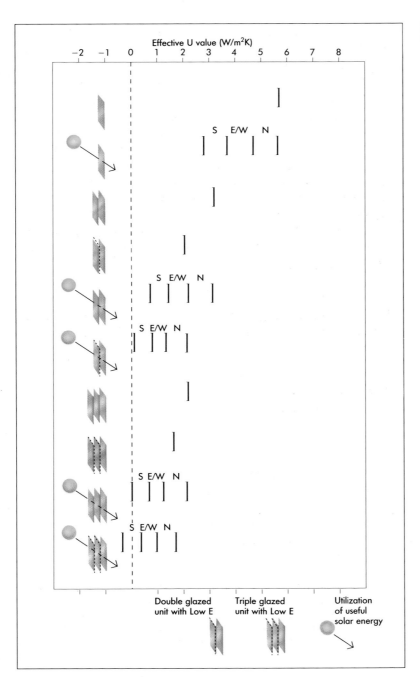

Figure 10.9
Range of effective U values

Figure 10.10 Energy rating index calculation method, USA

The energy rating index may be calculated using the following formula:*

$$ERI = 100 \left[(0.87 \times SC \times I) - (T_i - T_o \times U) - (\text{air leakage}) \right]$$

where

ERI = heating season energy rating (hundreds Btu per hour per ft^2)
SC = shading coefficient
I   = average solar insolation (22.9 Btu per hour per ft^2)
T_i = indoor temperature (average 70 °F)
T_o = outdoor temperature (average 31 °F)
U   = overall U value (BTU per ft^2 h °F)

	ERI	U	SC
Hard Low E	+ 329	0.36	0.87
Medium hard Low E	+ 212	0.39	0.87
Soft coat Low E	+ 148	0.34	0.74
Clear double glazed	− 98	0.50	0.93
Single glazing	−2376	1.12	1.00

*In the equation, 0.87 is a constant needed to normalize the shading co-efficient to air rather than 1/8 inch (4 mm) clear glass. Air leakage is included to demonstrate its relation to energy and to allow its inclusion if available.

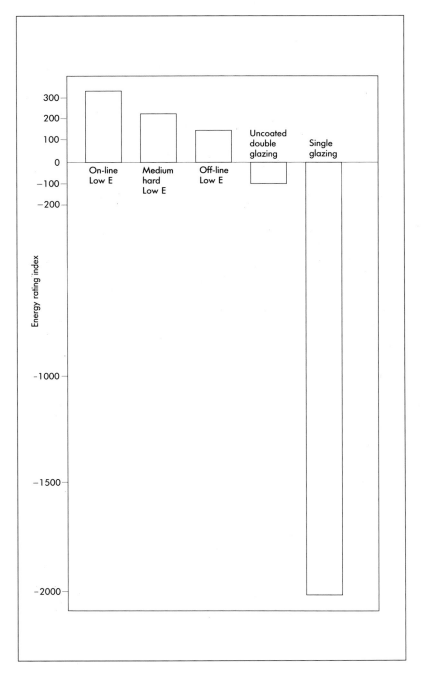

Figure 10.11
Energy rating index: a range of performances

BIBLIOGRAPHY

BRECSU *Best Practice Programme – Good Practice Case Studies*, Building Research Energy Conservation Support Unit, Building Research Establishment, Watford, UK, 1989–92

Commission of the European Communities *Building 2000 – a Series of Design Studies Illustrating Passive Solar Architecture in Buildings in the European Community*, CEC Directorate General for Science, Research and Development, Brussels, 1990–92

CSA Preliminary Standard A440.2-M1991, *Energy Performance Evaluation of Windows and Sliding Glass Doors*, Canadian Standards Association, Toronto, 1991

den Ouden, C. and Steemers, T. *Building 2000. Vol. 1: Schools, Laboratories and Universities, Sports and Educational Centres. Vol. 2: Office Buildings, Public Buildings, Hotels and Holiday Complexes*, Kluwer, Dordrecht, Netherlands, 1991

Gertis K, Hauser G, Künzel H, Nikoic V, Rouvel L, and Werner H, 'Heat gain because of windows', *Bautechnik*, 2, 1980 (in German)

NFRC 100– 91: Procedure for Determining Fenestration Product Thermal Properties. The National Fenestration Rating Council, Silver Spring, Maryland, USA, 1991

Owens, P.G.T. 'Energy conservation and office lighting', *Proceedings of the 1970 International Symposium of the Chartered Institution of Building*

Owens, P.G.T. 'Effective U value', *Building Services Engineering Research and Technology* 3(4), 1982

Pilkington Glass Ltd *Glass and Offices*, Pilkington Technical Advisory Service, 1979

Sullivan, Arasteh, Sweitzer, Johnson, and Selkowitz, *The Influence of Glazing Selection on Commercial Building Energy Performance in Hot and Humid Climates*, Lawrence Berkeley Laboratory, University of California, July 1987

UK Atomic Energy Authority, Energy Technology Support Unit, Department of Energy, Harwell, UK, various publications

'Energy conservation in the built environment', *Proceedings of the 1970 International Symposium of the Chartered Institution of Building*

CHAPTER 11

Durability of Glass

Bricks may crumble
Coloured glass endures.

Scheerbart, *Glasarchitektur*, 1914

Glass is one of the the most durable building materials. Much twelfth and thirteenth century glass is perfectly sound. The durability of modern architectural glass under ordinary conditions of exposure is excellent, and therefore the possibility of deterioration is usually ignored. However, 'ordinary conditions of exposure' must be clearly described.

The chemical structure derived from the melting and forming of glass affects the chemical durability (Figures 11.2 and 11.3).

The more random and complex the molecular structure, the more resistant to crystallization, the more durable, and the less soluble the glass becomes (Figures 11.4 and 11.5).

Figures 11.1a and b *(Previous double page)*
Bank of China Tower, Hong Kong
Architects: Pei, Cobb, Freed, and Partners
Glass: Spectrum, USA

The building's multiple facets mirror the ever-changing environment, providing a distinctive vertical axis to the towering Hong Kong skyline. The whole is supported by an innovative composite structural system strengthening the building against high velocity winds. The tower is clad in silver coated reflective glass that appears blue under sunny skies but grey when it meshes with Hong Kong's brooding clouds. Each storey is three panes high, the upper and lower spandrels having the same finish as the central vision band for a taut uniform surface. Each pane is part of a rigorous 1.333 metre modular system designed to unify the building and express its organizational logic. The building is 30 modules wide, its floors are 3 modules high, and its intermediate columns are 6 modules apart. Window washing is achieved by eight gondolas launched from concealed platforms that emerge and contact with the walls at strategic locations. (Pei, Cobb, Freed and Partners).

Figure 11.2
Raw materials for making float glass being fed automatically into furnace, Pilkington Glass Ltd, St Helens, UK

Figure 11.3 Materials for the manufacture of window glass (soda-lime–silica glass)

The main constituent, silica sand (SiO_2), can be melted to form a glass but the temperature required is in the region of 1800 °C and, even at this temperature, the melt is very viscous and like cold syrup. For practical and economic reasons, the high melting temperature and viscosity of silica are reduced by adding sodium oxide (Na_2O) as a flux in the form of soda ash. This can reduce the fusion temperature of the mix substantially to 800 °C. However, glass of such a composition would have poor durability. To achieve high durability and prevent crystallization in the melting and cooling processes, the amount of sodium oxide added is closely controlled, and further complexing oxides of calcium (CaO) and magnesium (MgO), in the form of limestone and dolomite, are added.

Aluminium and iron oxides are present as impurities in the sand and other ingredients. It is uneconomic to remove them, so care is exercised in sand selection to control their presence. Aluminium oxide, however, improves durability. Iron oxide aids melting and produces the greenish tint (as seen through the cut edge).

The main raw materials are:

sand	SiO_2	soda ash	Na_2CO_3
dolomite	$MgCa(CO_3)_2$	limestone	$CaCO_3$
salt cake	Na_2SO_4		

A typical glass analysis is as follows (%):

SiO_2	72.6	MgO	3.9
CaO	8.4	Na_2O	13.9
Fe_2O_3	0.11	K_2O	0.6
Al_2O_3	1.1	SO_3	0.2

Figure 11.4
Simplified two-dimensional representation of a glass network (after the model of Zachariasen and Warren)

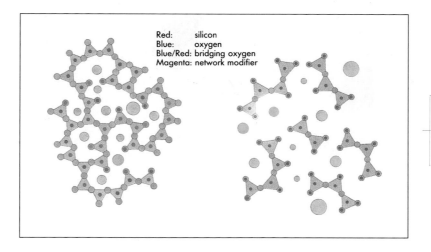

Red: silicon
Blue: oxygen
Blue/Red: bridging oxygen
Magenta: network modifier

Figure 11.5 Chemical structure of window glass and its durability

Many theories about possible structures of glass have been propounded to explain why it has certain properties and to predict how it may behave under specific conditions.

The structure is made up of oxides of various elements – mainly silicon, sodium, potassium, calcium, magnesium, and aluminium – which at high temperatures form a very viscous magma. The temperature is so high (above the melting point of simple silicates) that, with the high viscosity and short period of cooling, ions or molecules cannot orient themselves quickly enough into complete silicate or oxide configurations to form crystalline compounds. These randomly oriented molecular states are 'frozen' into the structure because of their lack of mobility in the highly viscous state of the mass.

If soda–lime–silica glass is held at temperatures in the region of 800–1100 °C for a long enough time, crystallization will take place and a variety of crystalline silicates and oxides will separate from the viscous mass. This process of crystallization is known as devitrification (devitrified glass is opaque) and is avoided by fairly rapid cooling of the molten glass through this temperature region.

One of the simplest theories about the structure of glass was propounded by Zachariasen and Warren in the 1930s: that glass is made up of network formers and network modifiers. Silicon and oxygen ions bonded together (formers) form the basic three-dimensional network structure; ions of sodium, potassium, calcium and magnesium (modifiers) are bonded in the holes in the silicon–oxygen former network. A simplied version of the glass structure is shown in Figure 11.4. By using a variety of elements as network modifiers, the glass structure is so complex that it possesses properties of high durability.

When soda–lime–silica glass is in prolonged contact with water, and the surface area of glass relative to volume of water is large, the bonding within the holes in the silicon–oxygen network (being weaker than the silicon–oxygen bonds) is broken and sodium followed by calcium and magnesium ions are released into solution. In small amounts of water the alkali concentration of the solution increases and further attack of the residual acidic silicon–oxygen network can take place, giving rise to severe corrosion of the glass surface. Alkali leaching by water does not readily take place in glazing and occurs only under severe conditions of misuse. Experience in service has demonstrated that soda–lime–silica window glass is a uniquely durable material.

GLASS SURFACES

The problem of how to form high quality 'polished' or 'fire' finished surfaces from molten glass, without the need for a grinding and polishing process, was eventually solved in the float process which revolutionized flat glass production. It is a process whereby a molten ribbon of glass can be formed and conveyed with 'polished' surfaces in a continuous flow process. The forming of the 'polished' surfaces is achieved by floating the glass ribbon on molten tin at a temperature of about 1000 °C. In the float chamber the atmosphere is controlled to prevent oxidation. The process is continuous, and a ribbon of glass typically 3.3 m wide in a range of thicknesses from 1.5 to 25 mm may be produced for architectural purposes.

The forming process influences the nature of the final surface. A surface which is fairly rapidly cooled, in the older rolled glass manufacturing process, can have different chemical characteristics from a float glass.

COATED SURFACES

The chemical and physical nature of coatings produced on-line and off-line can differ. Some are extremely weather resistant and hard, while others have poor durability and are soft (easily damaged). While some coatings are resistant to external environmental effects, others, having highly desirable properties, are less durable and need protection in double glazed units or in lamination.

On-line coated glass may be toughened, but with off-line coatings it is usual to toughen the glass before coating, as their nature is such that they usually cannot withstand the temperatures reached during toughening.

Coatings applied to glass usually consist of thin film deposits of metals, metal oxides or nitrides (Figure 11.6). Some of the more commonly used metals, oxides and nitrides are those of copper, lead, silicon, titanium, tin, cobalt, iron, nickel, chromium, indium, silver and gold deposited on hot or cold glass under controlled conditions.

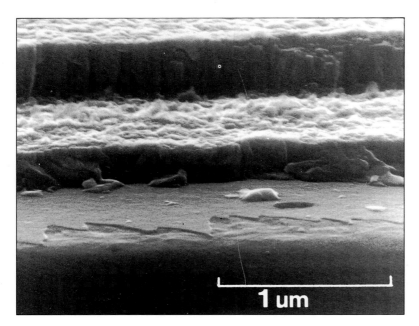

Figure 11.6
Three-layer coating on glass,
Pilkington Technology Centre,
Lathom, UK

The layers are
(1) thickness 200 Å, for adhesion;
(2) thickness 2250 Å, for emissivity;
(3) thickness 2400 Å, for reflectivity.

Precise control of thickness is essential as colour, principally that seen in reflection, invariably depends on the coating thickness. Normally, film thicknesses are in the region of a few hundred to a few thousand angstroms. Within these thicknesses a range of coloured and reflective coatings can be obtained. To produce thin films uniformly and consistently requires much development and an accumulation of knowledge which is guarded by licensing agreements and patents.

Pyrolytic coatings, deposited on-line, are chemically resistant because of the high temperature of formation and partial fusing or diffusion into the glass surface. They are often, but not always, very hard. Off-line cold formed coatings are generally less durable chemically and mechanically, but some can be tenaciously bonded to the glass surface.

The same metal oxide coating, deposited by different processes, can often have quite different chemical and mechanical properties. It is misleading to classify particular metal, metal oxide and metal nitride coatings as being either hard or soft *per se*.

Flat glass surfaces, either coated or uncoated, need to withstand conditions of:

- handling
- storage
- in service.

HANDLING

The main considerations in handling glass are usually not of chemical resistance but of mechanical damage and its prevention. The fundamental principle is that, if mechanical damage is to be avoided, contact between glass and metal (or other hard material) must be prevented.

Problems can also arise due to other materials coming in contact with glass surfaces, particularly if those materials are rubbed on the surface in handling operations. For example:

- Rubber sucker pads of handling equipment can impart modifications to the surface, which often are not visible until condensation forms on the surface. This reveals that specific areas, which have been in contact with sucker pads, have different characteristics.
- Rubber tyres of the conveyor rollers may rub the surface rather than produce movement.

Such effects, while not being detrimental in terms of surface deterioration, can be visually annoying. They can become detrimental when the glass is used for mirrors and other off-line coated products. The surface contaminants 'bond' tenaciously to glass and usually require a treatment with polishing powder or mild abrasive for removal.

STORAGE

Glass surfaces can be affected by:

- formation of condensation between closely stacked panes

- rain water or sea water lodging between panes, on site or in transportation
- incompatibility of materials used to separate panes in a pack.

Climatic changes can bring about condensation. When air and glass temperatures have been low, then, on a rapid warming up of the air, moisture saturation occurs at those glass surfaces of lower temperature and condensation is produced. A pack of interleaved glass, at a lower temperature, can become saturated with condensate drawn between panes by capillary action. The surface of flat glass is extremely durable in the window system, but the lodgement of moisture between panes in storage can have a severe surface effect after a relatively short period (months rather than years). Once moisture is between panes then it is retained by capillary forces and it is extremely difficult for the glass to dry out naturally.

Similarly when glass is stored uncovered, then rain water (or in transportation, sea water) may also wet the glass pack. Where packs have been left in the wet state for months, the panes may even have fused together with corrosion products.

For proper storage of glass there are two considerations. First, glass should be stored in warehouses, dry and free from condensation. Second, in the short term, glass in transport or on a building site should not be allowed to become wet. Corroded glass may only be apparent when glazed and viewed in reflection. The damage is characterized by 'oily' multi-coloured surface patches; these patches are very thin layers of corrosion, which interfere with the light reflection to give the appearance of iridescence. This is usually impractical to rectify, and necessitates replacement of the entire pane.

Interleaving materials are used by glass manufacturers to prevent mechanical rub between packaged panes during transportation and storage. If chosen with acidic characteristics (pH value in the region of 4.5 to 6.0) they have a further important role to play in protecting the surfaces from corrosion. They may be of a particulate nature (powder) or in the form of sheets. Where moisture is present, the acidic nature of the interleavant

Figure 11.7
Testing for environmental imposed conditions, humidity and temperature cycling, Pilkington Glass Ltd, St Helens, UK

inhibits the leaching out of alkali, so delaying the corrosive attack of the silica structure.

IN SERVICE

After installation, pure rain water will have little effect on the glass surface, as the surface is continually rewashed and dried.

The presence of sulphur dioxide (SO_2) in rain (acid rain) does not present a long term problem to glass surfaces, as it does to many other external building materials, since glass surfaces are resistant to most acids. However, some coated glass may not be resistant if glazed with the coating on the external surface and hence with the complex range of coatings available it is important to follow the manufacturers' instructions.

CONDENSATION

Condensation can occur on both external and internal surfaces. However, the surfaces will not be affected providing the condensation is free to evaporate and is not trapped.

If condensation is trapped, as in a sealed unit where the seal has broken down, surface deterioration can occur. The surfaces first become iridescent and then change through time with varying degrees of opacity.

Coatings on glass are tested to ensure that they are not affected by condensation (Figure 11.7). Where coatings are less resistant to moisture attack, manufacturers usually recommend that they are protected in a sealed unit system.

ATMOSPHERIC POLLUTANTS

These are many and varied, with some confined to local areas. The main types are:

- hydrocarbons
- sulphur dioxide
- atmospheric dust (containing sulphur or, chlorine; or carbonaceous based).

202

It is because of pollutants that cleaning of glass surfaces is necessary. Most of these contaminants sit on the surface as deposits rather than react with the surface to cause deterioration. Regular cleaning is necessary to remove contaminants since, should cleaning not be carried out, with wetting and drying conditions the deposits may become 'baked on' and removal made difficult. The contaminants can also retain moisture in close contact with the surface and in the long term, especially if they are alkaline, glass surfaces can suffer permanent damage. Film contaminants can also build up into layers which unacceptably affect light transmission.

Figure 11.8
Testing for environmental imposed conditions, weatherometer simulating solar radiation in the presence of humidity, Pilkington Glass Ltd, St Helens, UK

SOLAR RADIATION

Solar radiation can cause certain chemical constituents of some glass formulations to experience a colour change (a phenomenon known as solarization). Float glass compositions have been formulated so that such changes do not take place.

Solar radiation absorbed by glass raises the temperature of the glass: the greater the absorption, the higher the temperatures produced. Temperatures generated are usually below 100°C, and at these temperatures clear and body tinted glass products are chemically stable. Low temperatures that can be experienced in service (down to −40 °C) have no chemical or deleterious effect on glass or its surface condition.

Manufacturers of the wide range of coatings on glass carry out testing to simulate solar conditions. Measurements of colour and optical properties are carried out initially and at different times during exposure. Sample checks are made on coatings after exposure to elevated and low temperatures to ensure stability (Figure 11.8).

SALT LADEN AIR

Such air is experienced in coastal regions. There are conditions of wind and rain when the glass surfaces are left with a highly adherent salt containing film, which often is not readily washed off by rain. However, it is not harmful to glass surfaces and, where a regular programme of cleaning is in operation, these deposits will not cause any problems.

WIND AND GRIT

Wind and air borne grit can cause erosion rather than corrosion, and the main effect may be on glass surface strength. Wind blown stone chippings from flat roof finishes on tall buildings are a typically quoted cause of such erosion.

CONSTRUCTION SITES

Building site conditions probably constitute one of the most severe service environments for glass and coated surfaces, and any damage is often expensive to rectify. The adverse effects may only become noticeable under particular lighting conditions after final clean-up (often when the building is first occupied). A particular problem can occur in high rise projects, when glazing is carried out on lower floors while construction work continues on upper floors. Ideally for the glass, glazing should be the last operation.

There are so many materials on building sites that can affect the surface of glass and coatings that it is sometimes surprising that the surfaces survive as well as they generally do. Cement, concrete, plaster, sand, aggregate, water, spray organics, resins, plastics etc. are often splashed or fall on to the glass from upper floors to contaminate both inside and outside surfaces. Many building materials are of an alkaline nature and under wet conditions can cause severe deterioration to glass and coated surfaces.

Where the detailing of the design is poor and there is a lack of regular cleaning of the glazing, 'run-off' can slowly manifest itself from the concrete structure, lead flashing and sealants. Rain water washing over these materials can leach out, or wash from the surface, chemicals which form deposits on the glass surface in the wetting and drying cycles. Removal is often difficult if not carried out early; in the more severe cases, especially with alkaline run-off, damage can be caused to the surfaces and specialist cleaning will be required.

Welding or metal cutting operations are inappropriate in areas where glass has been installed. It is common for complaints about deterioration to be the result of these operations. Red hot metal and oxide produced by such operations can impinge on the glass surface causing pitting. In some cases spherical particles fuse into and are retained in the surface. This condition is impossible to rectify (Figures 11.9, 11.10).

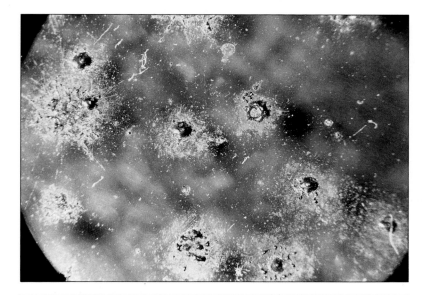

Figure 11.9
Weld splatter (magnification ×60)

Metal particles are splattered on to the glass surface. The heat in the particles causes pitting in the surface and the metal remains embedded. Damage is permanent.

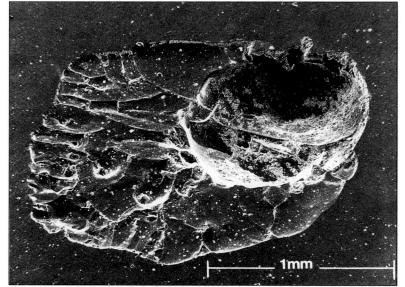

Figure 11.10
Crater damage from weld splatter

When the metal droplet is cleaned off the glass, it reveals the amount of subsurface damage and venting.

Surface contamination can take the form of film deposits or particles and, in any cleaning operation, the reagents used and method of removal should dissolve or lift contaminants from the surface (without rubbing the contaminants over the surface) and flush them away. Surface rubbing can cause serious damage, as particles of contaminant may readily cause scratching.

During external surface renovation of buildings (for example, aluminium frames) chemical cleaners are often used. Some contain fluorides, bifluorides or dilute hydrofluoric acid; these require great care because of the ease with which they can run down the glass or coated surfaces (leaving the surfaces permanently damaged) and because of the risks to personal health.

Compatibility of associated glazing materials with glass and coated surfaces is of importance. There are many formulations within any one type of glazing compound and sealant. The compound manufacturers will have carried out compatibility tests on their range of products with most glass types and will be able to provide guidance. Usually coatings have a high degree of durability, but it is known that sulphur from materials in some gaskets can diffuse into coatings and cause changes in appearance.

In silicone structural glazing systems, where the retention of the glass in the building relies solely on adhesion, it is imperative for the sealant to be compatible with the glass and the coated surface. Strict control of the condition of all surfaces to which the bond is to be made is essential, including the adhesion of the coating to the glass substrate. Glazing recommendations for these systems must be strictly followed.

Spandrel areas often have panels of reflective coated glass products to match the vision areas. Experience has shown that insulation, paints, plastics, adhesives or other materials may give off organic vapours, inside the spandrel, as temperatures may reach approximately 100 °C. The effect of these vapours on the coating, both physically and chemically, must be checked. Appearance changes have been experienced in service due to vapour, in thin film form, condensing on the coated glass surface.

HARDNESS

The concept of 'hardness' – resistance to mechanical surface damage – is of importance (Figure 11.11). Surface damage can be typically of three different types:

- scratch damage: individual line damage marks
- abrasion damage: many fine to coarse scratches close together
- penetration damage: spot penetration (indentation) of the surface.

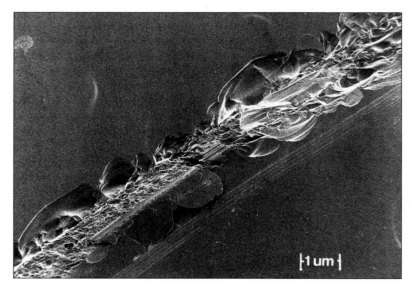

Figure 11.11
Scratch line on surface of float glass, Pilkington Technology Centre, Lathom, UK

This shows both the scratch line and the associated shelling and venting of the glass surface.

The ability of a surface to resist these types of damage is usually considered under the general term of 'hardness'. It is not a specific physical property of a surface, but is complex and needs qualification. With each type of damage, different mechanisms contribute to its formation depending on the loading level used. For example, light loads first produce scratches with some plastic deformation of the surface; this is different to the cracking effect resulting from scratches produced by heavy loads. Even when test conditions are standardized with specific loads and stylus, it is found that results are not always reproducible (Figure 11.12).

Figure 11.12
Abrasion test, Pilkington Glass Ltd, St Helens, UK

A typical apparatus usually consists of a machine with a reciprocating arm fitted with a head covered in felt or other fabric. The head has a constant load applied to it and a slurry of mild abrasive continuously feeds between fabric and glass. Usually the test method consists of a number of rub levels, i.e. 50 reciprocations, 100 reciprocations, 150 etc., after which the damage to the coating is assessed visually under controlled lighting conditions in reflection and transmission, against reference coated samples. From such comparative assessment of abrasion resistance, it is usual to draw up a league table with the most resistant coatings (least damaged) at the top and the least resistant (most damaged) at the bottom. Coatings which have been used satisfactorily in service (on surface 1 or surface 2 in exposed situations or in the internal surfaces of double glazed units) are used as comparators for new coatings.

Glass or coated glass surface hardness is a property which is difficult to measure, whether it is related to scratch, abrasion or indentation, and because of this it is rarely quoted. There is no international standard method of determining the hardness of glass or coated surfaces. While manufacturers have their own in-house test methods, they usually rely on subjective assessment rather than quantitative measurements.

Test information is used, in conjunction with the results of handling and processing trials, to determine how the coating has stood up to these processing conditions. One example is the use of normal hard brushes on washing machines for clear glass which will severely damage 'soft' coatings but will generally not damage 'hard' coatings. With 'soft' coatings, soft brushes have to be used in the washing of the coated surface, before it is incorporated within the cavity of a sealed double glazed unit.

BIBLIOGRAPHY

ASTM E774-88 *Standard Specification for Sealed Insulating Glass Units*, American Society for Testing and Materials, Philadelphia, PA, 1988

DIN 1249, *Chemical and physical performance*, Part 10, Deutches Institut für Normung e.V. (in German)

DIN 52347, *Examination of glass durability – abrasion wheel with scattered particles*, Deutches Institut für Normung e.V. (in German)

DIN 52348, *Examination of glass durability – sanddropping-process*, Deutches Institut für Normung e.V. (in German)

Holland, L. T*he Properties of Glass Surfaces*, Chapman and Hall, 1964

Jones, J.O. *Glass*, Methuen, London, 1956

Zachariasen and Warren, *Journal of the American Chemical Society*, 54, 3841, 1932

CHAPTER 12

Strength of Glass

In contrast to most other common materials such as metal or wood, glass exhibits brittle fracture. This can be both spectacular and frightening, yet glass for architecture can be designed safely. In order to do this, it is necessary to consider why glass is different and how it breaks.

GLASS MATERIAL STRENGTH

Glass is a liquid that has cooled to a rigid state without crystallizing. It is sometimes described as a 'supercooled liquid', which it is not. A supercooled liquid is still a liquid at a temperature below that at which it would normally solidify. Glass is a solid with an amorphous random or non-crystalline structure(Figure 12.2). The use of the term 'supercooled liquid' suggests the idea of flow, but in fact glass is far too rigid to flow at normal temperatures, however long a force is applied to it.

The application of a force to a material results in a slight deformation, whilst at the same time internal forces develop in order to resist this deformation. In engineering terms, the deformation induces strain (stretching or compression) while the internal forces per unit area are known as stress. These arise whenever a force is applied to a solid material.

When a material is stressed it deforms by the stretching of the interatomic and intermolecular bonds and, at low levels of

Figure 12.1 *(Opposite)*
Sculpture pavilion, Sans Beek, Netherlands
Architect: Bentham Cronwell, 1986

This minimal glass construction repetitive stepped boxes and fins is a striking application of the structural properties of glass.

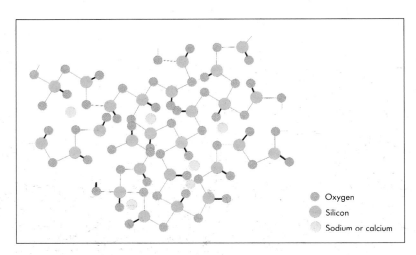

Figure 12.2
Structure of window glass

On an atomic scale, glass is a network of silicon–oxygen–silicon bonds, randomly modified by the presence of calcium and sodium. Their arrangement is completely random, as it would be in a liquid, and is not orderly or regular like the molecules in a crystal of sugar or ice. Because of this network arrangement, glass is non-ductile and it is this which sets it apart from most other materials.

Oxygen
Silicon
Sodium or calcium

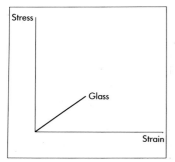

Figure 12.3
Stress–strain diagrams

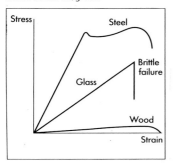

Figure 12.4
Plastic deformation

stress, the strain is proportional to the stress (Figure 12.3). At higher levels of stress most materials deform plastically, that is the atoms or molecules in the structure become rearranged or crystals slide past each other. These materials can often accommodate large strains without failure (Figure 12.4), although they may be permanently deformed. The structure of glass cannot accommodate this plastic deformation, so the stress–strain curve for glass (Figure 12.4) shows perfect linearity. This is rare among common materials.

Several conclusions about the physical properties of window glass can be deduced from the stress–strain graph:

- When glass is under stress, it deforms to a certain extent and then stops. There is no further deformation or creep with time.
- Glass is not subject to dynamic fatigue (from cyclic loading). The perfect linearity of its stress–strain curve means that reversals of stress leave the glass unchanged; for example, no work hardening can occur.
- Glass does not suffer from permanent deformation. When a stress is removed the glass returns to its original shape.
- The absence of any plastic deformation leads to susceptibility to local overstressing (due to its inability to yield locally) and a vulnerability to flaws.

A steel structure, for example, can accommodate local stresses and redistribute them by small plastic deformations; the structure is very 'forgiving'. Glass cannot do this. It deforms elastically up to the point where the interatomic bonds break. If there is sufficient stress applied then a crack will propagate through the glass and failure occurs.

TENSILE STRENGTH AND SURFACE FLAWS

The theoretical strength of a piece of flat glass should (on atomic bond strength calculations) be around 21000 N/mm^2. On freshly drawn glass fibres, tensile stresses of up to 5000 N/mm^2 have been measured and, even when incorporated into a resin to form glass reinforced plastic, glass fibres have a usable stress of about 1200 N/mm^2. However, window glass usually fails at stress levels less than 100 N/mm^2. In practice, therefore, the amount of stress needed to start a crack in glass is very much less than expected considering the forces needed to break the interatomic bonds. There is some form of stress concentration factor at work.

In 1921, A. A. Griffith first put forward the idea that the surface of any glass is liberally provided with invisibly small defects (Griffith flaws), any one of which may, under suitable conditions, concentrate the applied stress on to the interatomic bonds in the defect and cause them to break, thus propagating a crack and leading to failure (Figures 12.5). It is now understood that the stress needed to cause failure depends on the number of Griffith flaws and on the presence in the flaws of chemicals, including water, which may attack the strained atomic bonds. The presence of Griffith flaws appears to be attributable to contamination of the surface by particles of dust and moisture vapour.

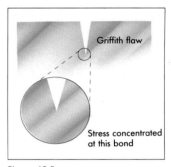

Figure 12.5
Griffith flaws on glass surface

The strength of glass is also modified by the presence of larger surface flaws. Under stress these can be the origin of cracks since the glass may be unable to accommodate the local stress concentrations they cause (Figure 12.6a). Also illustrated (Figure 12.6b) is a magnified scratch line on the surface of float glass and the associated shelling and venting of the glass surface. The presence of these flaws is one reason why the edge region of a piece of glass is usually weaker than the face surface. It is much more prone to damage from accidental contact with the surroundings. Methods of cutting glass and edge finishing may also lead to the presence of flaws at the edge.

The position is further complicated by a phenomenon known as 'static fatigue' of glass. This has nothing in common with the more widely known mechanism of dynamic fatigue in metals. The glass may withstand a stress for a short time, which, if it were maintained indefinitely, would cause failure due to corrosion of the strained interatomic bonds at a crack tip. In fact glass can sustain, for a short period, a stress more than double that which would cause failure if maintained for a long period (Figure 12.7).

Figure 12.6a Major surface flaws

The presence of major flaws, for example scratches, shells and vents, on the surface or the edges of the glass can generate local stress concentrations when the glass is put under strain, which may lead to crack formation. It is, however, not easy to predict whether any individual flaw is likely to do this. Vents in the glass (small surface fissures) are likely starting points for crack propagation as they produce unacceptable stress concentrations. Other sources of weakness, such as scratches and shells, may not necessarily form such high stress concentrations; only those that have vents associated with them are likely to do this.

Use is made of this principle during some manufacturing processes, where the edges of glass are arrissed (ground down) to ensure that there are no severe flaws in the edge. This controlled damaging of the glass has little effect on its usable strength because of the statistical variation in the strength of glass (Figure 12.9). The result of the controlled damage is to reduce the strength of the strongest pieces of glass to that of the weakest, but the weakest glass is not significantly reduced in strength.

Figure 12.6b
Surface scratch, Pilkington
Technology Centre, Lathom, UK

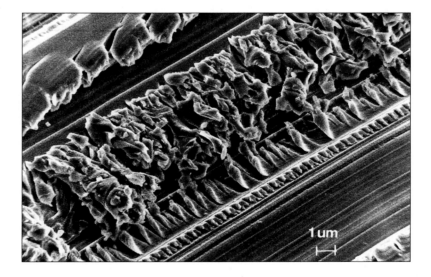

COMPRESSIVE STRENGTH

In theory, the compressive strength of glass should be around 21000 N/mm^2. In practice, it has not been measured. Any test which has been devised to measure compressive stress produces tensile stresses as a side effect. It has not been possible to measure only the compressive strength, because the test samples fail due to the tensile stress side effects. In effect, glass never breaks from the effects of compressive stress, always from tensile stresses.

Figure 12.7 Glass strength and load duration
Experiments to examine the relationship between time to failure and applied stress can be summarized by the formula s^nT = constant, where s is stress, T is duration of stress and n is a constant. This relationship shows that if the duration of stress is increased, the stress must be decreased. The value of the constant n is the important part of this relationship. Various researchers have obtained values between 12 and 20 for n, depending on conditions of test and glass composition.

The formula apparently suggests that, over extremely long periods, the allowable stress must decrease to a negligible level. In practice this does not occur, and the general formula no longer applies below a certain value of stress. There is a lower limit to the strength of glass, below which it will not fail, and research has suggested values between 25% and 40% of the short term strength. It is an important relationship, since glass can be subjected to both short term and long term loads (e.g. wind and snow loads).

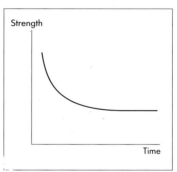

Figure 12.7
Glass strength and load duration

FRACTURE INITIATION

The mechanism discussed above enables some interesting conclusions to be drawn about fracture initiation:

- Glass fracture is highly unlikely to start from within the body of the glass. It is from the relatively weak surface that fracture is initiated.
- Breakage occurs only when a sufficiently large tensile stress is applied to open up a Griffith flaw. The numbers and distributions of the Griffith flaws differ for different kinds of glass surface (float or cast glass; the cut edge or the surface; newly manufactured or weathered).
- The stress level necessary to cause fracture initiation from a particular Griffith flaw depends on the length of time the

215

Figure 12.8a
Loaded toughened glass, Flachglas
AG, Germany

stress is applied and on the ambient conditions at the tip of the flaw. Water vapour, in particular, enables the strained interatomic bonds in the flaw to part more easily.

COMPRESSION EFFECTS

Since surface flaws only lead to fracture when a tensile stress opens them, any method of putting the glass surface into permanent compression is advantageous. An applied tensile stress would have to overcome this built-in compression before it begins to open up a flaw and the glass would be able to resist higher loads. Toughened glass and heat strengthened glass use this principle.

The stress distribution in toughened glass enables it to withstand bending stresses to much higher levels (Figures 12.8a, b) than ordinary annealed glass. During production of annealed glass, it is carefully cooled through the range of temperatures where the glass solidifies so that no significant residual stresses develop. This is necessary so that the glass can be cut or worked. Toughened glass cannot be cut or worked. If a crack penetrates the compressive layer of toughened glass into the central tensile region, there is enough tensile stress available to make the crack propagate violently through the glass. This forms the characteristic dice pattern of broken

Figure 12.8b
Stress profiles

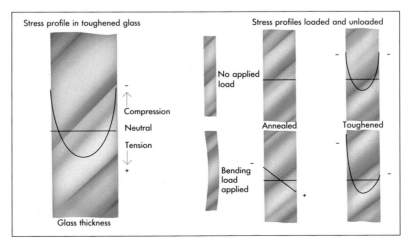

216

toughened glass. Heat strengthened glass is tempered to a lower level of stress so that it does not form the characteristic dice pattern, but it also cannot be cut or worked.

GLASS STRENGTH STATISTICS

The Griffith flaws, which control the strength of glass, are random in size, distribution and orientation. Such is the variation of Griffith flaws that the strength of apparently identical pieces of window glass tested under identical conditions can vary by a factor of 3. It is not possible to predict the strength of any particular piece of glass. The only way to establish a value is to mechanically load the glass to breakage. This then establishes the strength of that piece, tested at that time and in that particular way. Statistical analysis of a set of scattered values of glass strength measurements allows the derivation of a value below which there will be relatively few failures (Figures 12.9a, b).

However, no matter how many samples are tested, or what statistical treatments are applied to the results, it is only possible to arrive at a low risk value of stress such that, for example, there is '95% confidence that at least 95% of all possible test pieces would survive'. A higher confidence level may be used, but wherever the level is set there can never be 100% assurance that all specimens would survive.

DESIGN VALUES

Statistical treatment of test results can be used to obtain a design value at which there is a sufficiently low risk of the glass being weaker than that design value. This value can be used to select glass thickness for a given situation but with two provisos:

- It is not possible to be 100% certain that all glass panes will not break. The penalty for increased confidence will be the use of thicker glass.
- The result of any experiment measuring glass strength relates to particular conditions of size, glass history, type of

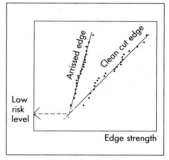

Figure 12.9a
Analysis of arrissed edges and clean cut edges

One method of analysing the results of glass strength tests is by the Weibull distribution function, where it is useful to plot the distribution of strengths on Weibull graph paper specially designed for this type of analysis. The vertical scale is non-linear and represents the distribution of results. The effect is to produce a straight line, which can be extrapolated down to any desired proportion; for example, 0.5% gives a strength value which would result in only 0.5% failures.

This graph shows why some types of deliberately induced damage to glass do not have a marked effect on the usable strength. Comparing the effect of arrissed edges with clean cut edges shows that, while the arrissed edges are on average weaker, the low risk values are very similar.

Figure 12.9b
Uniform loading glass test, Pilkington Glass Ltd, St Helens, UK

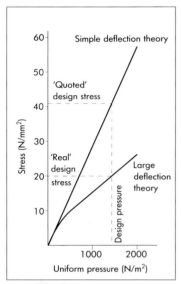

Figure 12.10
Large deflection theory and simple deflection theory

The effects of considering large deflection theory in contrast to simple deflection theory are shown by this graph of induced stress against applied pressure for 4 mm float 1200 × 1200 mm. The real stress induced in the glass is shown by the line 'large deflection theory' and deviates from that predicted by simple deflection theory. Using the real design stress with the simple formula would lead to 6 mm glass being specified instead of 4 mm.

stress etc. To use the results in other contexts involves assumptions about the behaviour of glass, some of which are empirical.

LARGE DEFLECTIONS

Most common engineering formulae, using simple deflection theory, assume that deflections are directly proportional to applied loads. This is a valid assumption for many applications, but it is not appropriate for thin plates supported on all four edges which are deflected by more than their own thickness.

Many applications for glass produce deflections larger than the thickness and stresses can be grossly overestimated when using simple deflection formulae. Thus the use of a 'design stress' (the stress in the glass which should not be exceeded in service) with simple deflection theory leads to overspecification of the glass thickness (unless the design stress is related to the application and the formula used) and is not a realistic value for the real strength of glass (Figure 12.10).

DESIGN STRENGTH

Design stresses which are associated with specific simple deflection formulae have a limited applicability due to the risk of them being used inappropriately. Manufacturers of glass therefore publish guides on the selection of glass for particular applications (e.g. wind load tables) which by experiment and experience have been shown to be suitable.

SUPPORTING SYSTEMS

When glass is glazed there are forces acting on it which need to be transferred to the supporting structure or frame.

As previously indicated, glass cannot accommodate local overstressing, so contact forces need to be kept to an acceptable level and concentrated forces need to be spread to avoid local overstressing. This concept is contained in such general good advice as 'avoid glass-to-metal contact'. While methods of fixing glass are dominated by this requirement to spread the application of loads and to insert softer materials between glass and its immediate surrounding, experience has shown that in a few special cases (for example, the aluminium spring wings of some patent glazing systems) glass can be fixed in contact with a relatively hard material.

Glass can be supported in many different ways; these can vary enormously, but all need to be correctly designed so that the glass is not overstressed.

Four-edge glazing is the most common method of supporting glass in frames, but sometimes three- and two-edge supporting frames are used. The major constraints to be considered are:

- Allow clearances around the glass to accommodate tolerances and thermal movements. These should be a minimum of 3 mm for single glazing and 5 mm for double glazed units, increasing with the size of pane.
- The edge of the glass should be covered by the rebate to a depth at least equal to the glass thickness, and never less than 6 mm for single glazing and 12 mm for double glazed units.
- The frame members should not deflect excessively under the applied loads.

In certain situations, glass does not need to be sealed around the edges and can be fixed with discrete clips. With clip fixing, glass needs to be designed as though fixed at discrete points. A glazing clip should cover an adequately large area of the glass. The method of designing the glass should take into account the positioning of the clips and the stress concentrations generated.

Glass can also be fixed using bolt fixings and spreader plates (frameless glazing). The use of bolt fixings will inevitably result in stress concentrations around a hole in the glass. This hole is a weak point in annealed glass and laminated glass, so toughened glass should be used. Bolt fixings consist of two metal spreader plates and one or more bolts passing through holes in the glass. These bolts clamp the glass between the spreader plates which are separated from the glass by a gasket (preferably incompressible, e.g. hard fibre, but not neoprene since it is too soft and creeps). A nylon or similar bush between bolt and glass should prevent the bolt from contacting the edges of the hole. The bolt size, spreader plate diameter and spreader plate thickness should be chosen to suit the loading (Figure 12.11).

Figure 12.11 Use of single bolt fixings

The relationship between the components of a bolted fixing can be determined after the appropriate size of bolt has been chosen. The thickness of the spreader plate should be about three-quarters of the bolt diameter, but not less than 6 mm. The diameter of the spreader plate should be about eight times its thickness.

Bolt diameter	Spreader diameter	Plate thickness
mm	mm	mm
6	50	6
8	50	6
10	60	8
12	75	10
16	100	12

OTHER CONSIDERATIONS

Glass surface quality influences the glass strength. Abrasive cleaning and scratches can introduce larger flaws, and even exposure to the atmosphere changes the strength. This is not always to its detriment. A 'sharp' crack tip may concentrate the stress on a few intermolecular bonds, forming a severe flaw. If the glass is left for a period without applied stress, water vapour diffuses into the crack, rearranges the bonds at the tip and diminishes the severe stress concentration. Thus glass may, in some circumstances, recover its strength. Window glass eventually reaches a virtually stable condition. Manufacturers base their recommendations for glass thicknesses on this condition, rather than on glass fresh from production.

It is a common misconception that wired glass and laminated glass are stronger than annealed glass. This is not so. Laminated glass is formed from annealed, unstrengthened glass and will break at much the same stresses as would single window glass. The virtue of laminated glass is that, when it is broken, the pieces tend to hold together (by adhesion to the interlayer). It is therefore potentially a safety glass (it may be suitable for some circumstances where a particular hazard can be foreseen), but it does not have enhanced strength in the way that toughened glass does.

Wired glass is usually weaker than other types of glass, since the presence of the wires causes additional flaws. However, when the glass is broken, the pieces tend to hold together owing to the presence of the wire. This is particularly useful in fire situations, since the wires do not melt. If the wires are sufficiently strong, wired glass is also a safety glass.

APPLICATIONS

The strength of glass is used to resist forces which generally fall into two main categories, natural and man-made:

Figure 12.12

Natural forces	Man-made forces
Wind pressure and snow loads	Human impact (accidental)
Thermally induced stresses	Other impact (accidental)
Loads on shelves or tables	Burglar attack
Hydrostatic (water) pressure	Bullet impact
	Explosion forces

It is not possible to provide a complete list, but in all the many applications the forces can be described in numerical or physical terms. They can be analysed to a greater or lesser extent. Even the natural disasters of the world can be described numerically or physically. For instance, hurricanes are strong winds, possibly containing impacting objects; earthquakes are vibrational loads, which can be described numerically. Design can thus be performed for both. The only things that cannot be designed against are those which are completely unpredictable, and for these there is no answer, whatever the material used.

As described, the nature of glass strength can also be explained numerically. All that engineering design requires is that the problem and potential solutions can be described numerically or physically. Chapters 13 to 19 indicate the ways in which glass can be designed to resist some of the applied forces.

The type of applied force may be revealed by the fracture characteristics which are exhibited in annealed glass on fracture (Figures 12.13–12.19).

Figure 12.13
Uniform loading fracture, Pilkington Glass Ltd, St Helens, UK

With the edges simply supported the fracture characteristics show radial cracks from the point of fracture origin together with many circumferential fractures concentrated in the areas of higher stress, for example wind loading.

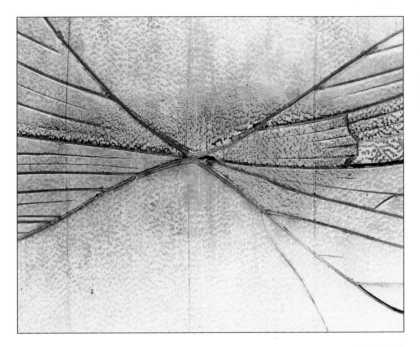

Figure 12.14
Bending fracture, Pilkington Glass
Ltd, St Helens, UK

With a uniform or concentrated
load and two edges simply
supported, the fracture
characteristics show the major stress
axis down the centre of the plate
and parallel with the edge support,
for example due to snow or wind
loading.

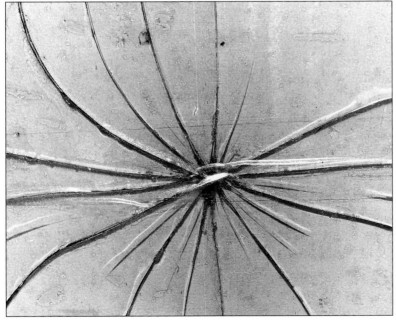

Figure 12.15
Hard body impact fracture,
Pilkington Glass Ltd, St Helens, UK

With the edges simply supported,
the fracture characteristics show
radials from the point of impact, for
example from a stone.

Figure 12.16
Soft body impact fracture,
Pilkington Glass Ltd, St Helens, UK

With the edges simply supported,
the fracture characteristics show
radials from the point of impact
together with circumferential
fractures due to local bending as
the impactor flattens and the
impingement area becomes larger,
for example a football.

Figure 12.17
Fast hard body impact, Pilkington
Glass Ltd, St Helens, UK

With a small impingement area, a
Hertzian cone (Figure 12.18) is
punched out from the opposite side
to the impact. The photo shows
point of impact in the centre of the
cone and the cavity left after the
cone is detached, for example air
gun pellets and bullets.

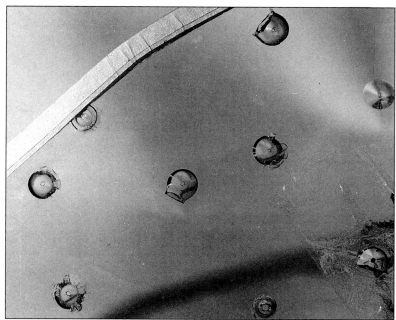

Figure 12.18
Detached Hertzian cone

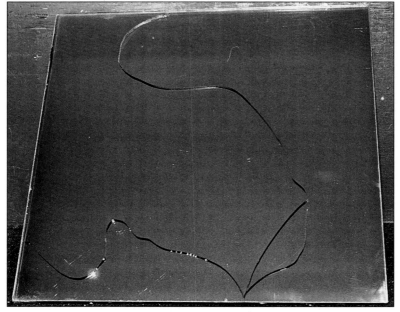

Figure 12.19
Thermal stress fracture

This form of fracture is discussed in Chapter 15. Its characteristic is an origin at right angles to the edge, with the single or bifurcated fracture propagating at a relatively slow speed and meandering through the stress zone. This is quite distinct from mechanical fractures which tend to travel in straight lines.

Figure 12.20
Glass stair tread, Joseph Shop,
London, UK
Architect: Eva Jiricna

The structural tread is composed of
thick float and thick sheet
polymethyl methacrylate.

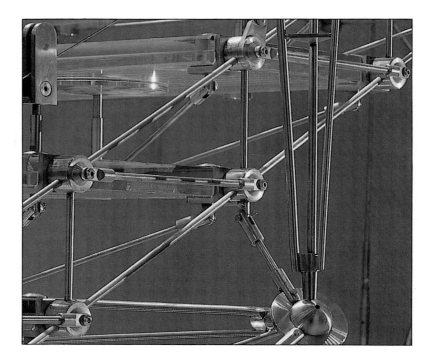

BIBLIOGRAPHY

ASTM E1300-89 *Standard Practice for Determining the Minimum Thickness of Annealed Glass Required to Resist a Specified Load*, American Society for Testing and Materials, Philadelphia, PA, 1989

CGSB-12.20-M *Structural Design of Glass for Buildings*, Canadian General Standards Board, Ottawa, 1988

Charles, R.J. 'Static fatigue of glass', *Journal of Applied Physics*, 29, 1549

Charles, R.J. 'Dynamic fatigue of glass', *Journal of Applied Physics*, 29, 1657

DIN 1249 *The Strength of Glass*, Part 10 'Chemical and physical performance', 8–90, Deutches Institut für Normung e.V. (in German)

DIN 52292 *Examination of Glass*, Part 1 'Regulation for bending strength', Part 2 'Double ringed flexible examination on flat formed samples', Deutches Institut für Normung e.V. (in German)

DIN 52303 Parts 1 and 2 'Proving test for Flachglas of the building property regulations for bending strength tests using twice normal conditions', Deutches Institut für Normung e.V. (in German)

Gordon, J. *The Science of Materials*, Scientific American Library, New York, 1988

Griffith, A.A. *Transactions of the Royal Society, London*, Series A, 221, 163, 1921

CHAPTER 13

Resistance to Wind and Snow

Wind is difficult to predict because it is never constant, in magnitude or direction. Statistically, however, it can be predicted that over a period there is low risk that the wind speed will be greater than a specific value.

THE WIND LOADING ENVIRONMENT

In many countries, research into wind speeds has produced sufficient data for the prediction of wind speeds which will be rarely exceeded. National standards and codes of practice contain maps showing wind speeds to be considered in design.

Even when the wind speed can be predicted, the value cannot be used directly for design because of the effects of several factors, related to immediate site topography, roughness of the terrain, height of the building and size of the component being considered. Modification of the wind speed taking into account these factors results in the dynamic wind pressure (Figure 13.3).

Figure 13.3 Factors influencing dynamic wind pressure

Effect of topography   Where the general topography is flat or gentle, it has little effect upon wind speeds. However, the presence of steep hills funnels the air as it passes, causing increased wind speed near their tops. The increase caused by even small but steep hills can be more than 30%. Altitude also affects the wind speed. At a height of 1000 metres the wind speed is twice that at sea level.

Effect of roughness of terrain   The terrain roughness relates to local obstructions to the wind, for example large trees/woods and surrounding buildings. These obstructions will block the wind, reducing its strength. Buildings in town centres will experience less wind than those in open country.

Height of building   Wind travels faster when it is further away from the drag influence of the ground. The higher the building the greater the wind pressure.

Size of component   Wind comes in gusts which have a size, duration and speed. The small size of gust which could affect an individual pane of glass can cause it to be much faster than the general wind, although its duration may be very short.

231

The dynamic wind pressure is modified by the building shape to produce the design pressure(s). Wind swirls around buildings exerting forces on their various parts. Pressure is exerted where the wind blows directly against a portion of the

Figure 13.4
Wind loading on a UK building

This curtain wall shows damage from the typically high suction loading on the corner of the building.

façade, but the stronger effects are experienced at the corners or eaves where large suction forces are generated. Factors involved in determining the local effects of wind on buildings can be expressed as pressure coefficients. These are used to modify the dynamic wind pressures and determine the design pressure on the building.

It is normal practice to calculate the worst design pressure (or suction) and use this as a single figure for design. However, if necessary, it is possible to calculate design pressures for different parts of a building.

DESIGN FOR WIND LOADS

The maximum average speed of the wind over a particular period is the general way in which design winds are described; the duration of loading chosen depends on the particular national code. In the UK, periods of three seconds, one minute and one hour have been used in different versions of the wind loading code. In other countries, periods of ten minutes and twenty minutes can be found.

Whilst all these provide reasonably accurate descriptions of the wind, they appear to give markedly different wind speeds. For instance, a wind speed of 40 m/s on a three second basis would be produced by a 23 m/s mean hourly wind speed. Similarly, if the mean hourly wind speed is 23 m/s, then gusts of 40 m/s over three seconds can be expected.

The apparent differences may be considerably less when wind loading design codes are followed through to obtain a dynamic wind pressure. This may be based on a different (shorter) time scale from the basic wind speed data. It is the time scale over which the dynamic wind pressure is calculated that is important for designing glass to resist wind pressures, because, as described in Chapter 12, glass strength is time dependent.

The magnitudes of design wind pressure vary from around 500 N/m^2 in low level sheltered areas to 8000 N/m^2 at the top of high rise buildings in the hurricane belt.

GLASS STRENGTH AND WIND LOAD

Depending on the time scale for the dynamic wind pressure, the design strength of glass will vary from country to country. Since wind load codes vary from country to country, glass should be designed according to the methods in practice in the country to which the code applies.

Wind loading can be considered as a uniform loading, that is the wind pressure is evenly distributed over the whole area of the glass.

The ability of glass to resist wind load depends on several factors:

- glass type or combination of glass types
- thickness
- area
- shape
- supporting systems (frames).

Under uniform loads, different glass types have different strengths. The following list begins with the strongest and ends with the weakest types:

- toughened glass
- heat strengthened glass
- float glass
- patterned (cast) glass
- wired glass.

The design strengths used for glass relate to local practice and depend on factors other than just pure strength. In order to limit deflections to visually acceptable levels, the design strengths may be lower than the stresses the glass can withstand. This is particularly the case with toughened glass.

The strength of laminated glass will depend on its component glasses. Where the component glasses are nominally identical, the laminated glass can be treated in design, for resistance to short duration loads, as a monolithic glass of the equivalent thickness, although some national standards do not permit this.

Glass thickness is taken into account in the formulae used to calculate stress and deflection. In calculations, the minimum tolerance for the glass thickness is used (Figure 13.5).

In sealed double glazed units the gas in the cavity is relatively incompressible under wind pressures, and a pressure on one pane will induce stresses and deflections in both panes. The effect is that the panes share the load, in proportion to the cube of their thicknesses.

Figure 13.5 Glass design thicknesses

Glass type	Nominal thickness mm	Typical minimum thickness mm
Float	3	2.8
	4	3.8
	5	4.8
	6	5.8
	8	7.7
	10	9.7
	12	11.7
	15	14.5
	19	18.0
	25	24.0
Patterned	4	3.5
	6	5.5
Wired	6	6.0
	7	6.0

Toughened glass will have the minimum thickness of the glass from which it was made. Laminated glass will have the minimum thickness equal to the sum of the minimum thicknesses of its component glasses. No allowance should be made for the interlayer thickness in laminated glass.

The effects of area, shape and support systems are taken into account in the formulae used to calculate design wind loads from given thicknesses.

THE SNOW LOADING ENVIRONMENT

Snow loading is the effect of the dead weight of snow lying on a structure. Records taken over many years indicate the maximum snow loading likely to occur in any location. This information is presented in national standards and codes containing maps showing the snow loading to be considered.

The amounts of snow which collect on various parts of a particular building may vary because of drifting. This will occur when there are multi-span roofs or abrupt changes of building height. The possibility of snow sliding from sloping roofs and reaccumulating on lower roofs should also be considered.

Roof glazing may be less insulating than other parts of a roof. Heat from the building may conduct through the glass and begin to melt the snow, although the increased use of high insulation glass will negate this. This has two effects. First, snow will not build up on the glass to the same extent as it does on other parts of the roof, because it is melting. The glazing snow load may not be as severe as the codes suggest and may last for a shorter time, but there are currently no methods of taking this into account in design. Second, the melting of the underlayers of snow on the glass roof, combined with the smooth surface of glass, can cause the snow to slide off a sloped glass roof much more quickly than it does off other parts of a roof.

DESIGN FOR SNOW LOADS

Snow load duration may be for a considerable period (days, weeks or even months). Therefore, with glass, it is necessary to consider snow loading as a long term loading and to use a reduced design stress.

Alternatively, it is possible to apply a factor to the snow load and consider it as an equivalent wind load. This procedure has been adopted in British Standard BS 5516 *Patent Glazing*, where the snow load is multiplied by a factor of 2.6 to equate it to an equivalent three second wind load.

Magnitudes of snow loads are usually taken as a minimum of around 500 N/m^2, but can range up to several times this value, depending on drifting conditions and climate.

GLASS STRENGTH AND SNOW LOADS

Snow loading normally applies a uniform pressure, but drifted snow can apply a load that is not uniformly distributed but of a triangular distribution. The load distribution should be taken into account when selecting appropriate formulae for calculating stresses and deflections.

Apart from this variation from a uniform load, the factors affecting the resistance of glass to snow loading are the same as those for wind loading.

BIBLIOGRAPHY

ASCE *Tall Building Criteria and Loading*, American Society of Civil Engineers, 1980

BS 6399 *Loading for Buildings. Part 3: Code of Practice for Imposed Roof Loads*, British Standards Institution, 1987

Cook, N.J. *The Designer's Guide to Wind Loading of Building Structures*, Parts 1 and 2, Butterworths

DIN 1055 *Resistance to Wind and Snow*, Parts 4(8-86) and 5(6-75), Deutches Institut für Normung e.V. (in German)

Macdonald, A.J. *Wind Loading on Buildings*, Halstead Press, Wiley, New York and Toronto, 1975

CHAPTER 14

Resistance to Water Loading

When glass is used in aquaria or as observation panels in swimming pools and large fish tanks, it can be subjected to high pressure by the water. If the glass should break the results could be catastrophic, so it is very important that the glass and glazing system are carefully designed.

Figure 14.1
Hippoquarium Toledo, Toledo Zoological Gardens, USA
Glass design: Toledo Mirror and Glass Co.

The laminate is composed of 4 × 12 mm toughened glasses in windows 1.83 m high and 3.05 m wide.

LOADS PRODUCED BY WATER

Water exerts a pressure in all directions, which is directly dependent upon the depth of the water. The total volume of water, for example in an aquarium, is not relevant.

The pressure at any depth in water, or any liquid, is given by the formula

$$p = \rho g h$$

where ρ is the density of the liquid (kg/m^3), g is the acceleration due to gravity (9.81 m/s^2), h is the depth (m) and p is the pressure (N/m^2). The pressure increases linearly with depth.

The density of water is 1000 kg/m^3 (1040 kg/m^3 for sea water). At a depth of 600 mm, typical of the bottom of a domestic fish tank, the pressure is about 6000 N/m^2. In comparison with pressures generated by wind (1000–2000 N/m^2, and up to 8000 N/m^2 for hurricanes), those generated by water are high. For large aquaria 4 m deep, the pressure generated at the bottom is nearly 40 kN/m^2 – a pressure comparable in size with that from an explosion.

Water pressure is a sustained pressure. Unlike wind pressure, it is not transitory. Since glass suffers from static fatigue (Chapter 12) the design stresses appropriate for designing against water pressure will therefore be much lower than those for wind pressure, resulting in (very) thick glass being required.

Whereas wind pressure could be considered as loading the glass uniformly, the pressure exerted by water varies with the depth. For example, in a 600 mm deep domestic fish tank, there will be zero pressure at and above the water level, and a gradually increasing pressure with depth on the sides of the

Figure 14.2
Forms of triangular load

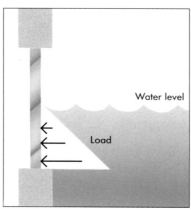

(a) Water loading on a glass aquarium
window may not be over the full depth
(a reptile tank may have only the bottom
portion in water).

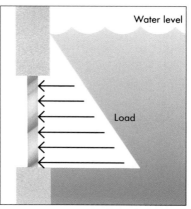

(b) There is already a significant pressure at
the top edge of the window and this
increases over its depth.

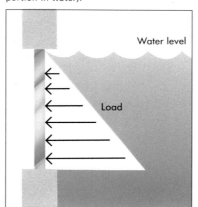

(c) More commonly, the water can be
considered to be loading the window over
its full depth, since the amount of unloaded
window at the top edge is relatively small.

tank to about 6000 N/m^2 at the base. This is a triangularly distributed load. These triangular loads take various forms (Figure 14.2).

GLASS PERFORMANCE

The combination of relatively high water pressure and relatively low design stresses results in thick glass being required for fairly small windows. Three glass types can be considered:

thick annealed glass, thick laminated glass and laminated toughened glass.

Thick annealed glass can be used for up to approximately 1 metre depth of water depending upon the shape of the pane and framing system, although some national standards preclude its use. If a thick annealed glass fractures in an aquarium window, it tends to suffer just one or two cracks and remain in place. Weeping will occur through these cracks. However, if the glass is not fully supported on all four edges, it may not exhibit this containment, so consideration should be given to the type of glass used in relation to the support conditions.

An advantage of using a laminated glass is that if one leaf of glass is cracked, the other(s) may remain intact and the pieces of cracked glass remain adhered to the interlayer material. Even if all the leaves are cracked, the laminated glass may still have considerable integrity. However, unlike its resistance to impulse loading, a laminated glass should not be considered to have the same load resistance as a monolithic glass of the same thickness for sustained loads owing to the shear creep of the plastic interlayers (Figure 14.3).

As an alternative to thick glass, or to resist loads where the thickest annealed glass is insufficient, single toughened (tempered) glass might be considered. Toughened glass has the strength to withstand higher pressures or to span larger distances than annealed glass. However, toughened glass, should it fracture, disintegrates into many particles leading to collapse of the aquarium window. Although this risk may be slight, toughened glass should always be laminated as a safety measure.

To accommodate the possibility of accidental damage to a leaf of the laminated toughened glass, the glass should contain at least one more leaf than the design load requires. For example, if the mechanical design indicates that two leaves are sufficient then three should be used, the extra leaf being ignored for design purposes. For this principle to work successfully, all leaves of the laminate should be the same thickness.

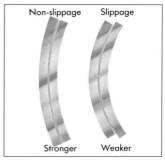

Figure 14.3
Laminated glass subject to short term and sustained loads

The interlayer is sufficiently stiff not to allow the panes of glass to slip over each other under short duration loads like wind pressure. Laminated glass can be assumed equivalent to a monolithic glass of the same thickness under short duration loads.
However, plastics, even relatively hard ones, tend to creep under long duration loads. This means that the assumption made for shorter duration loads is unlikely to be valid for permanent loads. It is necessary to assume that the leaves of glass can slide past one another and share the load between them in some way. Thus a laminated glass consisting of two 15 mm glasses would be assumed to take half the load on each pane. The effect on load capacity is that two 15 mm glasses are equivalent not to 30 mm monolithic but to 21 mm monolithic. If three 10 mm glasses are used, the effect is worse, being equivalent to 17 mm monolithic.

DESIGN OF GLASS AND SUPPORTS

Whichever type of glass is used, the design follows standard engineering practice and formulae. The stress induced in the leaves is limited to a safe design stress and the deflection of supporting structures is restricted to an acceptable level.

Some of the inhabitants in aquaria can be large and are able to inflict considerable force on the glass, and this possibility is taken into account at the design stage.

Since water will seep through any available gap at the high pressures involved, careful attention is also paid to jointing.

Failures in small aquaria are unlikely to cause significant risk to people and generally do not justify anything more than thick annealed glass. At the other extreme, an undersea observation room could be flooded very quickly by a single panel failure. Thus a considerable margin of safety is required in such windows.

The thickness of the windows in aquaria in relation to the span, combined with the lower design stress, means that deflections are small. Standard engineering formulae, based on simple deflection theory, are therefore suitable for designing against water pressure. The formulae used should be appropriate to the supporting system and load distribution. Design stresses for the types of glass should be according to national standards or obtained from the manufacturer where no standards are available.

Supporting structures should be regarded as giving only simple support to the glass. No clamping action or pinning of the glass edge should be considered, and the load from the glass should be transmitted uniformly to the supporting member. Point or local support should not be used, nor should there be the possibility of the glass coming into contact with another hard material (including other glass).

A supporting member can only be considered as such if the deflection sustained under the loading is sufficiently small, so that the glass is not excessively bent by conforming to the shape of the deflected supporting member.

The most common type of supporting system is where the glass is supported on all four edges. However, provided that the glass can be demonstrated as capable of resisting the water pressure, other supporting systems can be used. For instance, three-edge-supported glass (base and two vertical edges supported) may be appropriate e.g. for small domestic frameless aquaria (Figure 14.4).

Figure 14.4 Frameless aquaria

Small frameless aquaria with silicone sealant as the jointing medium can be constructed, provided the sealant has sufficient adhesive and cohesive strength and is correctly applied. The panes should form 90° corners, and edges adjacent to other panes can then be considered as fully supported by adhesion.

The top edge is usually unsupported, but panes more than 750 mm long should have a supporting strip of glass fixed from front to back of the tank near the top of the panels. Alternatively, a bracing strip of glass, at least 40 mm wide, should be fixed at right angles to the glass and near to the top of the glass to run along the full length.

It is recommended that frameless aquaria should not exceed 700 mm in depth (height).

Elimination of visually disturbing mullions may be achieved by supporting the glass only at the head and base to give long lengths of vision panels, but this may result in very thick glass panels being required. With two edges supported, a laminated glass or laminated toughened glass can be used. The supporting frames for aquaria windows are commonly steel members.

Glass fins can be used structurally as a means of increasing vision areas (Figure 14.5). However, because the edges of the glass would be exposed to possible impact damage, the fin must be designed as a laminate with extra panes, to safeguard against accidental breakage of one leaf of glass. Preferably, there should be one extra mullion leaf for each pane supported, implying a mullion with several laminated leaves.

Figure 14.5
Glass fin

BIBLIOGRAPHY

DIN 32622 *Resistance to Water*, 'Aquariums', 1-85, Deutsches Institut für Normung e.V. (in German)

CHAPTER 15

Resistance to Thermal Stress

When glass is directly exposed to solar radiation, it absorbs heat, rises in temperature and expands. The edges of the glass in the frame, which are shielded from the radiation, remain cooler than the exposed area. The force generated by the expansion of the central portion of glass stretches the cooler edges and causes stress which, should it reach the breaking stress of the glass, will result in thermal fracture (Figure 15.1; see also Figure 12.19).

Although thermal breakages are more often associated with solar radiation, a similar effect can be obtained during the hours of darkness. Thermal breakages have occurred in cold climates, where there has been a rapid decrease in the outside temperature. In these cases, the building has been heated internally, which has kept the exposed area of the glass relatively warm. The glass has fractured because the outside air has cooled the window frame and consequently the glass edge, causing excessive stress and fracture. This is more likely to happen to the inner glass of a double glazed unit, when the room heat keeps it warm but the glass edges are cooled to the outside by conduction through the frame. This problem should not occur if the frame has sufficient thermal insulation and thermal barriers are correctly positioned.

The risk of thermal breakage can be calculated by methods which are used by glass manufacturers and other designers. Set out below are the factors influencing thermal stress which are included in the consideration and calculation of the risk and its alleviation.

FACTORS INFLUENCING THERMAL STRESS

Any factor that encourages an increase in the hot-centre/cold-edge condition tends to increase the thermal stress (Figure 15.3). High intensity of solar radiation, high absorptance of glass, and any means by which radiation is reflected or reradiated back into the glass can increase the heat absorbed by the unshielded areas of glass and so increase the thermal stress. Low rates of air movement, and the insulation provided

Figure 15.1 *(Opposite)*
Test rig to reproduce thermal stress in glass, Pilkington Glass Ltd, St Helens, UK

Figure 15.2
Generation of thermal stresses

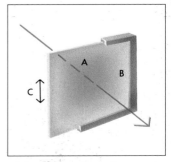

A Hot - trying to expand
B Cold - resisting expansion
C Tensile stress

Figure 15.3
Factors influencing thermal safety

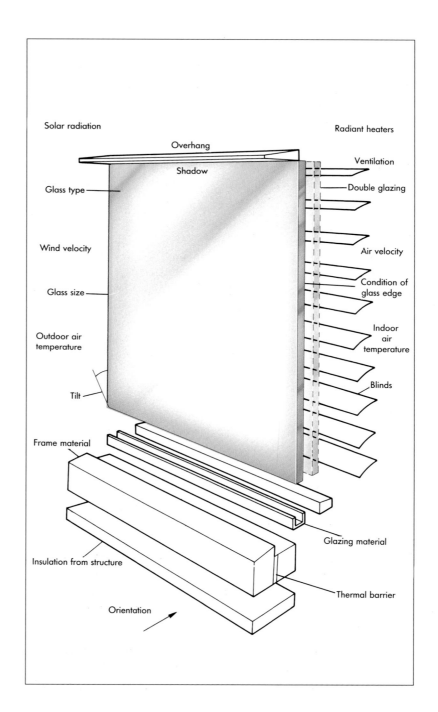

by internal blinds and multiple glazing, tend to reduce the loss of heat from the glass, sustaining its raised temperature.

Low temperatures at the edges are sustained by easy paths of conduction from the glass edges through the frame to a cold building structure with a high thermal inertia.

The magnitude of the thermal stress depends upon the temperature difference between the hotter central area and colder edge areas of the glass and also on the distribution of the temperature across the glass. The stress is generated by the large area of hotter glass forcing a much smaller area of cool glass to expand.

However, shading of part of the glass, which may be considered as reducing the area of hotter glass and increasing the area of cooler glass, does not necessarily reduce the thermal stress (Figure 15.4).

EFFECTS OF SOLAR RADIATION

The intensity of solar radiation on the glazing is determined by:

- geographic location of the building
- orientation and slope of the glazing
- season and time of day
- amount of cloud cover and atmospheric pollution
- reflection from the ground or adjacent structures.

EFFECT OF DIURNAL TEMPERATURE RANGE

The outdoor air temperature may vary considerably from a minimum just before dawn to a maximum around mid afternoon. The temperature of exposed areas of glass tends to follow the morning temperature rise, but the glass edges, because of the effect of the thermal inertia of the structure, shielded by the supporting framework and structure, may warm up much more slowly. This process increases the temperature difference across the glass.

Day and night time outdoor air temperatures change from day to day with known maximum and minimum values, but it is unlikely that the maximum and minimum temperatures will

247

Figure 15.4 Effect of shading on thermal stress

Additional thermal stresses may be induced in the glass if it is partially shaded from the sun by canopies, deep transoms, balconies, deep mullions, adjacent walls etc., and if the shadow so produced extends across the glass for more than 100 mm from its edge.

The duration of shadows depends upon conditions at the site as well as the latitude and the time of year. Shadows with a duration of four hours or more are classed as 'static shadows'; those with a duration of less than four hours are 'mobile shadows'. If a static shadow extends less than 100 mm across the glass it has no significant effect on the thermal stress. The effect of shading increases with increasing pane sizes. Shading factors which can be used to assess the increase in thermal stress are as follows:

Shading type	Factor
No shading	None
Mobile shadow	10% increase
Static shadow	Increase depends on the size of pane

occur on the same day. The diurnal range is determined on the basis of that month in a year which has the greatest difference between the daily maximum and minimum temperatures averaged over the month.

EFFECT OF ABSORPTION

Solar control glass products, such as heat absorbing glass and coloured coated glass, absorb more of the solar energy. Thus they will get hotter when exposed to solar radiation than will clear glass.

EFFECT OF MULTIPLE GLAZING

Thermal stresses induced in solar control glass that is combined with an inner clear glass in double glazed units are usually greater than those induced in the same glass when single glazed. This is because the insulating effect of the air space reduces the heat loss from the outer pane to the inside of the building. This effect is more pronounced in triple glazed units, especially for the centre pane.

Some opening windows allow glass units to pass in front of or behind one another. In the overlapping position, single glazing becomes double, and double becomes quadruple, thereby increasing the potential thermal stress in the panes.

EFFECT OF THE FRAME MATERIAL

Temperature differences in the glass are influenced by the types and properties of the framing. Its thermal properties are important in determining the temperatures of the glass edges.

If the frame is in good thermal contact with the surrounding building fabric, e.g. a heavy masonry structure, it will lose heat rapidly to it and stay cool. If the frame is insulated from the surrounding fabric, it will tend to warm up more quickly.

Where a metal frame incorporates a region of high thermal resistance (a thermal barrier) designed to reduce the heat transfer through the frame, the resistive region should be to the outside of the line of the glazing; this allows the temperature of the frame near the edge of the glass to rise. A thermal barrier to the inside of the glazing line encourages the cold edge condition in the glass (Figure 15.5).

Figure 15.5 Frame factors for assessing thermal stress reduction

The effect of the material in which the glass is glazed is indicated by the folowing factors:

Glazed directly into concrete or brick	no reduction
Wood frame	10% reduction
Light coloured metal frame	20% reduction
Light coloured metal frame with thermal barrier	25% reduction
Dark coloured metal frame	25% reduction
Dark coloured metal frame with thermal barrier	30% reduction
Metal frame where only gasket is visible externally	35% reduction
Plastics or rubber frame	50% reduction

EFFECT OF EDGE COVER

Edge cover is instrumental in keeping the edge cool and thus causing thermal stress in the edge of sunlit glass. However, when glass is glazed into a frame, sufficient edge cover to safely retain the glass is needed. This usually results in between 6 mm and 15 mm of the edge being concealed (depending on the type of frame and glass) and, within this range, variation of edge cover has little effect.

EFFECT OF INTERNAL SHADING

Blinds and other internal shading devices can interfere with the ventilation and free movement of air over the glass; they can also reflect and reradiate solar radiation, increasing the temperature of the glass according to their properties. For the space between the glass and the blind to be considered as ventilated, there should be 50 mm vertical gap between the blind and the glass, 50 mm gap over the top of the blind and 50 mm gap under the bottom of the blind (Figure 15.6).

Figure 15.6 Increases in temperature differences (°C) due to the presence of internal blinds, with and without ventilated space between glass and blind

Glass type	Light coloured blind	Dark coloured blind
Single, unventilated	11	9
Single, ventilated	5	3
Double, unventilated:		
Outer glass	4	0
Inner glass	8	5
Double, ventilated:		
Outer glass	4	0
Inner glass	6	4

EFFECT OF BACK-UP MATERIALS

The term 'back-up' describes a permanent structure close to the inside surface of the glass, such as back-up walls behind cladding, spandrel or infill panels. It can also be, for instance, a suspended ceiling, the ducts of a heating system, or the edge of an internal floor slab.

A back-up reduces the loss of heat from the glass and raises the glass temperature. The colour of a back-up surface facing the glass is important: a light coloured surface will reflect more of the transmitted energy back into the glass; a dark coloured surface may, by absorption, reach a higher temperature and radiate energy back into the glass. Both cause an increase in glass temperature and a corresponding increase in thermal stress, but by different amounts.

EFFECT OF INTERNAL HEATERS

Heat sources such as convection or radiant heaters can supplement the solar heating and increase thermal stressing, especially if the heat is directed on to the glass.

FACTORS AFFECTING THE THERMAL STRENGTH OF GLASS

The condition of the edges of a pane of glass is extremely important. Because the tensile stresses induced by temperature differences are located in the glass edges, the breaking stress of the glass is related to the extent and positions of flaws at the edges (Figure 15.7).

Figure 15.7 Edge condition

A clean wheel cut edge is the strongest edge that can easily be achieved in practice. When thick glass is cut, it is not always possible to avoid feather on the edges. Some types of glass, for example laminated glass, can be more difficult to cut. If arrissing of the edge is necessary, an acceptable edge can be obtained by using a wet arris parallel to the edge of the glass. Glass edges can be weakened by damage to them during handling, storage and glazing.

Size and thickness of panes affects the thermal safety of the glass. The probability of a critical flaw being present in the edge is less for smaller edge areas (the product of perimeter and thickness). The larger and thicker the panes, the more difficult they are to cut, handle and glaze without causing damage to the edges and introducing potential sources of fracture (Figures 15.8a, b, c, d).

The type of glass affects its resistance to thermal stress; glasses may differ in basic strength, and may vary in the standard of edge achieved. The most common type of glass used in building façades is annealed float glass of the thinner widths. The following table rates other types of glass in terms of their relative thermal strength, beginning with the strongest:

- toughened glass
- heat strengthened glass
- thin float glass
- laminated float glass
- thick float glass
- thick laminated float glass
- cast glass
- wired glass.

Figure 15.8

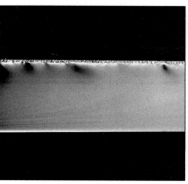

(a) Acceptable clean cut edge

(b) Acceptable good edge with little feather

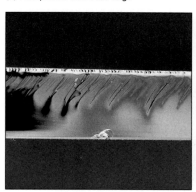

(c) Just acceptable severely feathered edge

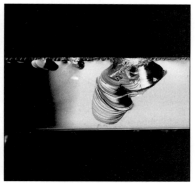

(d) Unacceptable vented edge

The relative thermal strength of heat strengthened glass means that it is highly unlikely to be subjected to excessive thermal stress. Toughened glass will never be subjected to excessive thermal stress (apart from a fire in the building) in architectural situations.

BIBLIOGRAPHY

DIN 1249 *The Strength of Glass*, Part 10, 'Chemical and physical properties', Deutches Institut für Normung e.V. (in German)

DIN 52308 *Boil test for Laminated Glass*, Deutches Institut für Normung e.V. (in German)

Pilkington Glass Ltd *Glass and Thermal Safety*, Pilkington Technical Advisory Service, 1982

CHAPTER 16

Resistance to Human Impact

The edges of glass, particularly broken glass, are often extremely sharp and can be a cause of serious injuries. Any pane of glass glazed with all edges in a frame is not a source of cutting injuries while it remains unbroken. However, if glass is subjected to accidental contact by a human being, the safety interest lies in reducing the possibility of cutting and piercing injuries, should the glass be broken. Since accidental means 'happening by chance, undesignedly, or unexpectedly', the loads cannot be easily quantified.

BIOMECHANICS

The human related variables in accidents with glass are:

- size and weight of the body
- parts of the body that impact the glass and their relative hardness
- velocity of the body on impact
- angle of impact.

A considerable amount of data has been collected on accidents, in particular the age and sex of those involved and the type and position of glazing impacted. This has allowed some quantification of the energy dissipated in an accident, indicating that impacts are from a semi-hard body acting over a small, unspecified area and of short, though indeterminate, duration.

Analysis of accident statistics has shown that a 45 kg (100 lb) boy was representative of glass breakage accident victims. It can been seen (Figure 16.2) that a 45 kg boy running at 6.7 m/s (22 ft/s) has about 1024 J (755 ft lb) of kinetic energy. The amount of energy delivered to the glass depends on the way he impacts the glass.

STANDARDS AND TESTS

One of the earliest standards produced was the US ANSI Z97. 1-1966: *Transparent Safety Glazing Materials used in Buildings*: Performance Specifications and Methods of Test. It was based on an attempt to classify the impact performance of products

Figure 16.1 *(Opposite)*
Impacting test bag, Pilkington Glass Ltd, St Helens, UK

A leather punch bag filled with lead shot to give weight and deformation characteristics similar to an impacting human body.

Figure 16.2
Human engineering data

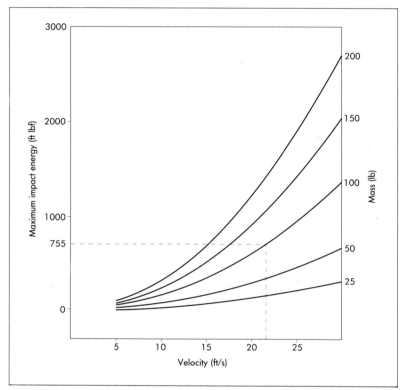

Current national test methods are based on these original data (ANSI 1966), using a 45 kg lead shot filled bag swung as a pendulum from various heights, for example:

Drop height mm	Impact energy J
300	132
450	199
700	309
950	419
1200	530

currently in service and used a test specimen which was the size of a large fully glazed door.

The impact energy levels were established from human engineering data (Figure 16.2). Two test values were originally selected, 136 J (100 ft lb) and 543 J (400 ft lb), as representative of the energy levels likely to be delivered in real situations. These test levels were set considerably below the 1024 J kinetic energy level of the typical victim, since the impact energy delivered to the glass – perhaps first by hands, then by the head, and then by knees – is much less than the full kinetic energy of the running boy.

Subsequently national standards have been developed from this basic model, using a greater variety of drop heights between 300 mm and 1220 mm for classification purposes. The pass criteria in these tests are directly related to the reduction of cutting and piercing injuries to persons who impact glass (Figures 16.3 and 16.4).

Figure 16.3   Test rig (Page 258), Pilkington Glass Ltd, St Helens, UK

A leather punch bag is used which is filled with lead shot to give it weight (45 kg) and deformation characteristics similar to the human body. The glass is impacted by the lead shot bag dropping from varying heights giving the required impact energies. There are two pass criteria:

- The glass does not break. (In some national standards this is not allowed as a pass criterion; the glass is required to be a type which breaks safely if it breaks.)
- If the glass breaks, it breaks safely.

The criteria for breaking safely depend upon the type of material tested. These criteria vary nationally. For example:

- Laminated glass, wired glass and glass with applied plastic film are deemed to break safely if 'no opening is produced through which a 75 mm diameter sphere can freely pass' and the weight of any glass falling off is below a 'limit'.
- Toughened (tempered) glass is deemed to break safely if 'the weight of the 10 largest crack free particles is less than the equivalent of (about) 6500 mm^2 of the original sample'.
- Annealed glass, if broken, does not break safely.

Figure 16.3
Test rig, Pilkington Glass Ltd, St
Helens, UK

 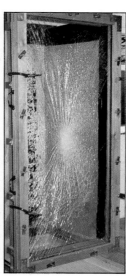 

(a) Impacted annealed   (b) Impacted laminated   (c) Impacted wired.

Figure 16.4
Impacted glass, Pilkington Glass Ltd,
St Helens, UK

HAZARDOUS AREAS

Since 1966 several studies have been made around the world gathering data on accidents. Figures 16.5 and 16.6 are produced from British data, but are typical of much international data.

From these and other research data a list of areas has been produced where there is an increased risk of accident:

- doors and glazed panels in the vicinity of doors
- low level glazing
- swimming pools and bathrooms (for example areas likely to have slippery floors)
- buildings with special activity (for example gymnasiums).

CONTAINMENT OR GUARDING

When the glass is being used to prevent injury to people 'falling through' a glass barrier from one level to another, then engineering design can be applied, together with knowledge of the impact performance of the glass (Figure 16.7).

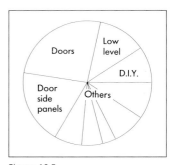

Figure 16.5
Hazardous locations

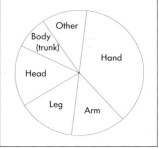

Figure 16.6
Body injuries

Figure 16.7
Balustrade, Landtag Building,
Dusseldorf, Germany

Architects: Hanig, Scheid and
Schmidt, Frankfurt

Balustrades, whether of glass or any other material, will be expected to carry a number of applied loads, for example, line load, point load, uniform load. Knowledge of the mechanical properties and impact performance of glass ensures that an appropriate type and thickness of glass can be designed and specified (Figure 16.7).

National regulations are very different and it is not possible to give recommendations concerning glass design for this purpose.

BIBLIOGRAPHY

ANSI Z97.1 *Safety Glazing Materials used in Buildings: Performance Specifications and Methods of Test*, American National Standards Institute, New York, 1966

BS 6180 *Protective Barriers In and About Buildings*, British Standards Institution, 1982

BS 6206 *Specification for Impact Performance Requirements for Flat Safety Glass and Plastics for Use in Buildings*, British Standards Institution, 1981

Department of Trade and Industry *Home Accident Surveillance Annual Reports on Glass Related Injuries*, DTI, UK, various years

DIN 52337 *Pendulum Impact Examination on Glass for Building Applications*, Deutches Institut für Normung e.V. (in German)

Organization Groups for Accidental Insurance Carriers in Public Hands, 'More Safety from Glass Breakage', (in German)

CHAPTER 17

Resistance to Explosive Loading

All building materials which are durable and obtainable in weather-resistant colours, have the right to be used. Brittle brick and inflammable wood have no such right; a brick building is also easy to shatter by explosives, which endanger the whole building equally. This is not the case in a glass-iron building; only partial destruction can be induced by explosives in the latter.

Scheerbart, *Glasarchitektur*, 1914

Figure 17.1 *(Opposite)* Urban explosion

Despite Scheerbart's enthusiasms, the glass building requires careful design against explosive loading. In this case only external explosions are discussed.

Explosions result from the ignition of explosive materials. There are two types, accidental and deliberate; some of the latter are malicious.

THE NATURE OF EXPLOSION LOADS

When an explosion occurs, the force exerted is directly proportional to the amount of explosive material and inversely proportional to the distance from the explosion.

A pressure wave in the air is produced taking the form of a pressure pulse followed by a partial vacuum (approximately two-thirds of the pressure), travelling away from the explosion in the shape of a spherical surface. The pulse is assessed on its pressure level (described as the overpressure) and its duration. Overpressure reduces with distance from the explosion, while the duration increases (Figure 17.2). There are other ways of describing an explosion; one is as an impulse load, since its effect is similar to that of a form of impact.

Figure 17.2 Explosion pressure wave

> The pressure wave dissipates and spreads out as it gets further from the source. An analogy can be drawn with the sound of thunder. If lightning is directly overhead, the thunder is extremely loud and of a very short duration. It is a crack of thunder. Further away from the lightning flash, the thunder is apparently less loud, for two reasons. First, the sound has spread over a much greater area, so it is proportionally reduced in loudness. Second, the sound wave becomes extended in the direction travelled, so that the sound becomes a rumble of thunder, lasting for a greater length of time. The pressure wave from an explosion is dissipated in a similar way.

If the source of an explosion can be predicted, it is feasible to estimate the overpressure and duration at any given distance from it. Thus the effects of explosions can be roughly assessed. However, the type of knowledge required to make some of these assessments may not be publicly available.

The forces in the pressure wave can cause material disintegration or can move extraneous items at high velocity. These can also cause damage and are often responsible for personal injuries.

Injuries can take three forms:

- burns from exposure to heat which can be generated in the explosion
- direct injuries from the pressure wave (usually to parts of the body in close proximity to the explosion)
- shrapnel damage (glass is one of the obvious hazards).

The design information required can only be obtained from tests. These can take the form of either tests with real explosives or simulated, explosion-like, pressure tests. Data from explosive tests are usually available only to official authorities. They can contain information on a variety of glass types, sizes, combinations and framing systems at a variety of blast overpressures and durations. Data from simulated tests are limited to material classification. They give little information as to the performance of different sizes of windows and different types of frames.

The required information which is relevant to glazing design is:

- expected blast overpressure (kN/m^2)
- duration of blast (of the order of 10 to 100 milliseconds).

Often the client may believe there is some risk of explosion but has no idea of the likely force or duration. Quantitative information relating to explosions may only be available from official authorities and some industries, for example the petrochemical industry.

DESIGNING TO RESIST EXPLOSIONS

The design can be for the glass either to remain unbroken or to remain in place when broken.

If detailed information about a blast is available it is possible to design for the glass to remain unbroken. Pressures below 10 kN/m^2 are little more than very severe wind pressures (in hurricane areas, design wind pressures of 8000 N/m^2 are not uncommon); they can be considered as a wind load and the glass designed accordingly. Where the pressures involved are higher than 10 kN/m^2, toughened glass will usually be required.

Whilst a single pane of toughened glass can resist the blast overpressure, debris is often carried by the pressure wave. Should this debris impact the toughened glass, it may penetrate the compressive surface layer causing fracture and failure. To keep the window intact, an extra sacrificial layer of toughened glass is laminated to the glass withstanding the blast pressure. Because the glass remains unbroken, the full blast pressure will be transmitted to the supporting structure which must remain structurally sound and intact.

Designing the glass to remain in position if broken usually results in more economic solutions. The procedure is to use laminated glass with a highly plastic interlayer (polyvinyl butyral) which absorbs the explosive energy in deformation and provides resistance whilst remaining in the frame. Also the broken pieces of glass adhere to the interlayer and are prevented from becoming shrapnel.

In double glazed units the laminated glass is placed on the side away from the anticipated explosion, normally the inner glass (Figure 17.3). The remaining glass can be any type, since shrapnel formed from it will be caught by the laminated glass. The presence of this shrapnel does not detract from the performance of the laminated glass; the outer glass, however weak, appears to assist the performance of the laminated inner glass.

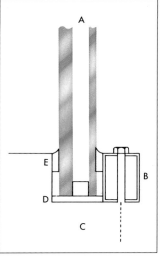

Figure 17.3
Blast resistant glazing, double glazed units

A Double glazed unit at least one glass, on the side away from the blast, must have 1.5 mm PVB interlayer.
B Bead must be fixed so that it remains in place during explosion (20–35 mm edge cover).
C Frame must be well connected to building structure. Both frame and connections must be designed to resist blast load forces.
D 5 mm setting blocks. Neoprene or similar material.
E Between 12–15 mm depth of silicone sealant.

267

FIXING METHODS

Fixing methods are important for the resistance of the glazing to blast pressure. Where the glass is intended to remain unbroken (except for the sacrificial layer), the fixing method can be one normally used for glazing, but must be designed to resist the forces transmitted through the glass (for example the full blast overpressure) whilst maintaining the glass in position. This may result in heavier duty fixings than those used to resist wind forces. Similarly the attachment of the frame to the building and the attachment of beads to the frame may need to be considerably stronger than for conventional fixings (Figure 17.4).

Where the glass is allowed to fracture, the fragmented laminated glass achieves its resistance from the plastic interlayer material being retained in the rebate (Figure 17.5). This requires a deep rebate for all four edges of the glass, augmented by either a clamping pressure (for single glazing) or a high bond strength sealant.

While the details of a framing system may vary, several general rules are suggested which will assist in producing a suitable fixing:

- Increasing the glass edge cover above that used in normal glazing frames can be beneficial to explosion resistance.
- The beads should be 'bolted' at frequent intervals in order to resist the partial vacuum after the blast.
- Clamping pressure or high bond strength sealants should be used.

If blast overpressure and duration have been specified, it is possible to design a laminated glass specifically to resist that level of explosion. Laminated glass with a 1.5 mm polyvinyl butyral interlayer will give resistance to relatively severe explosions provided it is effectively framed, but for very high explosion pressures it should be restricted in size.

When glass breaks and allows the plastic interlayer material to absorb energy from the explosion, the force transferred to the supporting structure will be significantly reduced. This allows lighter frames than might be required if the glass is designed not to break.

268

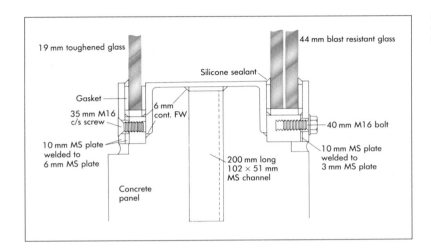

Figure 17.4
Glazing designed to resist 175 kN/m²
unbroken.

19 mm toughened glass

44 mm blast resistant glass

Silicone sealant

Gasket

6 mm
cont. FW

35 mm M16
c/s screw

40 mm M16 bolt

10 mm MS plate
welded to
6 mm MS plate

10 mm MS plate
welded to
3 mm MS plate

200 mm long
102 × 51 mm
MS channel

Concrete
panel

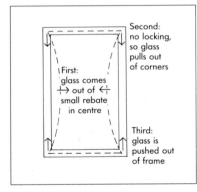

Second:
no locking,
so glass
pulls out
of corners

First:
glass comes
out of
small rebate
in centre

Third:
glass is
pushed out
of frame

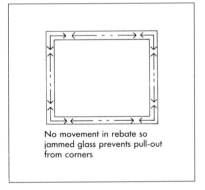

No movement in rebate so
jammed glass prevents pull-out
from corners

Figure 17.5
Retaining laminated glass in the
frame

Fractured laminated glass is very flexible because the plastic interlayer has no inherent bending strength and the shattered glass gives little support. Under blast pressure it will, if allowed, fold up and be pushed out of its frame.

However, the folding can only occur when the broken laminate can flex. This happens not in the rebate of the frame, but across the unsupported central span. If the interlayer is within a rebate on all four edges, the jamming of broken glass within the rebate stops the interlayer from pulling out of the corner. To work adequately, a deep rebate is required, augmented by adhesives or clamping, since, if the flexure of the broken laminate in the central span is sufficient to pull the laminate out of the rebate in the centre of an edge, the broken glass is no longer jammed in and the laminate will fold out of the corners of the frame.

OTHER CONSIDERATIONS

When there is a danger of flying glass shrapnel, protection can be augmented by the application of blast resistant films on to the glass or by the use of blast curtains.

Glass with applied blast resistant films, after fracture, tends to behave in a similar way to laminated glass and requires the same glazing methods. Blast resistant films do not strengthen the glass or prevent it from fracturing. Their effect is limited if the film is not continued right to the edge of the glass and clamped within the rebate.

A major difference between laminated glass and blast resistant films is the service life. Poor application, general wear and tear, and exposure to atmospheric agents may restrict the service life of films, requiring them to be replaced over time.

Blast curtains are designed to enfold and capture flying debris coming from a window, including external objects and glass shrapnel. The flexibility and strength of the curtain material allow it to absorb the energy of the debris and contain it in a cover which makes it far less dangerous.

BIBLIOGRAPHY

DIN 52290 *Resistance to Explosion*, Part 5, 12–1987, Deutsches Institut für Normung e.V. (in German)

Monsanto *Security Glazing Design Guide*, Monsanto Corporation, St Louis, MO, 1991

CHAPTER 18

Resistance to Bullet Impact

Glass may appear an unlikely material to form a bullet resistant screen, owing to its lack of ductility and its vulnerability to localized stresses. However, when combined in multi-layer laminates with ductile, energy absorbing, plastic interlayers, glass products can be very effective.

Figure 18.1 *(Opposite)*
Impacted laminated glass, Flachglas AG, Germany

A 23 mm laminated glass (4 + 8 + 6 + 4 mm) impacted by 0.357 Magnum revolver

STANDARDS AND TESTS

In principle, it is possible to design laminated glass against a particular firearm/bullet combination, but this has not yet been done satisfactorily. The more usual way to assess bullet resistance is by practical tests. These tests have been developed into national standards which differ slightly but apply similar principles (Figures 18.2).

Figure 18.2
Bullets impacting laminated glass, Pilkington Technology Centre, Lathom, UK

The tests require a particular size of glass pane and use specific weapons and ammunition selected to be representative of general categories of firearm. The tests also specify the range, angle of attack and particular strike patterns (for example, number of shots and where they hit the target). To obtain test repeatability, the weapons chosen may be modified to be particularly accurate and the ammunition selected by type and weight to achieve a particular strike velocity within close tolerances.

273

Figure 18.3
Bullet firing test, Flachglas AG,
Germany

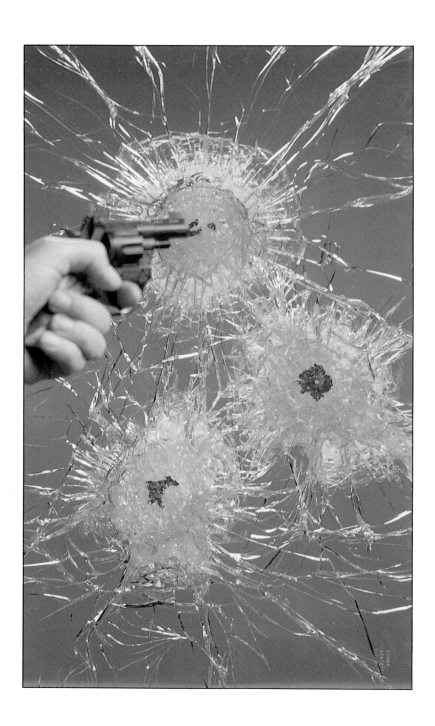

The weapons selected for tests range from handguns of various powers to standard military rifles and shotguns. The classification of bullet resistant glass products is based on the grade of weapon power, (Figure 18.3).

For a glass to pass a test, two criteria must be satisfied. The first is that the glass must not allow the bullet(s) to pass through. The second concerns the nature of the splinters ejected from the rear face of the glass. The impact of bullets can result in glass splinters being ejected from the rear side of the screen with considerable force, and these splinters may cause serious injury to anyone close to the glass. This ejection of splinters is referred to as 'spalling'.

The second criterion divides into three categories:

- No spall: no splinters are allowed to be ejected from the rear (protected) face. This may be best achieved by the addition of a zero-spall plastic layer, bonded to the glass, or by a separate pane behind the main bullet resistant glass.
- Limited spall: a quantity of very small, low energy splinters is allowed. These are detected in testing by a thin metallic foil behind the glass; no holes in the foil gives a pass.
- Unlimited spall: any amount of splinters is allowed.

National standards are likely to use only the first or second categories, since their purpose is to limit injury to superficial wounds. Products classified to meet the third category should only be used where it is unlikely that anyone will be close to the inner glass.

INSTALLATION

All components of the protective screen must offer equal bullet resistance.

Bullet resistant glass should be glazed with all the edges protected in strong rebates, so that the glass cannot be levered away to form a gap. The beading or retaining components should substantially overlap the glass and should not be accessible to the attacker. The fixing system should also be strong enough to prevent the glass being pushed out of the frame.

PERFORMANCE OF PRODUCTS

The performance of bullet resistant glass products is determined by detailed construction, i.e. the number and thickness of the individual leaves of glass, interlayer and (if used) polycarbonate (Figure 18.4).

Two fundamental groups of products are available. The first is inherently simpler (and hence cheaper), made from glass plies laminated together with polyvinyl butyral interlayers. The second incorporates polycarbonate plies within the construction (glass/polycarbonate composite) and offers significant weight saving potential.

Figure 18.4 Composite structure required for different levels of attack

	Parabellum	Magnum revolver	Nato rifle	Shotgun
	9 mm	44	7.62 mm	12 bore
Laminated glass (mm)	20–40	40–60	50–80	30–50
Glass/polycarbonate composite (mm)	15–25	25–30	30–50	–

BIBLIOGRAPHY

BS 5051 Part 1: *Specification for Bullet Resistant Glazing for Interior Use*, British Standards Institution, 1988

DIN 52290 *Resistance to Bullets*, Part 2, 5–1981, Deutsches Institut für Normung e.V. (in German)

Monsanto *Security Glazing Design Guide*, Monsanto Corporation, St Louis, MO, 1991

CHAPTER 19

Resistance to Burglar Attack

This chapter discusses the application and design of glass capable of resisting access through it by the 'non-casual' vandal.

The design problem is how to assess the type and nature of the applied load, particularly given the ingenuity in and range of methods of attack (hands, feet, bricks, hammers, axes, heat torches). It is not easy to predict the forces applied.

TEST METHODS

The simplest solution is to idealize these forces and to perform some form of graded test by which glass products can be classified.

An easily performed test is to drop heavy objects on to the glass. A steel sphere weighing up to 5 kg is dropped from a height sufficient to simulate the energy developed by an attacker. One such test uses a 4 kg steel ball dropped from heights up to 9 m. Glass products are classified according to the drop height at which they resist penetration (the sphere does not go through) from three successive impacts. The energy developed on impact from dropping a 4 kg steel sphere from 9 m height is as much as can reasonably be expected from a very strong person throwing a missile.

Attacks with instruments such as axes cause very different types of damage from those using a blunt, thrown object. The axe may be lighter, but its impact velocity is much higher than that of any thrown object. Simply dropping a steel sphere from greater heights does not simulate this type of attack.

It is therefore necessary to use other types of test. One such test simulates an axe attack by using a machine to idealize the axe stroke (Figure 19.2), keeping the velocity of the strike within close limits. Penetration of the glass in this test is defined as the cutting of a sufficiently large opening (400 mm square), and the glass is classified according to the number of blows taken to form the opening.

Figure 19.1 (Opposite)
Burglar resistance, Flachglas AG, Germany

Figure 19.2
Mechanical axeman test, Flachglas
AG, Germany

PRODUCT PERFORMANCE

The possible gain to the attacker and the time available to develop an entry both play an important part in determining how much resistance will be necessary to prevent access. A thin laminated glass will often deter the housebreaker, since the gains may be unknown and easier access may be obtained elsewhere. There are circumstances, however, where much higher resistance is necessary. In such cases there is a need for a graded system ranging from cheaper products with lower resistance, to more expensive products capable of resisting a sustained and severe attack.

Toughened glass is susceptible to impacts from sharp pointed objects, which can drive cracks directly through the compressive outer layer, thus propagating fracture. When the glass is fractured, access through the window is relatively simple and is unlikely to result in any serious injury to the attacker.

Annealed glass may be preferable, as it can leave jagged edges of glass protruding out of the rebate, making access difficult and potentially hazardous to the intruder. This is especially so where the panes are sufficiently small to make entry difficult. However, the objective in breaking the glass may be only to reach through to a door or window catch.

Laminated glass provides considerable resistance to penetration owing to the plastic interlayer material, which is difficult to penetrate without using a weapon, a sharp object or heat. The resistance to penetration relies mainly on the thickness and number of polyvinyl butyral interlayers. While 6.4 mm laminated glass (two pieces of 3 mm glass with a 0.38 mm polyvinyl butyral interlayer) will give some resistance against an opportunist housebreaker, shop windows require a more resistant glass, for example 11.5 mm laminated glass (5 mm glass, 1.52 mm polyvinyl butyral, 5 mm glass). For high security risk areas, much thicker laminates with more interlayers are appropriate.

An alternative to laminated glass, allowing reduced thicknesses for the same performance, is glass products incorporating leaves of rigid polycarbonate within the laminate. Polycarbonate has a much better impact performance than glass or polyvinyl butyral. Its incorporation into a laminate can give higher impact performance from relatively thin materials.

For instance, laminated glass either 18.1 mm thick containing polycarbonate or 29.8 mm thick without polycarbonate would give similar performance when subjected to the mechanical axe test.

ALARM GLASS

Further protection can be provided by glass products containing electroconducting circuits connected to an alarm system. When the glass is broken the circuit is interrupted, setting off an alarm.

Two types of circuit are normally used: ceramic loop and straight wire (Figure 19.3). In each case the conducting circuit is connected to the alarm system either at the surface or from the edge of the glass using sockets and connecting wire (Figure 19.4). These conducting circuits can be used with toughened or laminated glass and incorporated into double glazed units. It is usual that straight wired circuits are incorporated into laminated glass constructions.

Figure 19.3 Basic description of alarm glass circuits

	Ceramic loop	Straight wire
Material	conducting enamel	copper wire
Length	< 1200 mm	max. 2560 mm
Line width	0.4 mm	0.1 mm
Electrical resistance	35 Ω	2.2 Ω/ m

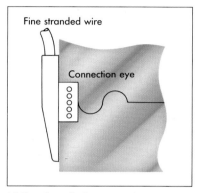

Fine stranded wire

Connection eye

(a) Elevation of edge connection at corner
of laminated glass

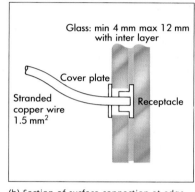

Glass: min 4 mm max 12 mm
with inter layer

Cover plate

Stranded
copper wire
1.5 mm²

Receptacle

(b) Section of surface connection at edge
of laminated glass

Figure 19.4
Alarm glass edge and surface
connections

Figure 19.5
Alarm glass display window with
straight wire, Flachglas AG, Germany

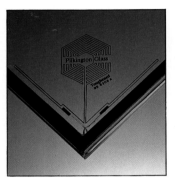

Figure 19.6
Alarm glass ceramic loop double
glazed unit with connection,
Pilkington Glass Ltd, St Helens, UK

A ceramic loop circuit fixed on to the surface of toughened glass and positioned on the air space side of a double glazed unit is shown in Figure 19.6. The alarm glass forms the outer pane of the glazed window. Connection to the loop is typically via a four-core flat plug attached to the edge of the double glazed unit.

The selection of glass type and connection method will depend on the level of security required and the type of glazing system used. When correctly designed, the window will meet the most stringent security requirements.

INSTALLATION

The frame itself, the method of fixing the frame to the structure and the method of fixing the glass in the frame need to be designed to resist a similar level of attack as the glass.

BIBLIOGRAPHY

BS 5544 *Specification for Anti-Bandit Glazing (Resistant to Manual Attack)*, British Standards Institution, 1978

BS 8220 *Guide for Security of Buildings Against Crime. Part 2: Offices and Shops*, British Standards Institution, 1987

DIN 52290 *Resistance to Burglars*, Parts 3 2–1989 and 4 6-1984, Deutsches Institut für Normung e.V. (in German)

Monsanto *Security Glazing Design Guide*, Monsanto Corporation, St Louis, MO, 1991

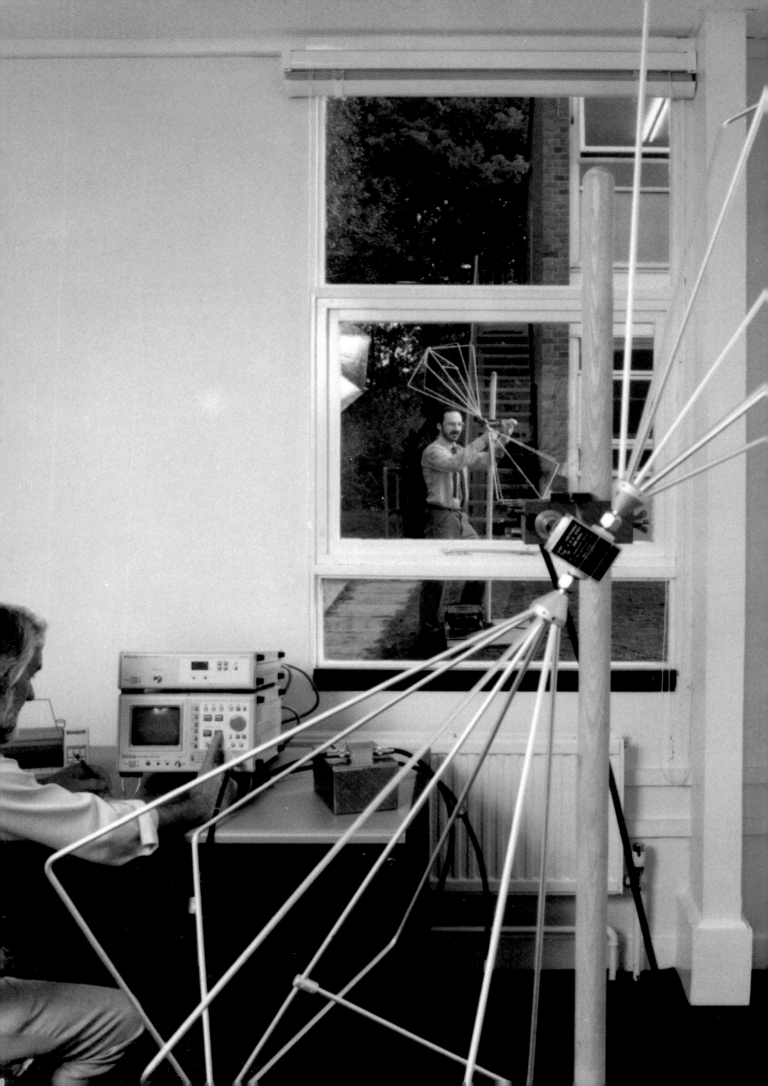

CHAPTER 20

Electromagnetic Shielding

Electromagnetic interference (EMI) is a well known phenomenon, best described as an electrical disturbance which interferes with the function of electric or electronic equipment.

The disturbance can be a result of natural occurrences (lightning discharges) or can be man-made, such as by the generation of radio and radar transmissions or unintentionally by the malfunction of electrical equipment. Once generated, interference can affect electrical equipment, either by conduction along the electrical mains supply line or by radiation in the form of electromagnetic waves, which then interact on equipment wiring components.

Electrical equipment itself can also be a radiator of electromagnetic waveforms, which can interfere with the operation of other non-shielded equipment or, if emitted from computer or data handling devices, can be interrogated (read) by sensitive detecting equipment.

To protect electrical equipment from interference, it is necessary to:

● suppress the interference at source, or
● protect components from interference, or
● enclose equipment within a shielded environment.

The building user may require that electrical signals are prevented from entering or leaving a building, whilst still wanting to take advantage of glass as part of the construction.

SHIELDING EFFECTIVENESS OF GLASS

The electromagnetic shielding of a building or facility involves the complete enclosing of an area within a continuous metal enclosure.

Building design in the future may have to consider a provision for incorporating a level of shielding to some or all buildings, in order to:

● exclude unwanted electromagnetic radiation, which may affect the operation of vital equipment

Figure 20.1 *(Opposite)*
Electromagnetic measurement of the unscreened office at the Building Research Establishment, Watford, UK
Crown copyright, 1992

- contain radiating signals from equipment, which may disrupt the operation of other equipment within the building
- prevent interrogation of computer and data handling systems by sensitive detecting devices.

The availability of glass based systems for shielding allows moderate levels of protection to be achieved, whilst at the same time utilizing the positive advantages of allowing heat and light into the building.

GLASS TYPES

Clear or tinted float glass provides little shielding when used as a barrier to electromagnetic waves. However, its shielding can be significantly improved by depositing a thin metallic coating on to the glass surface whilst controlling the coating resistivity properties.

The degree of electromagnetic signal attenuation achieved (shielding) depends on the frequency of radiation, the signal impedance, and the thickness and conductivity of the metallic coating. For the type of thin coatings deposited on glass, the electrical signal attenuation is effective only in the electric (E) field and not in the magnetic (H) field, and is achieved almost entirely by reflection of the electromagnetic radiation (Figure 20.2).

For maximum electrical signal attenuation, the special coatings on glass must be conductively connected to the window frame all round its periphery. The frame, in turn, should be connected to the wall screening (and where appropriate roof and floor) to produce a Faraday cage (an enclosure in which all surfaces are electrically conducting). A typical framing method is shown in Figure 20.3.

Figure 20.2 Nature of EMI radiation

Electromagnetic interference can be considered as an electromagnetic wave having two oscillating fields at right angles, the electric field (E field) and the magnetic field (H field).

Any barrier placed between an emitter and a receiver that diminishes the strength of the electromagnetic radiation can be thought of as an EMI shield. The efficiency of the shield to attenuate the electromagnetic field is referred to as its shielding effectiveness (SE), defined as the ratio of field strengths compared before and after shielding expressed in decibels (dB). The general formula is as follows:

$$E - field \;\; SE \; = \; 20 \log_{10} (E_1 / E_2) dB$$

$$H - field \;\; SE \; = \; 20 \log_{10} (H_1 / H_2) dB$$

Any loss in field strength resulting from a shielding barrier is a function of the barrier material (permeability, conductivity and thickness), the frequency of the electromagnetic radiation and the distance from the EMI source. Metallic coated glass provides shielding from electrical fields only. Little shielding is achieved from the magnetic field.

Metallic coated glass can be supplied either laminated or double glazed and can be combined with other glass panes to achieve the required electrical shielding and environmental performance specifications. Typical attenuation figures for different coated glass types across a wide frequency band are shown in Figure 20.4.

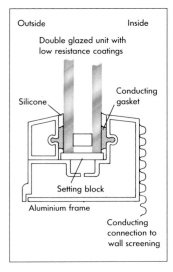

Figure 20.3
Typical frame conduction glazing method

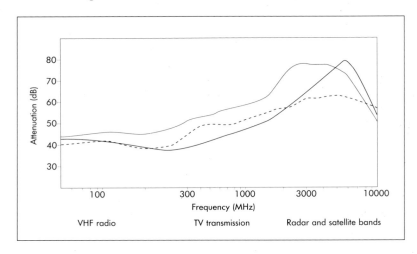

Figure 20.4
Typical attenuation figures for three different thicknesses of metallic coatings in double glazed units.

BIBLIOGRAPHY

Clarke, L.T. *The Use of Metallised Glass for RFI Shielding*, Pilkington Bros PLC, R&D Laboratories, Lathom, UK

Miedzinski, J. *Electromagnetic Screening Theory and Practice*, ERA report M/T 135, Electrical Research Organization, 1959

Monsanto *Security Glazing Design Guide*, Monsanto Corporation, St Louis, MO, 1991

Schwab, A. J. *Electromagnetic Compatibility*, Springer Verlag, Berlin, Heidelberg and New York, 1990 (in German)

White, D. A *Handbook on Electromagnetic Shielding Materials and Performance*, Don White Consultants Inc., 1975

CHAPTER 21

Fire Resistance

'A *glass house does not catch fire – there is no need for a fire brigade.*'
Scheerbart, *Glasarchitektur*, 1914

Figure 21.1 *(Opposite)*
Fire insulating glass in Dampfbier
Brauerei, Essen, Germany

The complete destruction by fire of the Crystal Palace in London in 1936 proved Scheerbart to be wrong in at least one of his 1914 prophesies: The Crystal Palace represented the high point in nineteenth century glass architecture. Its destruction by fire generated a reappraisal of glass and fire resistance.

Until recently, limitations were placed on the use of glass as an element of building construction in fire resistant applications. This was due to the natural property of glass to directly transmit radiation. When a fire is fully developed, high levels of transmitted radiation through glass may present a hazard to people escaping or possibly cause the ignition of combustible materials resulting in fire spread. Thus, a window in a fire wall could be a weak link. However, clear vision through a window in a door or a wall can also provide safety benefits in the event of a fire, enabling the location and safe evacuation of occupants from burning premises. This is particularly true in fire doors and has led to the extensive use of wired glass in these locations.

Figure 21.2
A building fire

Wired glass permits the transmission of heat radiation from the fire, yet provides specific resistance to the passage of flames and smoke; it is a non-insulating glass. Other non-insulating, non-wired glass products with similar properties have also become available in recent years owing to improvements in glass processing technology. Some glass products, as well as providing fire resistance, can also have a good impact performance.

A second, more recently developed range of glass products is able to offer enhanced fire performance characteristics. These glass products combine good impact safety performance with an ability to resist fire radiation transmission, by becoming opaque when subjected to heat above 120 °C. Such fire insulating glass products enable glass to be used in larger sizes and in locations which were previously served by traditional opaque fire compartment materials, such as brick and concrete. Fire resistant glass products can also be combined with other functional glass products to provide solutions for a range of different applications, such as security and thermal insulation, without compromising fire resistance.

Glass exhibits many different performance characteristics when exposed to fire. These characteristics vary with the type of fire exposure (the rate of temperature rise), the composition of the glass or the use of glass in conjunction with other materials (laminated glass, double glazed units). However, consideration must be given to the following areas to enable the most appropriate glass for the application to be selected:

- nature of fire hazard
- glass types and their performance in fires
- glazing details and maintenance.

THE NATURE OF FIRE HAZARD

Burning is often defined as a set of complex chemical reactions in which substances combine with oxygen to produce heat and (usually) light. These substances may be liquids, solids or gases which act as fuel and once ignited will generate heat, eventually resulting in the ignition of other combustible materials.

The size and intensity of a fire are determined mainly by the rate at which heat energy is produced and by the ability of that heat energy to ignite further combustible materials. It therefore follows that if non-combustible or low combustible products are used in a building, the rate of ignition and likelihood of fire spread will be reduced.

The rate of fire spread and growth is dependent primarily on three variables: fuel source (the material content of the room), air movement and supply, and ignition source. The variations in these ensure that no two fires are the same. The removal of any of the three variables results in the fire being unsustained.

Fires have defined phases of growth (Figure 21.3). As the fire passes through its different phases of development, over an unquantifiable period, it can be expected that the temperature in the room will rise. The time over which the temperature rises (the rate of fire growth) depends on the three variables above. To establish the behaviour characteristics of products or systems in a fire requires that they are subjected to one or more

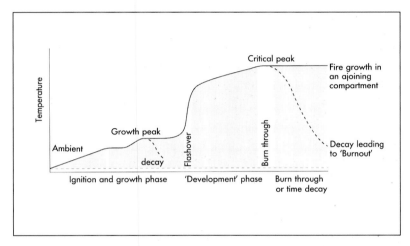

Figure 21.3
Description of stages of fire development in compartment of origin

Initiation   Fires start with the ignition of a fuel source by heat, the result being a continuous combustion.

Growth   During the early stages the fire will spread away from the point first ignited across the material. In order for the fire to propagate (spread), more heat than was initially required for ignition must be created. The rate at which fire spreads is related to the rate of heat release from the burning material. If a fire becomes established then, providing it has fuel and an air supply, it will continue to grow. When all the combustible material in the room is involved in the fire a condition known as 'flashover' has occurred. The fire is then fully developed.

Full development   When a fire is fully developed the temperature within the room will rise quickly, consuming the fuel and air supplies.

Decay   If the fire can be contained within the room or compartment it will exhaust the fuel and air supply and enter the decay phase. Alternatively the hot gases and flames may breach the surrounding room or compartment structure, resulting in fire spread to further parts of the building. This condition is know as 'burn through'.

Figure 21.4
Description of fire tests used to
assess fire development in
compartment of origin

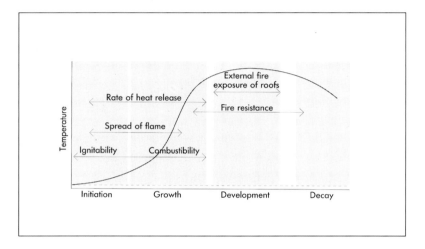

Figure 21.4
Description of fire tests used to
assess fire development in
compartment of origin

fire tests that can replicate the different degrees of fire exposures possible. This enables the burning characteristics of the
product or system to be assessed under standard reproducible
conditions. No fire test or combination of fire tests can
guarantee safety in a particular situation, but they do allow
product characteristics to be compared. Some of the fire tests
available in the UK are detailed in Figure 21.4. These tests can
be divided under two headings: those relating to the performance of individual products (reaction to fire tests), and those
used to determine the performance of systems (fire resistance
tests).

REACTION TO FIRE TESTS

A series of different tests is used to establish the fire performance of individual products and to determine, for example, the
'ease of ignition', the 'rate of fire spread across the surface' and
the 'rate of heat release' – all factors influential in the development of a fire in the period before flashover. A great diversity of
reaction to fire tests has been developed and forms the basis of
many national regulations.

Glass, because it is non-combustible, achieves the highest
level of performance in such tests.

FIRE RESISTANCE TESTS

Fire resistance tests are used to evaluate the ability of elements of a structure to withstand the effects of a fully developed fire.

When fire resistant glass is used as part of the fire protection of a building, the glazed system is designed and tested to determine its ability to contain the fire in the period following flashover. Systems can be tested to destruction to simulate a worst case of 'burn through', having resisted the fire for a measured period, or the test can be stopped when a required time has elapsed.

Existing national test procedures in this technology are often based on the International Standardization Organization codes ISO 834, ISO 3008 and ISO 3009. However, each country can have supplementary requirements. Thus, although the basic principles are shared, the results can vary from one country to another. These differences, in the long term, may be resolved by the development of unified testing systems based on an assessment of the real hazards and the increased risk associated with using the product in particular applications.

Fire resistance tests for glass involve the construction of a complete element of a structure, for example a glazed partition or door including all components. The fire resistance test evaluates the way in which all components work together and not just the performance of a single product or component.

To assess the ability of a structure to perform in a fire, it is necessary to test it against a defined procedure to meet certain criteria (Figure 21.5).

GLASS PERFORMANCE IN FIRE

The performance characteristics of glass vary with its composition. In order to achieve levels of fire resistance from glass, it is necessary to ensure that it is glazed and framed in ways that are specified for that particular product.

Figure 21.5 Fire resistance criteria

The fire resistance test procedure judges systems in accordance with their ability to meet certain criteria. Those applying in most of Europe are load bearing capability (R), integrity (E), insulation (I) and radiation (W).

Load bearing capability This criterion is not generally applicable to glazed structures, which are essentially non-load bearing. It determines the ability of the element to support its load during the fire resistance test without collapse. A load bearing capability is required of columns, beams and other structural components.

Integrity This is a measure of the ability of a separating construction to resist the passage of flames and hot gases from the exposed to the unexposed face of a test specimen. The specimen fails to meet this criterion when cracks or openings appear through which it is possible to pass gap gauges of a predetermined size, or when flaming on the unexposed surface exceeds 10 seconds, or when a cotton wool pad ignites when placed over cracks or openings.

Insulation This is a measure of the ability of a separating construction to restrict the temperature rise on the unexposed face to below specified levels. These temperature levels are intended to ensure that any combustible material in contact with the unexposed face will not ignite. The average temperature of the unexposed face should not rise more than 140 °C above ambient, nor should the temperature at any point on the unexposed face rise more than 180 °C above ambient.

Radiation The level of radiation hazard, either through the specimen or from the unexposed surface, is measured. High levels of heat radiation can inhibit means of escape or can cause the ignition of materials on the unexposed side of the specimen.

The methods of measurement for establishing compliance with the fire resistance test criteria are reasonably consistent between countries. However, the national regulations of each country do not always call for the system to be assessed against all the performance/test criteria detailed above.

Figure 21.6
A non-insulating wired glass under test, Pilkington Glass Ltd, St Helens, UK

The photographs show Georgian polished wired glass achieving 2 hour integrity. The temperature inside the furnace was 1039 °C and the glass temperature was 780 °C. As the furnace temperature rises, the non-insulated steel frame deflects in towards the furnace; the pressure in the upper part of the furnace causes the glass to bow out, away from the furnace. Thermocouples attached to the glass surface monitor its temperature rise. A heat flux meter located in front of the furnace measures the levels of heat radiation intensity.

NON-INSULATING GLASS PRODUCTS

These are glass products able to resist the passage of smoke, flames and hot gases (Figure 21.6) but not able to satisfy the insulation criterion. Regulations may place limits on the location or areas of non-insulating glass that may be used.

There are basically two types of glass which are considered non-insulating:

- Wired glass: on exposure to fire, the glass breaks due to thermal shock but the wire mesh within the glass maintains the integrity of the specimen by holding the fragmented pieces in place.
- Special composition glass: on exposure to fire, the glass does not break owing to its low coefficient of thermal expansion, and hence remains unbroken within its frame. The glass may also be thermally strengthened to minimize the effects of stress, thereby achieving a level of impact safety.

PARTIALLY INSULATING GLASS PRODUCTS

These have fire resistance properties which lie between the insulating and non-insulating glass products. They are usually multi-laminated panes incorporating one intumescent (swelling) interlayer which becomes opaque on heating. As a result of this intumescent interlayer, they are able to resist the passage of smoke, flames and hot gases and meet the insulation criterion for up to 15 minutes. The temperature on the unexposed face, after this time, then rises beyond the accepted criterion level, but less quickly than for a non-insulating glass.

INSULATING GLASS PRODUCTS

These are glass types which are able to resist the passage of smoke, flames and hot gases and meet the insulation criterion for at least 30 minutes. National regulations generally require 30, 45 and 60 minutes compliance. An insulating glass with an intumescent interlayer under test is illustrated in Figures 21.7.

There are two types of insulating glass available. The first is intumescent laminated glass formed from multi-laminated layers of float glass and clear intumescent interlayers. The fire resistance

Figure 21.7
Insulating glass under test, Flachglas
AG, Germany

The photographs show single panes
of intumescent glass in insulated
frames reacting to fire after 6
minutes and 60 minutes on test.

depends on the special composition of the interlayers, which react to high temperature by intumescing to produce an opaque shield that resists the transmission of radiant and conducted heat. On exposure to the fire the glass fractures, but remains bonded to the interlayer. The level of fire resistance achieved is directly related to the number of interlayers.

The second is gel interlayered glass formed from a clear, transparent gel located between sheets of toughened glass separated by metal spacer bars and sealed at the edges. The level of fire resistance achieved is related to the thickness of the gel interlayer. On exposure to fire, the gel forms a crust and the evaporating water from the interlayer absorbs the heat energy. This process continues until the gel has burnt through.

GLASS DURABILITY

All of the non-insulating fire glass products exhibit surface durability characteristics similar to those of float glass. However, all partially and fully insulating glass products may require protection from UV light if glazed externally. This is typically achieved by using a cast-in-place resin added to the external face of the product and further protected with an additional pane of glass; this technique is known as cast-in-place lamination. They additionally require the intumescent materials to be protected from contact with moisture at their edges in all glazing situations.

GLAZING DETAILS

Glass by itself is not fire resisting. The level of fire resistance achieved is that of the system, glass, beads, glazing materials, frame and frame restraint detail. The system is as strong as its weakest components.

Although the requirements of each system should be considered individually, certain key factors apply.

GLASS

The type of glass used influences the design of the frame and bead and the choice of glazing material.

Non-insulating glass products will allow the transmission of radiant heat, possibly resulting in the ignition of combustible material on the unexposed side of the system (including the timber frame). The use of appropriate glazing materials and bead design will reduce the possibility of ignition of the unexposed face bead.

Insulating glass (Figure 21.7) significantly reduces the degree of radiant heat transmission. Therefore the choice of glazing materials and bead design may differ for this group of glass products.

The size and shape of glass, known as aspect ratio, affects the performance of non-insulating glass when fire resistance periods in excess of 30 minutes are required. When the temperature of some non-insulating glass exceeds about 600 °C, they start to soften and slump. As the glass slumps, it slips out of the top edge rebate if sufficient pressure is not exerted on the glass to clamp it in place. The shape and size of the glass influences the time and rate at which the glass slumps (Figure 21.8). For most non-insulating glass products the frame design for systems intended to have a fire resistance of longer than 30 minutes has to take slumping into consideration, by using appropriate fixings or clamping methods along the top edges of the glass (Figure 21.9).

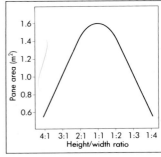

Figure 21.8
Effect of aspect ratio on fire resistance performance of non-insulating glass

As the shape and size of the glass can influence its performance, glazing systems have been developed which address the particular issue of slumping. Manufacturers of the systems offer guidance on how to achieve the best result for a given pane size and shape. The graph shows one method of determining a given pane size for a particular aspect ratio when one hour fire resistance is required in timber frames.

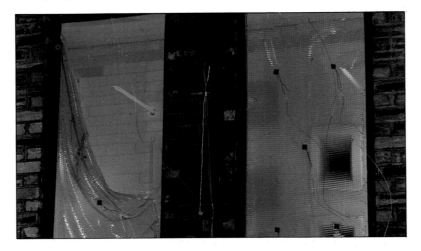

Figure 21.9
Non-insulating fire test with clamped and unclamped glass edges

The left hand glass shows non-insulating wired glass slumped out of the frame along the top edge at 91 minutes into the fire test. The glass starts to flow at about 600 °C (40–50 minutes in the fire test). As the glass becomes soft it naturally wants to flow (slump) and in doing so can pull out of the top edge of the frame, resulting in integrity failure.
The right hand glass shows non-insulating wired glass still contained within the frame (the top edge is clamped). Although glass softening has occurred, the clamping pressure exerted on its top edge has prevented slumping from the frame.

GLAZING MATERIALS

The glazing material in a fire resistant system is required to perform a number of functions. It must prevent movement and contact between glass and bead and may intumesce on exposure to heat, filling the voids around the glass so restricting the passage of smoke and fire to the unexposed face. The degree and type of expansion of intumescent materials vary; some materials have a large degree of expansion but are not pressure forming, whereas others exert pressure and help to clamp and/or cool around the edges of the glass to give extended periods of fire resistance. The selection of materials may depend on whether the frame material is steel or timber (Figure 21.10).

FRAMING

Frames used in fire resisting applications are usually made of timber or steel.

Timber for fire resisting systems should be selected on the basis of a proven fire performance, in accordance with national test standards. Its performance in fire is influenced by the timber density (which determines the rate at which it chars) and on its ability to resist warping or splitting. As insulating glass products are thicker (and therefore heavier), it may be necessary to increase timber thickness to ensure that the glass continues to be supported by the frame as it is weakened by burning (Figure 21.11).

Unlike timber, which is naturally insulating, steel fire resisting frames can be either insulating or non-insulating. Insulating steel frames are typically more complex in design, needing to accommodate a barrier which resists the passage of heat (Figure 21.12). Non-insulating steel frames conversely are usually much simpler in design (Figure 21.13), as thermal barriers are not required.

To provide overall fire protection, the glass and frame usually have the same level of fire resistance. However, if insulating glass is put into non-insulating frames, the glass will prevent the transmission of radiant heat, but this will be negated by the transmission of heat through the frame. The fire resistance

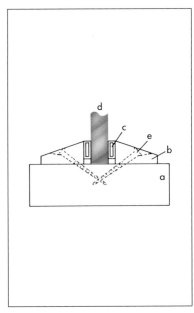

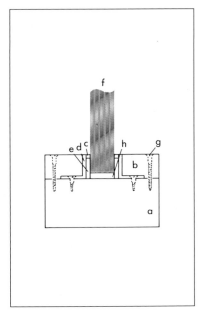

Figure 21.10
Hardwood timber glazing detail

The figure illustrates a 60 minute glazing detail in a hardwood timber frame. The graphite based intumescent strip, between the glass and the bead, swells when heated to create sufficient pressure on the edge of the glass to prevent it from slumping. The size and aspect ratio are significant contributors to performance with this system.

a 80 mm wide by 25 mm high hardwood frame (minimum density 650 kg/m³)
b 25 mm wide by 15 mm high hardwood bead with chamfer away from the glass
c Intumescent strip 10 × 3 mm Pyroglaze
d 6 mm Georgian polished wired glass
e 38 mm no. 8 steel wood screws

Figure 21.11
Hardwood timber frame and insulating glass

Timber is a naturally insulating material and has been used with insulating glass to achieve over 60 minutes integrity and insulation.

a 40 mm wide by 92 mm high hardwood frame
b 20 mm wide by 15 mm high hardwood bead
c Fire resistant silicone
d 20 x 20 x 3 mm steel angle
e Intumescent or fire resistant material
f 20 mm thick 'Pyrostop' glass
g 38 mm no. 8 steel wood screws
h 5 mm hardwood setting block

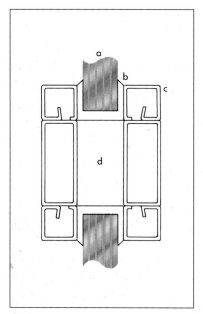

Figure 21.12
Section through an insulating steel frame

Insulating steel frames often contain an insulating core between two outer metal skins as shown or on either side of a central metal core. The thickness of the insulating barrier will depend on the level of insulation required.
a   20 mm Pyrostop insulated glass
b   Fire resistent glazing material
c   Bead
d   Insulated core: Promatect block

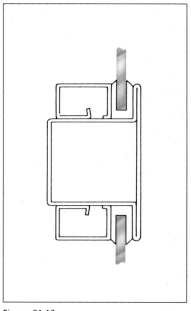

Figure 21.13
Section through a non-insulating steel frame

The metal sections pass through the full width of the frame, providing a path for the conduction of heat from the exposed face of the frame to the unexposed face. Neither the frame nor the glass achieve any measure of insulation protection.

claimed is that of the element which first fails to meet the test criteria, in this case the frame.

FRAME RETENTION AND DEFLECTION

Fixings appropriate to the surrounding wall and suitable for use in fire conditions should be used to retain the overall frame within its opening (Figure 21.14).

BEADS AND FIXING DETAILS

For timber systems, the bead should be of sufficient size to retain the glass for the desired period of fire resistance. As timber beads are usually small in relation to the size of the

Figure 21.14
Frame deflection and
disengagement
The photograph shows the degree
of deflection possible with a non-
insulating steel frame. Along the
verticals, fixing bolts have been
pulled from the surrounding wall.

overall frame, high density timber (usually hardwood) is specified, even if the door or frame are in softwood.

For non-insulating glass, chamfered beads are usually specified. By chamfering the bead away from the glass, the risk of
bead ignition by radiant heat is reduced. As insulating glass
allows little radiant heat to pass through the glass, the risk of
bead ignition is highly unlikely (Figure 21.15).

When glazing most non-insulating glass products into timber
frames, for periods in excess of 30 minutes, it is necessary to use
special glazing channels or high pressure intumescent strips.

For steel frames the beads can snap on or be held in place by
one of a variety of mechanical fixings. Some steel non-insulating framing systems use pressure plates to clamp the glass for
longer periods of fire resistance (Figure 21.16).

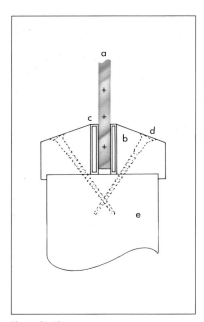

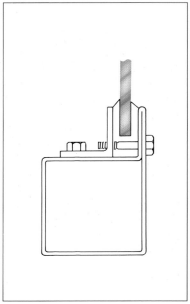

Figure 21.15
Section through bead detailing

This section was tested with Georgian wired glass and achieved 37 minutes integrity. To reduce the risk of bead ignition, the timber beads were chamfered away from the glass at an angle of 20°. The screws were splayed towards the centre of the frame, to ensure that they were secured into uncharred timber for as long as possible. A high volume intumescent strip was used between the glass and the bead. This helped to protect the bead on the unexposed face from the effects of radiant heat and to reduce the risk of fire spread underneath the glass.

a   6 mm Georgian polished wired glass
b   25 × 25 mm hardwood beads with 20° chamfer
c   25 × 3 mm intumescent seal (Pyroglaze 500 P)
d   58 mm no. 8 steel or brass wood screws
e   Hardwood frame (minimum density 650 kg/m³)

Figure 21.16
Pressure glazing system

The pressure glazing system is used to increase the length of time that non-insulating glass will remain in place in a fire. The clamping effect is achieved by pressure plates imposing a mechanical restraint on the perimeter of the glass. This fixing method is not suitable for intumescent laminated glass.

Figure 21.17
Wired glass screen, Neue
Staatsgalerie, Stuttgart, Germany
Architect: James Stirling

BIBLIOGRAPHY

BS 476 *Fire Tests on Building Materials and Structures*, Parts 3–8, Part 20, Part 22,
Part 23, 1972-1987

PD 6512 *Use of Elements of Structural Fire Protection with Particular Reference to the
Recommendations given in BS 5588: Fire Precautions in the Design and Construction of
Buildings*, Provisional Draft Parts 1–3, 1987

DIN 4102 *Fire Resistance*, Parts 5, 9-1977 and 13, 5–1990 Deutsches Institut fur
Normung e.V. (in German)

ISO 834 *Fire Resistance Tests, Elements of Building Construction*, International Organization for Standardization, 1975

ISO 3008 *Fire Resistance Tests, Door and Shutter Assemblies*, 1976

ISO 3009 *Fire Resistance Tests, Glazed Elements*, 1976

CHAPTER 22

Sound Insulation

In the last decade more effort has been devoted to the measurement and control of noise in the environment than ever before. Attempts have been made to reduce noise at source by better mechanical design, to improve the insulation of buildings, and to investigate the reactions of people to noise in their environment at home and at work. Legislation has been passed dealing with various aspects of noise, ranging from the emission of noise by motor vehicles to grants for sound insulation of houses. In spite of all this effort, noise levels inside and outside some buildings are so high that they disturb many people.

SOUND GENERATION AND RECEPTION

Sound is produced when something vibrates. These vibrations produce local variations in air pressure due to a squeezing of the air in immediate contact with the object in vibration, and this motion is then transmitted to adjacent air molecules. With increasing distance from the source, there is a loss of energy and the sound decays.

Within a well defined range, the ear is able to detect these changes from normal atmospheric pressure (the reference at all times) even when they are minute, that is above 0.00002 N/m^2 at 1000 Hz, the threshold of human hearing.

The dominant parameters of sound are frequency, wavelength and energy level (Figure 22.2).

Frequency is the number of complete vibrations which occur in each second. Subjectively, high frequencies are high pitched sounds (treble) and low frequencies are low pitched sounds (bass).

Wavelength is the distance occupied by one complete vibration. Low pitched sounds have longer wavelengths than those of high pitch.

Energy level is a consequence of the amplitude of sound vibrations. Loud sounds produce greater amplitudes (bigger pressure changes) at normal atmospheric pressure than quiet sounds. These amplitudes are indicative of the energy levels,

Figure 22.1 *(Opposite)*
Urban traffic, Manhattan, USA

Figure 22.2
Frequency, wavelength and energy level

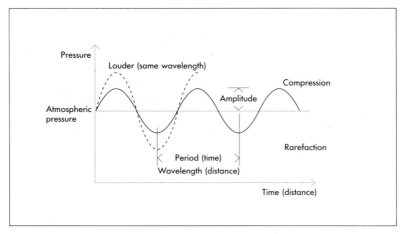

measured in decibels (dB); the range of interest is from 0 dB (threshold of hearing) to around 120 dB (threshold of pain) (Figure 22.3a).

The human ear is able to detect sound frequencies in the range from 20 to 20 000 vibrations per second (hertz, symbol Hz). The corresponding wavelengths in air are from 17m down to 17mm (Figure 22.3b).

With older persons, it is the discrimination of high frequencies which is impaired; the low frequency response remains virtually unchanged. Frequencies above and below the human range are detected by some animals, for example dogs.

Sound level dB	Environmental conditions
134	140
	130 Threshold of pain
	120 Pneumatic drill
114	110 Loud car horn (1 metre)
94	100 Inside tube train
	90 Inside bus
	80 Average traffic (kerbside)
74	70
	60 Conversational speech
54	50 Typical business office
	40 Living room, suburban area
34	30 Library
	20 Bedroom at night
14	10 Broadcasting studio
	0 Threshold of hearing

Figure 22.3a
Acoustic spectrum

Figure 22.3b
Graphical representation of acoustic spectrum

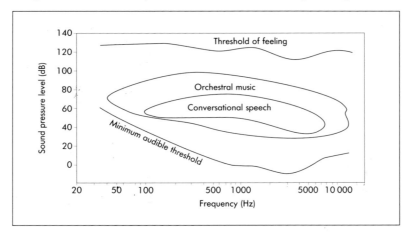

312

Even though people are able to detect sounds within the broad frequency range of 20 to 20 000 Hz, their reception of them is not uniform. Because of the physiology of the ear, the corresponding response is not linear. The ear is more sensitive to high frequency sounds than to lower ones, so that when measuring sounds with equipment, such as a sound level meter (Figure 22.4), corrections must be built in to mimic the ear's response. The readings thus obtained can then provide a reliable guide to human subjective reaction to sounds of different mixes of frequencies. Sound readings, so modified, are measured in dBA, the letter A signifying the application of this selective frequency modification. The units dB and dBA should not be confused, or used together in calculations; consistent units are essential (Figure 22.5).

Some important approximate relationships between changes in sound pressure level and the corresponding changes in apparent loudness are as shown in Figure 22.6.

Figure 22.4
Measuring traffic noise, Pilkington Glass Ltd, St Helens, UK

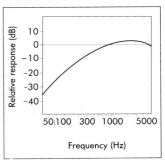

Figure 22.5
Comparison of dB and dBA

Figure 22.6 Relationship between sound pressure changes and loudness

Change in dB or dBA	Apparent loudness change
3	just noticeable
5	clearly noticeable
10	doubling (+) or halving (−) of loudness

THE CHARACTER OF SOUND AND SUBJECTIVE RESPONSE

All the preceding comment has been relevant to sound in general, but noise may be simply stated as 'unwanted sound'. Sound is the process of generating acoustic energy and of its reception by the ear, whereas noise is our subjective reaction to it. Music may be enjoyable, but when intruding in a conversation it can be distracting and so become a noise.

Loud noises do not always produce complaints, and neither are quiet environments always preferred. Reactions are influenced by factors other than energy level and include frequency

313

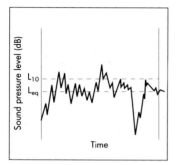

Figure 22.7
Comparison of L_{10} and L_{eq}

of occurrence, frequency mix of the sound (its spectrum) and other environmental signals (too hot, too cold, glare etc.). These factors are often as important as the more easily measured and defined parameters.

Subjective response in any noise environment is not best related to the average or mean noise level which prevails. Research has shown that the L_{10} level (the noise level exceeded for 10% of the relevant or chosen time) is a much more reliable indicator. Often, as in the case of UK legislation on sound proofing grants for dwellings, the L_{10} 18 hour index is used as the best descriptor. This is the L_{10} value established over the period from 6 a.m. to midnight (Figure 22.7).

The L_{10} value is useful in defining the relevant noise climates for a wide variety of situations but is gradually being superseded by another concept, the equivalent noise level L_{eq}. This is the notional continuous noise level whose total energy over a given period is equal to that of the real varying sound (or noise) over the same period. This index is better able to compare noises which differ in level and in their variation with time. Thus the impact of continuous road traffic noise can be compared with that from intermittent aircraft or railway noises.

Because transportation noises are the main offenders in buildings, it is of interest to compare the different characteristics of the principal sources (Figures 22.8a, b).

Figure 22.8a Road, railway and aircraft noise

Road traffic noise   The noise spectrum of road traffic noise will be influenced by factors such as the percentage of heavy vehicles, speed, nature of road surface, road gradient etc., but the overall typical spectrum will always exhibit the strongest components at low frequencies. City centre noise is typically at around 80 dBA, as is the noise close to motorways.

Railway noise   This is principally influenced by wheel/track interactions, track type (welded or jointed), sleeper type (timber or concrete), local terrain, cuttings etc. Peak noise can be high, perhaps of the order of 100 dBA, but reaction to this is not as adverse as might be expected. The noise is intermittent sometimes with long periods of silence. Also, trains warn of their approach by gradual noise build-up, and arrival is followed by a predictable decay. Hence people's tolerance to train noise is around 10–15 dBA higher than for the road traffic spectrum, i.e. 95 dBA of railway noise generates a similar level of disturbance as 80–85 dBA of road traffic noise.

Aircraft noise   The spectrum of aircraft noise varies widely according to aircraft type, load ratio, and whether taking off or landing, and is critically dependent on the location of the hearer with respect to the aircraft's flight path. Aircraft in flight generally have an even mix of sound frequencies. On the ground, their noise is most often dominated by the high pitched whine of the auxiliary power unit from the tail of the aircraft. This variability of aircraft noise makes it difficult to define typical noise levels. Until recently, contours of noise and number index NNI were prepared for all major UK airports to aid the planning of development around them. The composite index NNI takes account of peak noise level and also the number of occurrences. The L_{eq} is now considered to be more indicative of annoyance and is gradually superseding NNI.

Industrial and other noise sources   Because of the wide variability of industrial machinery and processes, it is impossible to adopt a single noise spectrum as representative for design purposes. Expert advice is necessary in order to establish the dominant components to be attenuated.

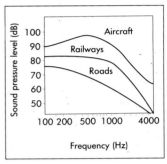

Figure 22.8b
Spectra noise for aircraft, railway and road

INDICES OF ACOUSTIC PERFORMANCE

Analyses of acoustic problems involve measuring the level and frequency of all the noise components and determining their modification by the glazing at all frequencies, in order to derive a residual transmitted spectrum. This may then be judged against notional targets or criteria. These procedures are time consuming and may involve expertise.

As expedient alternatives, single figure indices have been developed which give quick, approximate indications of the acoustic efficiency of materials, including glazing. They should be used with caution and should not be regarded as complete substitutes for full analyses.

In considering the definition of these indices it should be noted that the range of frequencies encompassed varies nationally. Typically the British Standard range covers 100–3150 Hz (16 values) in third octaves and 125–4000 Hz (6 values) in full octaves; the American standards cover 125–4000 Hz in both third octave (16 values) and full octave (6 values) analyses.

MEAN SOUND INSULATION R$_m$

This index is the arithmetic average of the 16 third octave band

315

values of the measured sound insulation of the glazing. Because of the slight difference between the British Standard and American Standard frequency ranges (namely a shift upwards by a third octave in American data compared with British) there may be a small discrepancy in their comparison. Typically, the American R_m is 1 dB higher than the corresponding British R_m derived from the same data.

R_w INDEX (ISO 717, BS 5821)

To take account of the ear's response, this more complicated index has evolved. It involves plotting the sound insulation curve on a series of reference curves, whose shape approximates to that of the 'A weighting' or ear's response curve. By finding the reference curve which is closest to that under investigation, the R_w index is derived according to prescribed rules, the main one of which is that the total shortfall (where the actual sound insulation is less than the reference curve chosen) must not exceed 32 dB. The R_w index is characterized by the sound insulation of this matching reference curve at 500 Hz (Figure 22.9).

STC VALUE

The sound transmission class index originated in the USA and formed the basis of the R_w index calculation procedure. The main difference is in the frequency range considered, so that typically STC values are about 1 dB greater than R_w indices derived from the same data.

R_{TRA} INDEX

The R_m, R_w and STC indices are derived from the basic sound insulation performance of the glazing across the frequency bands. In order to obtain better correspondence with people's reaction to the transmitted noise, it is also necessary to take account of the dominant components of the incident noise. The R_{TRA} index is calculated by adopting a spectrum shape of typical road traffic noise, and then modifying it, frequency by frequency, according to the sound insulation data of the glazing. The residual aggregate level, in dBA, is the R_{TRA} index. Unlike the indices above, it may be used directly in simple calculations to yield approximate levels of interior noise in dBA:

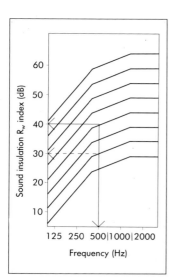

Figure 22.9
R_w index

Outside level – R_{TRA} = inside intrusive level

It has also been found that simple correction factors may be applied to R_{TRA} to derive realistic estimates of corresponding attenuation to railway and aircraft noises. This is currently under consideration as part of a European (CEN) standard.

INTERIOR NOISE LEVEL CRITERIA

Rooms are not necessarily designed to have the lowest possible background noise levels, since this could lead to unsatisfactory environments and would be costly. The glazing should attenuate the outside noise to a level which does not annoy, but is still sufficient to mask the ambient, internally generated noises. This target noise level will be dependent upon the nature of the activity inside the building (workshops do not demand as high attenuation from the glazing as would conference rooms). Recommended background noise levels are identified in national standards for a wide range of situations, for example in BS 8233:1987, which adopts the La_{eq} (equivalent noise level, measured in dBA) as an appropriate index. Approximate conversion to L_{10} (dBA) is simple:

$L_{10} = La_{eq} + 3.$

Examples of the La_{eq} targets for common locations are shown in Figure 22.10

Figure 22.10 La_{eq} targets for common locations

Large offices (including open plan)	45–50
Private offices, small conference rooms	40–45
Living rooms	40–45
Bedrooms	30–40
Classrooms (15–35 people, with communication distance not more than 9 m)	40

SIMPLE ASSESSMENT OF GLAZING REQUIREMENTS

Because it is usual to derive ambient outside noise levels in dBA, the required acoustic performance of the glazing may be determined by comparison with the appropriate recommendation of background noise level. For example, if an open plan office is located in a city centre where the ambient traffic noise is 80 dBA, the glazing needs to provide an attenuation of 80 minus 50 dBA (or 80 minus 45 dBA if preferred), i.e. R_{TRA} must be 30 (or 35) dBA. Reference to glazing performance data is then able to establish satisfactory alternatives.

THE PERFORMANCE OF GLASS

The fundamental principle of the sound insulation of glass and windows is the Mass Law, which demonstrates that, with each doubling of glass thickness, the corresponding sound insulation is increased by about 4 dB. This is not exact and takes account of intrinsic resonance phenomena which impair the acoustic performance at certain frequencies.

Single glazing shows two main types of resonance. One is related to its size (low frequency) and the other to its thickness (medium to high frequency). This latter resonance is very sensitive, the frequency being inversely proportional to thickness, so that, for example, 12 mm float glass resonates at 1 kHz whereas 6 mm float glass resonates at 2 kHz (Figure 22.11).

One means of suppressing some of the characteristic resonances is to laminate two or more glass panes together with resilient plastic interlayers, which absorb some of the incident sound energy, reducing that which passes through it. The most common laminating material for this purpose is polyvinyl butyral, and it reduces the loss in sound insulation at the resonant frequencies (Figure 22.12).

Other materials, including polymethyl methacrylates, are even 'softer' and so are able to reduce further the losses of sound insulation at the basic frequencies and the component glass panes are decoupled so efficiently that the associated

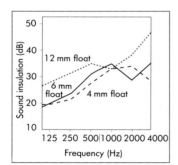

Figure 22.11
Resonance effects

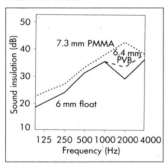

Figure 22.12
Attenuation spectrum of laminated glass

resonant frequencies are shifted to a higher position in the noise spectrum, where they are less troublesome.

Double glazing units or secondary sashes exhibit two additional resonances. One is caused by the interaction of vibrations of the two individual panes, which may be enhanced or suppressed by the precise distance between them. The other is produced because of inter-reflections of sound trapped between the two panes, and is a high frequency phenomenon. If dissimilar glass thicknesses are used in double glazed units, there are acoustic benefits, because as one pane tends to resonate, the other provides acoustic stability. High acoustic performances for double glazed units are achieved when lamination and asymmetric construction are employed simultaneously. The addition of more panes of glass to form glazed units with more than two panes may impair the corresponding acoustic performances owing to the generation of further resonances with each extra pane.

Other gases may be used as the cavity fill in place of dry air, for their thermal benefits. For example, argon filled units show no change in acoustic performance from standard air filled units, for the same basic construction. Sulphur hexafluoride (SF$_6$) gas, however, may be used for acoustic purposes. Its heavy molecular structure tends to enhance the middle frequency performance (about 630–2000 Hz), but it introduces a resonance at low frequencies (around 200 Hz) which limits its effective application where low frequency insulation is the dominant requirement (transportation noises).

Potentially the highest acoustic insulation may be attained by separating the two main glass components with a large air space in excess of 100 mm, creating a double window. The interactions between the panes are minimized and each acts more independently as an effective barrier. However, unless all air gaps are fully sealed by employing either fixed lights or hinged windows which have compressible seals and multi-point locking to avoid the frames twisting, the actual in-service performance of these windows is likely to be no better than that of a sealed double glazed unit. For this reason, sliding sashes are not compatible with high acoustic performance (Figure 22.13).

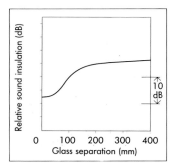

Figure 22.13
Double glazed air space width

If the internal reveals of a double window are lined with a sound absorbing material, the inter-reflections of sound between the panes may be reduced, and thereby contribute further to the overall attenuation by up to 5 dBA. Performance data for a range of typical products are shown in Figure 22.14.

Figure 22.14 Key indices for common glazing arrangements

Single glazing

	4 mm	6 mm	6.4 mm PVB laminate	10 mm	12 mm	8 mm	17 mm acoustic laminates
R_m	28	29	30	33	34	33	38
R_w	31	32	33	36	37	37	41
R_{TRA}	27	28	29	32	33	31	36

Double glazed units

	6/12/6	10/12/6	10/12/6.4 PVB laminate	10/12/17 mm acoustic laminate
R_m	30	34	36	41
R_w	33	38	40	45
R_{TRA}	26	32	34	37

Double windows (secondary sash)

	6/150/4	10/200/6
R_m	44	47
R_w	47	49
R_{TRA}	39	45

OTHER DESIGN FACTORS

EFFECT OF AREA

The larger the window area, the more acoustic energy is able to pass through it. However, because of the way in which sounds add together, this is not a dominant effect. If the opaque parts of

320

a façade (walls) are considered to have a sound insulation at least 10 dB higher than the window, then each halving of window area increases the effective sound insulation by 3 dB. If, for example, a 100% (fully) glazed façade had a sound insulation of 30 dB, changing to 50% and 25% glazed façades would secure corresponding aggregate sound insulations of 33 dB and 36 dB, respectively.

EFFECT OF DISTANCE

With increasing distance from a noise source, there is a corresponding decrease in noise level. The decay rate is dependent upon whether the source originates at a point or over an area, which, in turn, depends on its shape and the distance at which the sound is heard.

Noise from an aircraft or a single vehicle may be considered to be a point source, and the decay rate approximates to 6 dB per doubling of distance. Noise from a line of traffic or railway train does not diminish as rapidly; 3 dB per doubling of distance is a typical decay rate.

For example, if a roadside noise measurement, 5 metres from the vehicles, indicates a level of 78 dBA, this would reduce correspondingly to 75 dBA at 10 metres, to 72 dBA at 20 metres and to 69 dBA at 40 metres. This 9 dBA drop in level from the initial measurement is almost equivalent to a halving in its perceived loudness at the kerbside.

EFFECT OF HEIGHT

With increasing building height, there should be an associated decrease in received street noise level, but the acoustic horizon of the upper floors is correspondingly increased. These are opposing trends, and the result is that the vertical noise field is almost uniform.

BARRIERS

Sound waves have long wavelengths, as mentioned earlier. Therefore diffraction effects are significant; that is, bending around obstacles is relatively easy. Fences, earth mounds and screens are therefore relatively ineffective, unless positioned either close to the source or close to the reception point. Window furniture, like blinds, has no influence on the noise transmission through windows.

OTHER GLAZING TYPES

Apart from lamination, other glass types do not exhibit any departures from the sound insulation of ordinary clear float glass. Thickness for thickness, toughened, wired, coated and tinted glass products have exactly the same acoustic performance. Patterned glass products, which have surface indentations, behave identically to ordinary clear float glass of the same average thickness.

FIXING EFFECTS

Better sound insulation is achieved by installing glass in resilient gaskets instead of tightly clamping it with beads. Any structural vibrations are then less able to be transmitted to the glass, thus maintaining its acoustic integrity.

Figure 22.15
Aircraft noise, Flachglas AG,
Germany

BIBLIOGRAPHY

ASTM E413-73 *Standard Classification for Determination of Sound Transmission Glass*, American Society for Testing and Materials, Philadelphia, PA, 1973

Barry, C.J. 'How glass controls acoustics', *Glass Digest*, May 1989

BS 5821 Part 3, *Methods for Rating the Sound Insulation in Buildings and of Building Elements – Airborne Sound Insulation of Façade Elements and Façades*, British Standards Institution, 1984

BS 8233 *British Standard Code of Practice for Sound Insulation and Noise Reduction for Buildings*, British Standards Institution, 1987

Derner, P. 'Sound Protection – Insulating Glass' and 'Functions – Insulating Glass' in *Glass*, Expert-Verlag, Ehningen, 1992 (in German)

DIN 4102 *Sound Protection in Structural Engineering*, 11-1989, Deutsches Institut für Normung e.V. (in German)

Inman, C. 'Noise control and double glazing', *Glass Age*, November 1985

Monsanto *Acoustical Glazing Design Guide*, Monsanto Corporation, St Loius, MO, 1991

Schultz, T.J. 'Variation of the outdoor noise level and the sound attenuation of windows with elevation above the ground', *Applied Acoustics*, 12, 1979

The Noise Insulation Regulations 1975, Statutory Instrument 1763, HMSO, London, UK, 1975

Utley, W.A. and Sargent, J.W. *The Insulation of Dwellings Against External Noise*, Building Research Establishment information paper IP12/19, 1989

VDI (Verein Deutscher Ingenieure, Association of German Engineers) *Sound Insulation of Windows*, guideline 27190,3-1987 (in German)

Appendix A

Structural Glass Systems

Structural glazing is included as this appendix since it concerns the exploitation of glass rather than the fundamental properties of glass which are the subject matter of previous chapters.

Two methods of structural glazing are described:

- structural sealant glazing (stuck-back glazing)
- mechanical fixing, subdivided into bolt and plate fixing (suspended assemblies) and countersunk bolt fixing (Planar system).

STRUCTURAL SEALANT GLAZING

Structural sealant glazing, or simply structural glazing, is a system of bonding glass to a frame using structural (silicone) sealants without an external cover bead.

There are two principal types of glazing in use, both of which originated in the USA. These are normally referred to as two-edge and four-edge structural sealant glazing. The two-edge system is where the glass pane has the head and sill contained in a conventional glazing rebate, while the two remaining sides are bonded to a mullion with structural sealant. A four-edge system is where all four sides of the glass pane are bonded to the framing system, using structural sealants, either with or without mechanical fasteners to retain the glass in the framing. A typical glazing detail and typical installations are shown in Figures A.2, A.3 and A.4.

INSTALLATION

The successful installation and longevity of any structural sealant glazing system relies entirely on the structural sealant maintaining adhesion and cohesion during the building's life. Any structural sealant must therefore be capable of withstanding severe environmental conditions, including stresses from wind loading, exposure to UV radiation, weathering and stresses from thermal expansion. Adhesion and cohesion tests are carried out on all metal/glass samples to confirm compatibility between the structural sealant and all other materials. Care needs to be taken where the structural sealant is bonded to a coated glass surface.

Figure A.1 *(Opposite)*
Clear single glazed Planar, Lots Road, London, UK
Architect: Goldstein Ween

Figure A.2
Typical structural sealant glazing

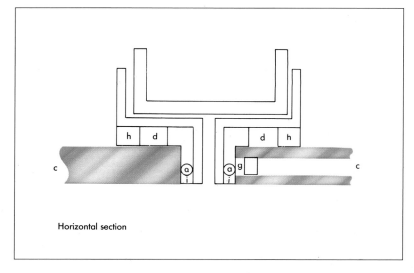

Horizontal section

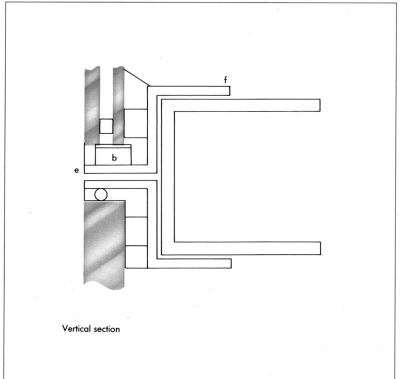

Vertical section

Key to Figure A.2

a   Backer rod: a strip of polyethylene or other suitable foam material, used to limit the depth of the weatherseal joint.

b   Setting blocks: blocks of a resilient precured silicone or other compatible material of 70 to 90 degrees Shore A hardness used between the bottom edge of a panel and the support fin (or other support) for setting up and spacing purposes.

c   Panels: comprise glass in single or multiple panes.

d   Spacer tape: a tape which when placed around the edges of a panel will determine the distance between the panel and its frame. It limits the bite (or depth) of the sealant joint and holds the panel until the sealant is cured.

e   Support fin: a small horizontal ledge in a frame transom which bears up the panel weight on two setting blocks.

f   Sealant support frame: any member(s) adjacent to panel edges to which sealant is bonded and which are independently supported by and fixed to the building structure or substructure.

g   Hermetic seal: a means of providing an airtight seal at the perimeter of an insulating unit. It also resists the ingress of water or vapour and is resistant to ultraviolet light and ozone, whilst remaining compliant to the glass displacements due to wind or other loading.

h   Structural seal: sealant material which is extruded into place and when cured provides a durable weather resistant structural seal.

i   Weatherseal: sealant material which is extruded into place and when cured provides a durable weatherseal but which is not required to assist with the maintenance of structural stability within the system.

Figure A.3
Sunpark 2, Johannesburg, South Africa.

Structurally glazed laminated solar control glass

It is also necessary to consider how each pane of glass is supported, in order to ensure that the dead weight of each pane is not transferred to those below. It is recommended that each glass pane is supported on setting blocks (in some countries this method of support is a requirement), but designs vary from country to country.

For four-edge structural glazing systems, in order to ensure good adhesion between all components it is recommended (and can be a requirement) that all components are factory glazed, so that good environmental control can be maintained during construction. Metal framing members used to support the glass are designed so that any torsional, twisting or bending stresses should not be transmitted to the glass edge, or to the structural sealant.

Great care in surface preparation of all components to be bonded is essential for successful glazing installation. Continuous sampling of the structural sealant for strength tests and surface preparation is necessary to ensure consistent quality.

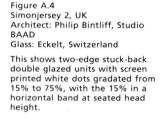

Figure A.4
Simonjersey 2, UK
Architect: Philip Bintliff, Studio BAAD
Glass: Eckelt, Switzerland

This shows two-edge stuck-back double glazed units with screen printed white dots gradated from 15% to 75%, with the 15% in a horizontal band at seated head height.

MECHANICAL FIXING

BOLT AND PLATE FIXINGS (SUSPENDED ASSEMBLIES)

One method of providing a frameless glazing façade is to fix together a matrix of toughened glass panes, hung from the building structure. A system of this type, commonly referred to as a suspended glass assembly, was designed and developed in the 1960s by Pilkington Glass Limited. It allowed designers to glaze large openings in buildings, without the use of metal frames or mullions, providing the creation of light and space in buildings with a minimum of visual barriers (Figure A.5).

The system comprises a series of specially processed and toughened glass panes, bolted together at their corners by means of small metal patch fittings. Pane to pane joints are sealed with a silicone building sealant, and toughened glass stabilizers are used at each vertical joint to provide lateral stiffness against wind loading. The assembly so produced is suspended from the building structure by hangers bolted to its top edge, and is sealed to the building in peripheral channels by means of neoprene strips or non-setting mastic.

The concept of the design ensures that the façade is, at all times, 'floating' in the peripheral channelling, and problems which might arise due to differential movement between component parts are eliminated. Assemblies can, therefore, be used to advantage when vibratory or seismic forces must be taken into account in the design.

Weather sealing is carried out at all joints in the façade using a structural silicone building sealant. In the design calculations the structural properties of the sealant, in providing greater stiffness to the façade, are not recognized. However, from extensive laboratory and on-site testing it is known that the sealant does improve the load bearing capabilities of the façade, and its use is therefore an added safety factor in design.

The principle behind the design of the fittings for a suspended glass assembly is that all in-plane forces transferred between components are resisted by friction developed at the metal/gasket/glass interfaces, arising from the tension developed in the fixing bolts.

329

Figure A.5
Suspended assembly design

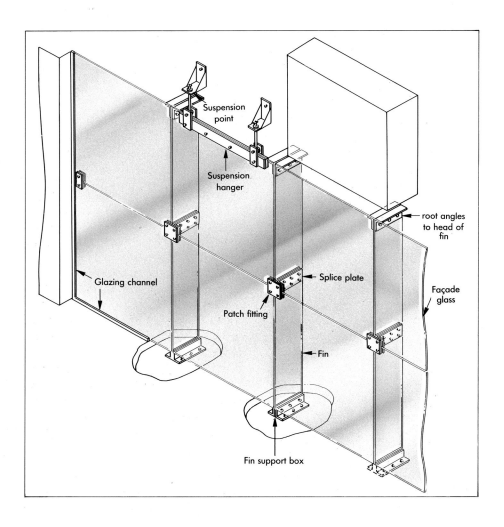

The use of friction to transfer forces between glass and fittings makes it essential that bolts of the correct size and quality, tightened to the specified torque, are used. Although the holes in the glass can resist considerable bearing forces from the bolt, through the hard bush, this is only taken into account in the height limitation for assembly constructions. The friction grip is of particular importance in the design of the splice joints and root support of the stabilizers, where the bearing strength of the holes is unlikely to be able to resist the turning moments generated in the stabilizers when an assembly is subjected to wind forces.

If required, the coefficient of friction at the metal/gasket/glass interface can be enhanced by the application of a suitable adhesive.

The façade panes resist lateral wind forces through the small metal patch plates, 165 mm square, supporting the four corners of adjacent panes off the stabilizers. These metal patch plates clamp the glass at the corners of each pane, developing significant stress concentrations at the edges of the patch plate and around the bolt hole. In order to safely design panes supported in this way, it is essential to have a detailed knowledge of the stresses generated around and under the patch plates, for various shapes of pane subjected to different levels of lateral load. Equally essential is knowledge of the strength of the toughened glass at and around the fixing holes.

The size of suspended assembly façade panes is rarely limited by deflections. The clamping effect of the patch plates, which reduces deflections, together with the relatively high stresses generated, dictates that most assembly façade panes are stress limited rather than deflection limited in design.

Extensive research into both stresses and strengths enables Pilkington to be confident in the successful design of large façades built using this system. Single assemblies can be designed up to 20 m in height on a 1.5 m module, and up to 23 m on a 1.2 m module. Assuming an adequate main building structure, any height can be specified using multiple assembly design. Any length is possible, and curved façades are not

Figure A.6 *(Opposite)*
Planar system, *Financial Times*
Building, London, UK
Architects: Nicholas Grimshaw and
Partners

unusual, as exemplified in the Willis Faber Dumas Building by Sir Norman Foster Associates (1975).

COUNTERSUNK BOLT FIXINGS (PLANAR SYSTEM)

In order to meet designers' requirements and achieve a more flush and uninterrupted glass surfaced façade, Pilkington developed the Planar system with the use of countersunk bolt fixings (Figures A.8, A.9 and A.10).

One of the features of a suspended glass assembly was that it could not be used in conjunction with double glazed units or for non-vertical applications. The Planar system can be used for both. It is capable of fixing toughened glass either single or double back to any structure. In some cases, glass mullions are used to form part of the substructure to which the glass is attached. The system is used for vertical or sloping glazing and can be incorporated as a complete cladding system.

The principle behind the design of the Planar fittings is almost exactly opposite to that of suspended assembly fittings. The fittings are designed to support the weight of the glass by direct bearing of the bolt, through the bush, on to the hole in the glass. This feature is made possible by each pane being fixed separately, and not supporting the weight of those below it. The fitting is also designed to give minimal clamping, by the attachment of the fixing bolt to a spring plate, which is sufficiently flexible to allow rotation of the glass. The overall effect is to significantly reduce the stresses developed in the glass in the region of the Planar fitting, compared with those developed around patch plates.

Since frictional forces, and hence the clamping forces needed to generate them, do not play a key role in the design of the Planar system, it has proved possible to develop a double glazed version. In this the outer pane provides the main load bearing capability, while the inner pane is located, by ingenious design of the Planar fixing components, in a way which avoids crushing the unit edge seal.

Figure A.7
Exploded axonometric of Planar
bolted double glazed fixing

334

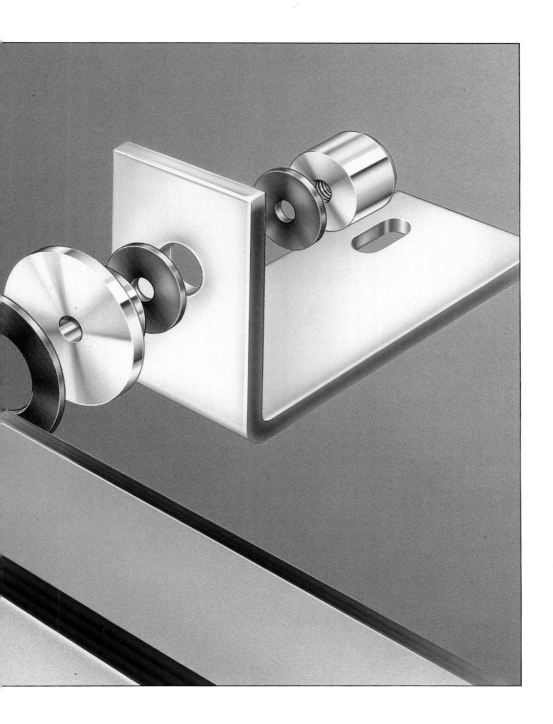

Figure A.8
Sterling Hotel, Heathrow Airport,
London, UK
Architects: Manser Associates

Clear single glazed Planar with some
screen printing.

Careful research into the stresses developed in the Planar façade panes, especially around the fixing holes, in both single glazing and double glazing of various shapes and fixing arrangements, is required in order to successfully design the Planar system.

The size of the Planar façade panes, particularly in single glazing, is more likely to be deflection limited than the façade panes in a suspended assembly. This is due to the flexibility, or lack of clamping, provided by the Planar fixing, combined with a reduction in the stresses generated around the fixing.

Because the glass panes are individually fixed to the structure, there is no restriction on the height of building which can be glazed. The specially engineered bushes, bolts and fittings are standard for all designs, while spring plates may be designed and fabricated to suit each specific application.

Figure A.9
Planar construction with external
shading, Knowle Green, Staines, UK
Architects: Nickolas Hare Associates

Figure A.10
Planar system with cascading water
on outer surface. UK pavilion at
Barcelona Exhibition, 1991
Architects: Nicholas Grimshaw and
Partners

Figure A.11
Research and development, Planar,
Pilkington Glass Ltd, St Helens, UK

Figure A.12
Planar Building, Museum of the
Moving Image, London, UK
Architects: Avery Associates

BIBLIOGRAPHY

Breukelmann, A. 'Structural glazing', Deutche Bauzeitung No. 2/89 (in German)

Rice, P. and Dutton, H. *Le Verre Structurel*, Editions du Moniteur, Paris, 1990

Rückeshäuser, K.-H. ' A Vision...' *Glaswelt* No. 9/88 (in German)

Stacey, M. 'Maximum Vision', *Habitat International*, 14 (2/3), 227–233, 1990

Appendix B

Glass and the Environment

In discussing the Willis Faber Dumas Building, Rayner Banham (1981) commented:

Now 'everybody knows' that glass is an energy wasteful material. Yet Foster Associates have the gall and (tough luck, herbivores) the figures to show that this is a reasonably energy efficient structure – partly because its very deep plan four storey format gives a low ratio of glass to internal volume (and the glass is deeply bronzed as well) and partly ... because the roof is clad in ... growing turf!

Had Pilkington Glass developed double glazed Planar in the early 1970s, Foster Associates might have considered this system to make the building even more energy efficient.

Because building energy conservation is a key issue in alleviating global warming (not such a well known or important fact in the 1970s). The amount of energy required to manufacture the additional pane of glass for an insulating unit is recoverable, through its additional insulation, in less than one heating season in a temperate climate such as the UK.

Figure B.1a *(Opposite)*
Industrial pollution

Figure B.1b
Willis Faber Dumas Building,
Ipswich, UK, 1975
Architects: Foster Associates

343

Ozone depletion, global warming (the greenhouse effect), deforestation and other global issues are of growing importance for the specifiers of building materials in their dealings with clients and occupiers. New legislation, directives and world-wide agreements to protect the environment are dictating the use of materials.

Specifiers are beginning to consider the full environmental effects of their designs on the locality, the building occupants and the building performance. This introduces considerations of 'conception to exhumation' for both building design and use. The obtaining of raw materials, manufacture, construction, building use, demolition, material recycling and final disposal are all now for consideration. Legislation is being discussed in Europe which will mandate that a large percentage of new buildings 'must be recyclable'.

For all materials, components and activities there will be both negative and positive points for consideration. Nothing is purely 'green'.

ENERGY CONSERVATION AND GLASS USE

The principal contributor to global warming is the emission of carbon dioxide (CO_2) (Figure B.2). This arises primarily from the burning of fossil fuels. Energy conservation must be a major part of any global warming control strategy. Reduction of energy consumption by 40% in the industrialized countries will be necessary to balance increases in the Third World, so that the world as a whole can meet the 20% reduction of emissions by 2005 agreed at the 1988 Toronto Conference. The European Community has committed itself to the Toronto agreement.

Figure B.2 Main gases contributing to global warming (Shorrock and Henderson 1990)

> The main greenhouse gases being emitted are carbon dioxide (from burning fossil fuels), methane (largely from agricultural activities), chlorofluorocarbons (used in aerosol sprays, refrigeration equipment and certain insulants) and nitrous oxides (mainly from internal combustion engines and boilers). The CFCs, besides being potent greenhouse gases, are also implicated as being responsible for the depletion of the earth's protective ozone layer and urgent action has already been taken to curtail their emission. Of the remaining greenhouse gases, the one which causes most concern is carbon dioxide (CO_2), the production of which is inexorably linked to maintaining and improving standards of living because it is directly related to the use of fossil fuel derived energy. CO_2 is the largest single waste product of modern society and it is thought to account for about half of the temperature rise associated with greenhouse gas emission. Such is the concern over CO_2 emissions that there have been calls for the industrialized nations to reduce their emissions by 20% by the year 2005.

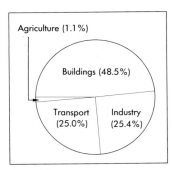

Figure B.3
Sources of CO_2 emission in the UK, 1990

Total 606 million tonnes.

In most industrialized regions, including North America and Europe, buildings and building use are deemed to be a major target for CO_2 reduction – a more important target than the more publicized emissions from vehicles (Figure B.3). Energy used in buildings, as in many industrialized countries, accounts for about half the UK's total CO_2 emissions (currently just over 600 million tonnes per year). The efficient use of energy has found new emphasis in building regulations and codes around the world. Such emphasis brings pressure on investors and designers to produce what they might see as innovative and expensive solutions. In reality, the efficient use of energy may be achieved simply and inexpensively.

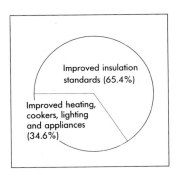

Figure B.4
BRE data: potential CO_2 reductions through cost effective energy efficiency measures in housing, 1990

Total reduction 44 million tonnes.

In the UK, as a typical example of an industrial nation seeking CO_2 reductions, the Building Research Establishment (BRE) estimates that national CO_2 emissions could be reduced by 17% by the application of energy efficient measures (Shorrock and Henderson 1990). About two-thirds of these savings could be achieved by higher insulation standards, and the remainder by improved efficiency in electrical appliances, lights and heating systems. These figures are based on the assumption that energy consumption and pattern of use in buildings remain at present levels.

The BRE estimates that the emissions of CO_2 due to energy use in dwellings can be reduced by 25% solely by applying energy efficiency measures already considered to be cost effective (Figure B.4). A further 10% cut can be achieved by using other proven energy saving techniques.

Detailed assessments of CO_2 emissions, attributable solely to the housing stock, demonstrate that the greatest reductions would result from improved insulation of walls, insulated glazing, the use of passive gain and the replacement of conventional gas boilers by condensing types. Considerable reductions can also be made through improving the efficiency of electrical lighting (influencing window design) because of the high CO_2 emissions associated with generated electricity.

The implications for glass are important. The provision of heat, light and insulation by the window become of paramount importance.

Low emissivity coatings are an energy efficient product since they reduce CO_2 emissions, through increased insulation, where double glazed products are installed, and through the utilization of passive solar gain. If the 15 million existing homes in the UK currently without double glazed products were to be fully double glazed with low emissivity glass, the amount of CO_2 released into the atmosphere would be reduced by 6%, or 10 million tonnes per annum.

A study in Germany confirms the relevance of insulation and passive solar gain for CO_2 reduction. There, improvements to the already good window insulation, by means of Low E coatings in new and existing dwellings, would achieve an estimated 10% reduction of total CO_2 released to the atmosphere. The effect of south facing glazing areas, of varying U values, on the overall average U value of the whole dwelling, assuming a fixed U value of the walls and roof of 0.3 W/m^2 K, is shown in Figures B.5a, b. These figures indicate that for window U values below a threshold of approximately 2.0 W/m^2 K, south facing windows in larger sizes benefit the dwelling average effective U value and energy conservation.

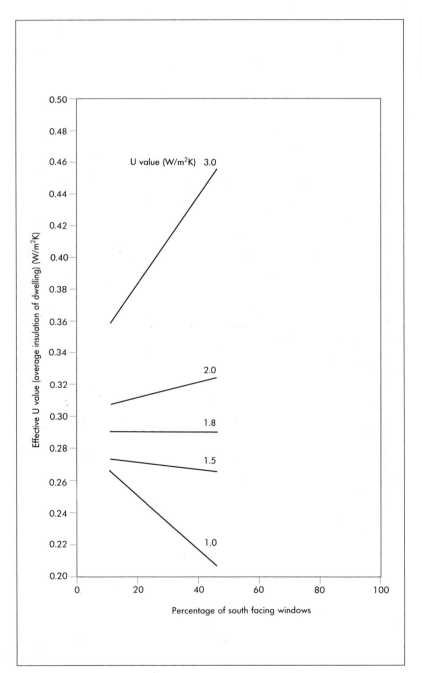

Figure B.5b
Relationship between percentages of
south facing windows of various U
values and overall house U value for
detached family houses

U values: wall 0.3 W/m² K
roof 0.3 W/m² K.

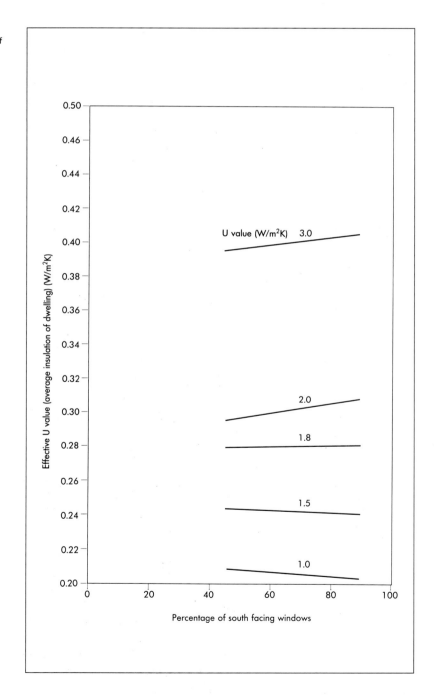

The German study also examined the effect of a national implementation of window U values of 2.1 W/m^2 K, using Low E coated glazing in the entire housing stock (Figure B.6). This showed that the national energy saving in Germany would be equivalent to 10% of the required future annual CO_2 reductions.

Figure B.6 Potential for reducing energy consumption and CO_2 emissions by using glazing with U value of 2.1 W/m^2 K

	Glazing conversion W/m^2 K	Savings per year from 2005 millions of litres of oil
Western Germany dwellings		
New	- 3.0 to 2.1	2184
Renovated 50%	- 5.8 to 2.1	
Renovated 50%	- 3.0 to 2.1	5977
Eastern Germany dwellings		
New	- 3.0 to 2.1	628
Renovated * 50%	- 5.8 to 2.1	
Renovated * 50%	- 3.0 to 2.1	887
Apartments post 1945	- 3.0 to 2.1	305
Total		9981

*One-family houses before 1945, apartments before 1918.

The future development of high performance thermally insulating solar control glass products, described as 'smart glazings' in the USA, is signalled for a key role. Selkowitz and Lampert (1989) conclude:

There is growing evidence that current international attention to major global environmental threats (for example global warning, CFCs and the ozone layers, acid rain) will result in coordinated worldwide response. Most studies suggest that, in the short term (20 to 30 years), the most cost effective option to slow environmental degradation is an aggressive energy efficiency programme, that substantially reduces energy use and related emissions, while permitting real growth in needed energy services. Smart glazing, along with many other advanced building technologies, would become an important element in such a future scenario.

GLASS MANUFACTURE AND GREEN ISSUES

Many glass manufacturers are carrying out environmental audits of all operations, from handling of raw materials to transport of the finished product. These audits direct improvements in manufacture, promote glass recycling and generate educational programmes involving staff, customers and specifiers.

In Germany, large manufacturing companies must have a legally required appointee for environmental affairs (Konzern Beauftragter für Umweltschutz); currently 40 types of manufacturing plant, including glass plants, require such an appointee who is responsible to the chief executive. The role of the appointee is creative: to find the best economic fit of manufacturing process to the strict regulatory requirements, and to ensure the requirements are met.

The most important issue in glass manufacture is to reduce CO_2 emissions from fossil fuels. Glass manufacture, which involves heating the batch to high temperatures, makes use of oil, gas or electricity. All these fuels involve, at some point, the release of CO_2 and other gases. The flat glass manufacturing industry is not unlike other high temperature heavy industries. It can claim to have contributed, as much as any, in cutting 90% of the pollutants released into the skies over the past three decades, to levels within the World Health Organization's current targets (Figure B.7).

Figure B.7
Pollution improvements in the manufacturing town of St Helens, UK, 1959–1989
WHO: World Health Organization

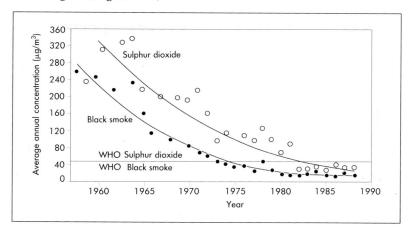

350

The key to the improvements is improving the efficiency of manufacturing technology by investment in R&D. Energy used in flat glass manufacture has been reduced from around 300 gigajoules per tonne (GJ/t) in the nineteenth century to around 5 GJ/t in 1992 as a result. The theoretical minimum is 2 GJ/t (a gigajoule is roughly equivalent to 10 therms) (Figure B.8).

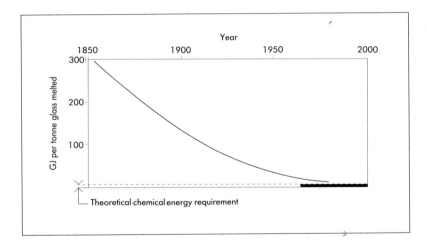

Figure B.8
Thermal performance of typical flat glass furnaces 1850–1976

New technology for R&D is being introduced which includes flue gas desulphurizing plants. This technology is expensive and might cost as much as 10% of the total capital expenditure of the float tank.

The principal raw material used for glass manufacture is silica sand (one of the world's most abundant and naturally occurring minerals). The majority of the other raw materials are also among the world's most abundant. These materials are converted into glass. The float glass manufacturing process produces minimal waste products. The amount of toxic wastes from manufacture is very small.

The float process recycles virtually all its glass waste during production. This glass (known as cullet) is reintroduced to the float batch mix to aid melting. It takes half the amount of energy to produce glass from cullet as it does to produce it from raw materials.

351

RECYCLING

All glass can be recycled, although its degree of reuse will depend on its purity. Flat glass manufacturers, as indicated above, recycle virtually all their own waste glass during the manufacturing process.

Whilst bottle banks are prominent in most shopping precincts and municipal refuse sites, there appear to be few collection points specifically for flat glass (windows from domestic sources). With the aim of creating an infrastructure for flat glass recycling, Pilkington have commissioned an independent investigation to develop means to increase the amount of flat glass recycling in the UK, concentrating on the commercial sector, i.e. using glass from window replacement, building demolition and vehicle windscreen breakage.

In Germany, centres to collect automobile glass are being further developed to take architectural glass, with the collaboration of window frame manufacturers' organizations.

DESIGN GUIDANCE

There is no universal and comprehensive method of auditing environmental impact. There are, however, several national initiatives to provide guidance.

The American Institute of Architects started a three year project in 1990 to give guidance on the energy, pollution and recycling implications of products and materials concerned, and has published an *Environmental Resource Guide* (1992).

The Royal Institute of British Architects, London, has published *Building and Health* (1990), a green guide to healthy buildings. It provides the beginnings of an environmental impact assessment in which most of the issues may be considered. At a practical level, the UK BRE environmental assessment method analyses the environmental quality of a building (Baldwin *et al.* 1991). Initially developed for assessing new offices at the design stage, it now includes other building types. It uses independent assessors to evaluate the environmental effects of the building at the design stage, and a certificate is issued to confirm the criteria the design has satisfied.

BIBLIOGRAPHY

American Institute of Architects *Environmental Resource Guide*, 1992

Baldwin, R., Leach, S., Doggart, J. and Attenborough, M. BREEAM 1/90: *An Environmental Assessment for New Office Designs*, Building Research Establishment, Watford, 1991

Banham, R. *Design by Choice*, Academy, London, 1981

Royal Institute of British Architects, *Building and Health*, 1990

Selkowitz, S. and Lampert, C. *Application of Large Area Chromogenics to Architectural Glazings*, Lawrence Berkeley Laboratory, Applied Science Division, University of California, June 1989

Shorrock, L. and Henderson, G. *Energy Use and the Greenhouse Effect*, Building Research Establishment, London, 1989

Shorrock, L. and Henderson, G. *Energy Use in Buildings and Carbon Dioxide Emissions*, report BR 170, Building Research Establishment, 1990

Glass Terms, Products and Processes

GLASS MANUFACTURING PROCESSES

More than 90% of the world's flat glass is made by the float glass process, invented by Pilkington in 1959. Previously the common method of producing flat glass was the sheet drawn process, which now accounts for a diminishing proportion.

SHEET GLASS

Because of the long usage of the term, much thin float glass is still incorrectly referred to as sheet. Sheet glass suffered to some degree from surface distortion and, for applications where this was unacceptable, plate glass was used.

PLATE GLASS

The plate glass process was used to produce higher quality glass, by grinding and polishing of both sides, but has now been completely superseded by the float process. Again, because of the long usage of the term, much currently made float glass is sometimes still incorrectly referred to as plate glass in many specifications.

FLOAT GLASS

In the float glass process, molten glass at approximately 1000 °C is poured continuously from a furnace on to a large shallow bath of molten tin. The glass floats on the tin, spreading out and forming level parallel surfaces on both sides. Thickness is controlled by the speed at which the solidifying glass ribbon is drawn off the tin bath. The surfaces of the glass do not come into contact with any rollers or mechanisms which could damage them until the glass has solidified.

ANNEALED GLASS

The glass is then passed down an annealing lehr where the cooling continues under controlled conditions. It emerges at handling temperatures as a flat 'fire polished' product with virtually parallel surfaces.

GLASS THICKNESS

Float glass thicknesses range from below 2 mm to over 25 mm

for architectural purposes. They are usually 3, 4, 5, 6, 8, 10 and 12 mm thick, with 15, 19 and 25 mm for special uses. There is only one architectural quality of float glass.

GLASS SIZES

Most float lines have ribbon widths just over 3 metres; available sizes depend on handling and shipping limitations rather than the manufacturing plant. Sizes which can be manufactured are not necessarily the sizes which can be directly used.

Clear float is generally available in a maximum size of 3180 × 6080 mm for all thicknesses of 3, 4, 5, 6, 8, 10 and 12 mm. For thick clear float (15, 19 and 25 mm) the maximum size will sometimes be smaller.

CUTTING GLASS

The extreme edges of the ribbon, known as selvages, are scored longitudinally, and pane sizes are determined and scored, usually with tungsten carbide cutting wheels, whilst the ribbon is still moving. Panes and edges are snapped apart automatically (usually computer controlled).

CULLET

The waste glass from the edges and from defective broken panes is known as cullet. This is further broken down and passed to the feeding end of the float process, where it is returned to the tank together with fresh raw materials. The proportion of raw materials to cullet is controlled to give advantage in melting.

CLEAR GLASS

Architectural clear glass is almost invariably of the soda–lime–silica type. Composition varies with manufacturer but is generally silica (SiO_2) 70–74%, lime (CaO) 5–12% and soda (Na_2O) 12–16%, with small amounts of magnesium, aluminium, iron and other elements.

BODY TINTED GLASS

Body tinted glass is produced by small additions to the melt of metal oxides, which do not materially affect the basic properties except for the solar energy transmission – and hence the colour.

In the main the oxides used are iron, cobalt and selenium and, depending on the ratios of each, a range of shades of bronze, grey, blue and green can be produced. The colour is homogeneous throughout the thickness. From one source of manufacture to another, the coloration may not be the same, although in recent years there has been some degree of standardization.

Body tinted float is generally available to a maximum size of 3210 × 6000 mm in a range of colours – green, grey, bronze and blue.

ROLLED GLASS

Patterned, figured, obscured, cast and rolled are all terms used to describe glass made by a rolling process, whereby the semi-molten glass is squeezed between metal rollers to produce a ribbon with controlled thickness and surface textures or patterns.

PATTERNED GLASS

Patterned or figured glass is formed by a reversal of a pattern on the roller (the other roller being nominally flat) so that a repetitive design is impressed into the glass surface.

WIRED GLASS

Wired glass is made by the rolling process. A steel wire mesh is sandwiched between two separate ribbons of glass, the whole then being passed through a pair of rollers which consolidate the material and may impress a required pattern.

POLISHED WIRED GLASS

Polished wired glass is now the only product which is still subjected to a grinding and polishing secondary process to remove surface irregularities produced by the rollers.

Patterned wired glass is usually available in 7 mm thickness and polished wired glass in 6 mm thickness. Typically maximum sizes are 3700 × 1980 mm for patterned and 3300 × 1930 mm for polished wired glass.

SURFACE COATINGS

Because changing the basic composition in a glass tank to produce body coloured glass products is a lengthy and large scale operation, modified properties are produced from basic clear glass by surface coatings applied during manufacture on-line or subsequently off-line.

ON-LINE COATINGS

On-line modifications are made while the glass is hot and still in the annealing lehr. They may still be considered as basic products, and size and tolerance constraints are similar to those for clear float glass.

Surface coatings, either for solar control purposes or for reduced emissivity (a property to improve thermal insulation), are called pyrolitic coatings because they are generally applied to the hot glass during its passage through the annealing lehr. They involve the thermal decomposition of gases, liquids or powders sprayed on to the glass to form a metal oxide layer which fuses to the surface.

On-line coatings have advantages of hardness and durability over off-line coatings and are suitable for bending and toughening. They tend to be limited in variety of colour.

OFF-LINE COATINGS

Off-line coatings are those which are applied to individual panes of glass once the glass has been manufactured and cut. The application of coatings, by dipping panes into chemical solutions, drying and firing, or by evaporation of metals on to glass surfaces under conditions of vacuum, has been known for many years, but in the last decade application by magnetron sputtering of materials has come to the forefront. This process is capable of giving a wide range of coatings of different colours, reflectivities and thermal properties.

In magnetron sputtering, the material to be sputtered is made the cathode of an electrical circuit at 500 volts. Argon gas is introduced into a vacuum chamber, and a glow discharge plasma occurs. Electrons are removed from the argon and leave positively charged ions. These ions are attracted to, and impact with, the target cathode. They have very high momentum and eject atoms of the cathodic material which recondense on the glass below.

Fine tuning enables uniform coatings to be laid on large substrates. Panes 3000×2000 mm can be sputter coated at a rate of one every 60 seconds or so. Virtually any non-magnetic metal or alloy can be sputtered. If argon is in the chamber, a metallic coating results; if oxygen or nitrogen, the result is an oxide or a nitride. A large number of designed coatings is available. Light transmission depends on the nature and thickness of coating. Colour depends on coating thickness material and configuration. The product ranges are under continuous development.

LOW EMISSIVITY COATINGS

Energy conservation products use low emissivity (or Low E) coatings produced off-line and on-line. These reduce emissivity from a value of 0.9 for uncoated glass to less than 0.1. The infrared reflectivity of an appropriately coated glass in the wavelength region of 3–30 µm increases to over 80%. It is in this waveband that radiation emitted from walls and objects in a room is normally lost to clear glass.

Coatings specifically for energy conservation can be tailor-made to allow maximum daylight and short wavelength infrared radiation to enter the building and warm it, but at night to reduce heat loss by reflecting long wavelength heat back into the room. Typical of such coatings is the three-layer Low E coating. Its important component is a thin metal layer, usually of gold, silver or copper, sandwiched between layers of tin oxide to increase adhesion and reduce corrosion. The thickness of the dielectric layer is chosen to give maximum visible light transmission.

Coatings of silver, copper and gold are less transparent to radiation in the near infrared. Their attenuation of radiation of this near infrared occurs by reflection and, since about 50% of the total radiation from the sun occurs in this waveband, such coatings are useful for solar control glass which reflects rather than absorbs.

DIELECTRIC COATINGS

The range of performances available from the use of metallic coatings is limited because of the thickness of coating which has to be applied. The use of dielectric coatings, which produce interference effects, allows higher light transmission with increased selectivity; the range of colours is also increased.

The maximum sizes of coated glass are dependent on the various facilities, and manufacturers' literature should be consulted.

It is not possible to toughen or bend most off-line coated glass; such work must be carried out before coating. It is possible to combine coatings in double glazed and laminated products.

DICHROIC COATINGS

These are composed of multi-layered coatings which exhibit different colours by reflection and transmission as a function of viewing angle.

MIRROR SILVERING

Mirror silvering is a chemical process depositing a coating of metal, mostly silver, on to the surface of clear glass. This deposit is usually protected by a layer of copper which in turn is protected by a paint backing. The silver gives the mirror its reflective properties. The controlled use of stannic solution can produce decorative 'oil-stain' patterns which can be painted with a coloured transparent varnish.

TOUGHENED (TEMPERED) GLASS

Toughened or tempered glass is produced by heating annealed glass to approximately 650 °C, at which point it begins to soften. The surfaces of this heated glass are then cooled rapidly.

The technique creates a state of high compression in the outer surfaces of the glass. As a result, although most other characteristics remain unchanged, the bending strength is usually increased by a factor of four or five times that of annealed glass. When broken, the toughened glass fractures into small pieces (dice). As these particles do not have the sharp edges and dagger points of broken annealed glass, toughened glass is regarded as a safety glass and safety glazing material.

Toughened glass must be cut to size and have any other processing, such as edge polishing and hole drilling, completed before being subjected to toughening, because attempts to 'work' the glass after toughening will cause it to shatter. The toughening process imposes limits on the maximum glass sizes. Wired glasses cannot be toughened.

VERTICAL TOUGHENING

In vertical toughening the glass is held vertically by tongs along the upper edge and suspended in a furnace to raise its temperature. The glass is then cooled rapidly by placing it between an array of nozzles, which blast cold air on to the glass surfaces, cooling it rapidly. The process introduces a slight distortion called tong marks where the tongs have gripped the glass.

All float and sheet glass products can be toughened, as can many patterned glass products depending on the pattern profile.

ROLLER HEARTH TOUGHENING

The roller hearth process supports the glass horizontally on rollers, passing it first into a heating chamber and then into a cooling area. The roller hearth can produce an effect known as roller wave.

CHEMICAL TOUGHENING/TEMPERING

A process of chemical toughening by ion exchange is available but is little used in architecture.

COLOURED CLADDING GLASS

Coloured opaque materials can be fired into the surface of the glass during the heating cycle of the toughening process.

SPONTANEOUS BREAKAGE

Spontaneous breakage is a term applied when toughened glass fractures for no immediately obvious reason. The breakage is usually caused by impact damage, edge damage, poor glazing or incorrect design, but occasionally it is due to foreign particles in the glass. The reason is often not obvious because toughened glass disintegrates after fracture, making the cause difficult to ascertain.

Minute nickel sulphide inclusions when present in the base glass can cause breakage of toughened glass. The risk of breakage from nickel sulphide inclusions can be virtually eliminated by a post-toughening quality control process called heat soaking. Many float glass manufacturers have taken steps to reduce the occurrence of nickel sulphide inclusions in the base glass.

HEAT STRENGTHENED GLASS

Heat strengthened glass is produced by a process similar to that used for toughened glass, but the cooling process is slower. The strength developed is about half that of toughened glass and distortion is generally less. The product has many uses, but it does not meet the criteria for safety glazing because its breakage pattern resembles that of an annealed glass.

LAMINATED GLASS

This is produced by bonding two panes together with a plastic material or a resin. The interlayer, which is usually polyvinyl butyral, can be either clear or tinted. The bonding is achieved by heating the glass/interlayer sandwich under pressure in an autoclave.

CAST-IN-PLACE LAMINATION

When a resin is used as the bonding medium it is poured between the two pieces of glass, which are maintained at the correct separation whilst pouring and curing take place. This process, referred to as cast-in-place, is appropriate to smaller scale production of special glass products.

Laminates can incorporate most thicknesses and many combinations of glass types to give a selection of products with the required range of mechanical and optical properties. They can incorporate other materials such as polycarbonate to achieve specific performances; toughened and heat strengthened glass can also be included.

When a laminated glass is broken, the interlayer tends to hold the fragments of broken glass in place. It is regarded as a safety glass and safety glazing material. Its breakage pattern and strength depend on the glass components and the load duration.

BENT GLASS

Bent glass is produced by heating annealed glass to the point where it softens and then can be pressed or sag bent over formers. Bends can be created in one or two planes. Bending can be incorporated in the toughening process to produce curved glass. Bent glass can be laminated.

Glass bending is a specialist operation. Manufacturers' literature indicates availability of standard items and special orders.

INSULATING GLASS UNITS OR MULTIPLE GLAZED OR SEALED UNITS

Insulating glass units or multiple glazed or sealed units incorporate two or more panes, separated by a spacer or spacers, to create a cavity between each successive pane in the unit. The cavity is usually filled with air. They can be constructed from various combinations of glass and usually incorporate two panes and one spacer. Additional panes and air spaces can be incorporated.

GAS FILLING

Dehydrated air is normally used to fill the cavity of the unit. Argon can be used to enhance the thermal insulation properties. Heavy gases such as sulphur hexafluoride can be used to improve acoustic insulation.

SPACERS

The spacer is usually attached to the glass by a sealant, with further additional sealant material to prevent air and water penetration. The spacer is normally a metal extrusion but can be made from low thermal conductivity plastics. Spacer widths of

5 to 20 mm are available, depending on the performance required.

DESICCANTS

The spacers are often hollow and incorporate a dehydrant or desiccant to ensure a low water vapour pressure in the unit, reducing the likelihood of condensation forming in the unit under extreme temperature conditions.

DECORATIVE EFFECTS

ACIDING

Aciding or acid etching consists of producing varying degrees of etched surface texture on the glass surface by successive flotations of dilute hydrofluoric acid. Texture is produced by interposing acid resistant substances during the aciding.

STIPPLING

Stippling is achieved by floating grades of mica before the aciding.

BROMESH

Bromesh is a grained effect produced by scraping an acid resist before further aciding. Multiple designs can be produced by screening the resist through silk screen or photographic stencils.

SAND BLASTING

Sand blasting consists of blasting an abrasive at the surface of the glass, under pressure. Matt and peppered effects are achieved using different pressures. Shading is achieved by changing the distance and pressure of blasting during application. Designs can be produced by using an adhesive plastic covering resistant to the abrasive. The sand blasted surface can be brightened by the application of varnish or strong acid. Further decoration is achieved by the application of gold or silver leaf.

FIRING

Permanent colours can be produced by firing ceramic colour on to the glass surface at high temperature (600 °C).

ENGRAVING

Engraving consists of abrading the surface of the glass to achieve decorative designs by means of copper wheels, diamond points, carborundum pencils and other flexible drive tools. The engraving can consist of 'brilliant' cutting of various geometric shapes in the glass surface which can be further polished.

SILK SCREEN PRINTING

Silk screen printing is the application of design and patterns to a glass surface through a screen of fine stainless steel or nylon mesh used in combination with paint, sand blasting and other media.

EDGE WORKING

Edge working consists of abrading or polishing the edge of the glass to achieve decorative profiles. It is also used to minimize flaws in the edges of glass, obtaining greater edge strength.

BIBLIOGRAPHY

Balkow, D., Von Bock, K., Krewinkel, H., Rinkens, R., *Glas am Bau*, Deutsche Verlagsanstalt, Germany, 1990 (in German)

Klindt, L.B. and Klein, W. *Glas als Baustoff*, Veragsgesellschaft Rudolf Müller Cologne, Germany, 1977 (in German)

Libbey Owens Ford Co. *Architectural Products Binder*, Toledo, 1992

Pfaender, H. *Schott-Glaslexikon*, MVG-Verlag, Munich, Germany, 1980 (in German)

Tooley, F.V. *Handbook of Glass Manufacture*, 3rd edn, Ashlee, New York, 1984

Photographic Credits

Cover photographs and Figures 1.14, 3.1, 3.10, 6.6 and 6.7: James Carpenter

Figures 1.1, 1.6, 1.7, 2.8, 2.11, 2.12–2.14, 4.2, 4.7, 4.10, 4.12, 4.15, 4.22, 4.23, 5.2, 5.7, 5.26, 7.1, 8.1, 8.9, 9.11a, 9.15, 9.20, 9.21, 10.1, 12.8a, 13.1, 16.7, 18.1, 18.3, 19.1, 19.2, 19.5, 21.1, 21.7 and 22.15: Flachglas AG

Figure 1.3: David Carnwath – Architectural Association Slide Library, London

Figures 1.8, 1.11, 4.1, 12.20, and 21.17: Richard Bryant – Arcaid

Figures 1.9 and 5.21: The National Gallery, London

Figures 1.10, 4.3, 5.14 and 6.11: Robert Byron

Figure 1.12: Mike Davies – Richard Rogers and Partners

Figures 1.13, 9.27, 11.6, 11.9–11.11, 12.6b and 18.2: Pilkington Technology Centre

Figures 4.13 and 5.3: Nathaniel Lieberman – I M Pei, Cobb, Freed and Partners

Figure 4.17: Alfred Wolf

Figure 4.24: Paul Birkbeck

Figure 5.1: P Bond – Architectural Association Slide Library, London

Figure 5.13b: Lawrence Berkeley Laboratories, California

Figure 6.1: Brian Clarke – The Mayor Gallery

Figure 6.2: Brian Clarke

Figure 6.3 and 6.4: Radford and Ball

Figure 6.5: H G Esch

Figure 6.8: Ian Richie Architects

Figure 8.11: Pilkington Energy Advisors

Figure 9.1: Robert Kristofik – The Image Bank

Figures 10.5 and 20.1: Building Research Establishment; Crown copyright 1992

Figure 11.1: Paul Warchol – I M Pei, Cobb, Freed and Partners

Figure 12.1: Heinz W Krewinkel

Figure 13.2: Pictor International

Figure 13.4: Nottingham Evening Post

Figure 14.1: Libbey Owens Ford

Figure 17.1: The Telegraph Colour Library

Figure 22.1: Chuck Mason – The Image Bank

Figures A.1, A.6, A.8, A.9 and A.11: Jim Wheeler – Industrial Image

Figure A.4: Jeremy Cockayne – Arcaid

Figure B.1a: The Stock Directory; The Telegraph Colour Library

All other photographs by Pilkington Glass Ltd

Index

Note: Page numbers in bold type indicate a reference to a figure.